T0235264

Lecture Notes in Computer Science 10479

More information about this series at http://www.springer.com/series/7408

Alexander Romanovsky · Elena A. Troubitsyna (Eds.)

Software Engineering for Resilient Systems

9th International Workshop, SERENE 2017
Geneva, Switzerland, September 4–5, 2017
Proceedings

Editors
Alexander Romanovsky
Newcastle University
Newcastle-upon-Tyne
UK

Elena A. Troubitsyna
Åbo Akademi University
Turku
Finland

ISSN 0302-9743 ISSN 1611-3349 (electronic)
Lecture Notes in Computer Science
ISBN 978-3-319-65947-3 ISBN 978-3-319-65948-0 (eBook)
DOI 10.1007/978-3-319-65948-0

Library of Congress Control Number: 2017948643

LNCS Sublibrary: SL2 – Programming and Software Engineering

Printed on acid-free paper

This Springer imprint is published by Springer Nature
The registered company is Springer International Publishing AG
The registered company address is: Gewerbestrasse 11, 6330 Cham, Switzerland

Preface

This volume contains the proceedings of the 9th International Workshop on Software Engineering for Resilient Systems (SERENE 2017). SERENE 2017 took place in Geneva, Switzerland on September 4–5, 2017. The SERENE workshop is an annual event that brings together researchers and practitioners working on the various aspects of design, verification, and assessment of resilient systems. In particular it covers such areas as:

- Development of resilient systems;
- Engineering processes for resilient systems;
- Requirements engineering and re-engineering for resilience;
- Frameworks, patterns, and software architectures for resilience;
- Engineering of self-healing autonomic systems;
- Design of trustworthy and intrusion-safe systems;
- Resilience at run-time (mechanisms, reasoning, and adaptation);
- Resilience and dependability (resilience vs. robustness, dependable vs. adaptive systems);
- Verification, validation, and evaluation of resilience;
- Modelling and model-based analysis of resilience properties;
- Formal and semi-formal techniques for verification and validation;
- Experimental evaluations of resilient systems;
- Quantitative approaches to ensuring resilience;
- Resilience prediction;
- Case studies and applications;
- Empirical studies in the domain of resilient systems;
- Methodologies adopted in industrial contexts;
- Cloud computing and resilient service provisioning;
- Resilience for data-driven systems (e.g., big data-based adaption and resilience);
- Resilient cyber-physical systems and infrastructures;
- Global aspects of resilience engineering: education, training, and cooperation.

SERENE 2017 featured two invited speakers – Miroslaw Malek and Jorge Cardoso. Miroslaw Malek is the Director of the Advanced Learning and Research Institute (ALaRI), which is part of the Faculty of Informatics of the University of Lugano, Switzerland. He is a well-known expert in the areas of dependability and fault tolerance. He has carried out pioneering work in the area of dependable, parallel network design and proactive fault tolerance. Jorge Cardoso is a Chief Architect for Cloud Operations and Analytics at Huawei's German Research Center (GRC) in Munich. He is also a Professor at the University of Coimbra, Portugal. In 2013 and 2014, he was a Guest Professor at the Karlsruhe Institute of Technology (KIT) and a Fellow at the Technical University of Dresden (TU Dresden). Previously, he worked for major companies such as SAP Research (Germany) on the Internet of services and the Boeing

Company in Seattle (USA) on Enterprise Application Integration. His research interests focus on dependable and secure cloud computing and service-oriented systems.

The workshop was established by the members of the ERCIM working group SERENE. The group promotes the idea of the resilient-explicit development process. It stresses the importance of extending the traditional software engineering practice with the theories and tools supporting modelling and verification of various aspects of resilience. We would like to thank the SERENE working group for their hard work on publicizing the event and contributing to its technical program.

SERENE 2017 attracted 16 submissions, from which 11 papers were accepted. Every paper received three rigorous reviews. All submissions were of a high quality, which has allowed us to build a strong and technically enlightening program. We would like to express our gratitude to the program committee members and the additional reviewers who have actively participated in reviewing and discussing the submissions.

Since 2015 SERENE has become part of a major European dependability forum – the European Dependable Computing Conference (EDCC). We would like to thank the Organizing Committee of EDCC 2017 for their help in organizing the workshop.

July 2017

Alexander Romanovsky
Elena A. Troubitsyna

Organization

Steering Committee

Didier Buchs	University of Geneva, Switzerland
Henry Muccini	University of L'Aquila, Italy
Patrizio Pelliccione	Chalmers University of Technology and University of Gothenburg, Sweden
Alexander Romanovsky	Newcastle University, UK
Elena Troubitsyna	Åbo Akademi University, Finland

Program Chairs

Alexander Romanovsky	Newcastle University, UK
Elena Troubitsyna	Åbo Akademi University, Finland

Program Committee

Rami Bahsoon	Birmingham University, UK
Michael Butler	Southampton University, UK
Nelio Cacho	UFRN, Brazil
Andrea Ceccarelli	University of Florence, Italy
Vincenzo De Florio	VITO, Belgium
Nikolaos Georgantas	Inria, France
Anatoliy Gorbenko	Leeds Beckett University, UK
Felicita Di Giandomenico	CNR-ISTI, Italy
Lars Grunske	Humboldt University of Berlin, Germany
Jeremie Guiochet	LAAS, France
Dubravka Ilic	Space Systems Finland, Finland
Rolf Johansson	SP, Sweden
Mohamed Kaaniche	LAAS-CNRS, France
Linas Laibinis	Vilnius University, Lithuania
Istvan Majzik	BUTE, Hungary
Miroslaw Malek	University of Lugano, Switzerland
Henry Muccini	University of L'Aquila, Italy
Andras Pataricza	BUTE, Hungary
Patrizio Pelliccione	Chalmers University of Technology and University of Gothenburg, Sweden
Andreas Roth	SAP, Germany
Juan Carlos Ruiz	Technical University of Valencia, Spain
Cristina Seceleanu	MDH, Sweden

Jüri Vain	Tallinn University of Technology, Estonia
Marco Vieira	University of Coimbra, Portugal
Wilhelm Hasselbring	Kiel University, Germany

Subreviewers

Simin Cai	MDH, Sweden
Bryan Knowles	Western Kentucky University, USA

Cloud Reliability: Decreasing Outage Frequency Using Fault Injection (Invited Talk)

Jorge Cardoso

Huawei Germany Research Centre (GRC), Munich, Germany
Jorge.Cardoso@huawei.com

Abstract. In 2016, Google Cloud had 74 minutes of total downtime, Microsoft Azure had 270 minutes, and 108 minutes of downtime for Amazon Web Services (see cloudharmony.com). Reliability is one of the most important properties of a successful cloud platform. Several approaches can be explored to increase reliability ranging from automated replication, to live migration, and to formal system analysis. Another interesting approach is to use software fault injection to test a platform during prototyping, implementation and operation. Fault injection was popularized by Netflix and their Chaos Monkey fault-injection tool to test cloud applications. The main idea behind this technique is to inject failures in a controlled manner to guarantee the ability of a system to survive failures during operations. This talk will explain how fault injection can also be applied to detect vulnerabilities of OpenStack cloud platform and how to effectively and efficiently detect the damages caused by the faults injected.

Keywords: Cloud computing • Software reliability • Failure diagnosis • Fault injection • OpenStack

Summary

The reliability and resilience of cloud platforms (e.g., Amazon AWS, Microsoft Azure, Open Telekom Cloud from T-Systems, Google GCP, and Huawei HWS) are acquiring an increased relevance since society is relying more and more on complex software systems. Cloud computing is becoming as important as the other established utilities (e.g., water and electricity).

The new type of software systems supporting cloud platforms is extremely complex and new approaches to resilience and reliability engineering are needed. In fact, Netflix has developed Chaos Monkey, Google has implemented DiRT, and Amazon has developed GameDay. The complexity and dynamicity of large-scale cloud platforms requires automated solutions to reduce the risks of eventual failures and new intelligent components for an automated recovery. Problems, which need to be handled, include the transient unavailability of services, scalability difficulties, demand spikes (i.e., the Slashdot Effect), correlated failures, hot upgrades, and interference between tenants.

These software platforms cannot be tested only during their software development; they need to be tested during realistic operations. A data center with 40.000–80.000 physical servers supporting a public cloud platform cannot be only tested during the development of the underlying software. Its reliability needs to be constantly tested in near-real settings and during operations while hundreds or thousands of tenants are connected.

As with most software, the validation of all the modules of a cloud platform is done through a test suite containing a large number of unit tests. It is a part of the software development process, where the smallest testable part of an application, called unit, along with associated control data are individually and independently tested. Executing unit tests is a very effective way to test code integration during the development of software. They are often executed to validate changes made by developers and to guarantee that the code is error free.

Although unit tests are extremely useful for the purpose of development and integration, they are not meant to diagnose failures resulting from injecting faults. The use of unit tests for failure diagnosis presents a set of challenges. First, unit tests do not provide any information about the nonresponsive or failed services in cloud platforms. The execution of unit tests generates a list of passed and failed tests. This list can help to locate software errors or to find issues with individual modules of the code but cannot diagnose failures as there are no relationships between unit tests and services running on a cloud platform. Second, a cloud platform is a large system with a high number of unit tests. With the increase in codebase of cloud platforms, the number of unit tests also increases. Thus, it takes a considerable amount of time to execute them.

Because of these challenges, cloud operators often develop new sets of tests to diagnose failures. But as mentioned before, cloud platforms are continuously evolving. They undergo modification and frequent updates, and have periodic release cycles. Hence, the tests developed become outdated and there is a constant need to modify them when a new release is available. Therefore, this approach is costly for the cloud operators.

In the experiments we conducted with OpenStack (openstack.org), we experienced all the problems mentioned above. OpenStack is a cloud operating system for building public and private clouds consisting of more than 1500 unit tests. Currently, these unit tests are used for the purpose of development and integration and to test OpenStack deployment. They perform all the operations that a user can perform. But they only validate the functioning of OpenStack APIs and are not able to directly detect services that are not functioning as expected. Moreover, many of the unit tests are time consuming. For example, unit tests involving creation of a virtual machine, uploading a large operating system image, etc., need a few minutes to execute. Therefore, it can take up to 3 to 4 h to execute all unit tests. Considering the reliability requirements of 99.95%, cloud platforms can have a downtime of only 21.6 minutes per month. Hence, the time required to execute unit tests is considerably high. Lastly, OpenStack has a very active open source community with a release cycle of 6 months. Therefore, developing new tests for failure diagnosis is very costly since modification in the tests would be required for every new release.

A different approach is therefore needed to diagnose failures in cloud platforms after injecting faults. The solution should be efficient (fast) and should be able to establish relationships between unit tests and the services they are capable of testing. The solution should also be able to cope up with the fast release cycle of cloud platforms. Through our research, we found out that with the integration of several techniques, the challenges associated with unit tests could be overcome to efficiently diagnose failures. It has several benefits. First, unit tests are developed along with cloud platforms. Hence, there is no additional cost of development required. Second, unit tests can be executed with minimal effort as they are automated. This property of unit tests can be utilized to diagnose failures automatically. Lastly, with every new release, unit tests are also updated. Therefore, there is no need to modify the tests for a new release.

Our approach uses existing unit tests and is composed of 3 phases. In the first phase, it reduces the number of existing unit tests. Second, it establishes relationships between the reduced unit tests and all the services responsible for the functioning of cloud platforms. It then further reduces the unit tests based on these relationships. In the last phase, it generates a decision tree to efficiently diagnose failures in cloud platforms. Test results have shown that executing only 4–5 % of the original unit tests can efficiently detect failed services.

Acknowledgments. This research was conducted in collaboration with Deutsche Telekom/T-Systems and with Ankur Bhatia from the Technical University of Munich to analyze the reliability and resilience of modern public cloud platforms.

Contents

Fault Tolerance, Resilience and Robustness

Invited Talk

Predictive Analytics: A Shortcut to Dependable Computing

Miroslaw Malek(✉)

Advanced Learning and Research Institute (ALaRI),
Università della Svizzera italiana, Lugano, Switzerland
malekm@usi.ch

Abstract. The paper lists three major issues: complexity, time and uncertainty, and identifies dependability as the permanent challenge. In order to enhance dependability, the paradigm shift is proposed where focus is on failure prediction and early malware detection. Failure prediction methodology, including modeling and failure mitigation, is presented and two case studies (failure prediction for computer servers and early malware detection) are described in detail. The proposed approach, using predictive analytics, may increase system availability by an order of magnitude or so.

Keywords: Failure prediction · Feature selection · Malware detection · Modelling · Predictive analytics · Proactive Fault Management

1 Introduction: Three Tyrants and the Permanent Challenge

With ever-growing system complexity, ever more stringent timeliness requirements and the uncertainty on the rise due to failures and cyber-attacks one should consider three tyrants[1] that impact not only computer and communication systems operation but also our lives. They are:

1.1 Complexity

The growth of complexity cannot be stopped in practice due to permanent strive for new features and applications and continuously growing number of users and objects (things). In fact, the Internet of Things (IoT) is turning into the Internet of Everything where virtually trillions of devices will be connected ranging from self-driving vehicles to coffee machines. The continuous strive for improved properties such as higher performance, low power, better security, higher dependability and others will continue with further requirements for system openness, fading cries for privacy and flow of incredible volumes of data, yes, big data. This situation seems to be beyond control and is simply part of our civilization.

[1] Inspired by a quote from Johann Gottfried von Herder (1744-1803): "Die zwei größten Tyrannen der Erde: der Zufall und die Zeit" (Two biggest tyrants on Earth are: the chance and the time).

A. Romanovsky and E.A. Troubitsyna (Eds.): SERENE 2017, LNCS 10479, pp. 3–17, 2017.
DOI: 10.1007/978-3-319-65948-0_1

1.2 Time

Many individuals, especially our professional friends and colleagues, have an illusion that the time can be controlled and manipulated. There are two major problems destroying this illusion:

a. Time can neither be stopped nor regained
b. Disparity between physical and logical time is evident and in many applications cannot be reconciled.

This creates an insurmountable challenge as creating a real-time IoT is simply beyond our current capabilities.

1.3 Uncertainty

Since occurrence of faults is frequently unpredictable, we have to deal with uncertainty which can be controlled to a limited extent but, all in all, we have "to cope" with it. Furthermore, the new failure modes, new environmental conditions and new attacks further increase uncertainty.

In view of ever-increasing complexity, ever more demanding timing constraints and growing uncertainty due to new cyber-attacks and new failure modes, the dependability is and will remain a permanent challenge. There is no hope that one day it will go away. In fact, it will become ever more pervasive and significant as impact of faults or attacks may range from minor inconvenience to loss of lives and economic disasters.

2 Failure Prediction and the Paradigm Shift

Knowing the future fascinated and employed millions throughout the centuries. From fortune tellers and weather forecasters to stock analysts and medical doctors, the main goal seems to be the same: learn from history, assess the current state and predict the future.

Analysing the historical record on our ability to predict, we may admit that in long term predictions we have miserably failed. Stellar examples include cars, phones, mainframes, personal computers, radios. There are some notable exceptions such as Moore's Law on processor performance but, in principle, especially with respect to breakthrough technologies we were more often wrong than right.

Since a long term future is so difficult to predict, we focus on short, 1–5 min predictions which, as practice shows, have much higher probability of success. In fact, a spirit of this paper can be succinctly summarized by a Greek poet, C. P. Cavafy (1863–1933) who wrote: "Ordinary mortals know what's happening now, the gods know what the future holds because they alone are totally enlightened. Wise men are aware of future things just about to happen."

We have demonstrated that, in fact, such short term predictions may be very effective in enhancing computer systems dependability regardless of the root cause of failure, be it software or hardware.

Not surprisingly, a plethora of methods for short term prediction has been developed [1], and many of them perform very well. Take a method based on the Universal Basis Function [3], for example. We have developed a data-driven, dynamic system approach using modified radial basis function which is able to predict performance failures for telecommunication applications in 83% of cases.

Knowing even a short term future may help us to avoid a disaster, better prepare for an imminent failure or increase the system performance.

Predictive analytics, is the processing of algorithms and data which result in prediction of user's behaviour, system status or environmental change. Knowing the future system state or user's behaviour can significantly increase performance, availability and security.

With predictive analytics a drastic paradigm change is in the making. While in the past, we have mainly analysed a system behaviour, and currently, in most cases, we observe the status and behaviour to react to changes in the system, the next big trend is to predict the system behaviour and construct the future (see Fig. 1).

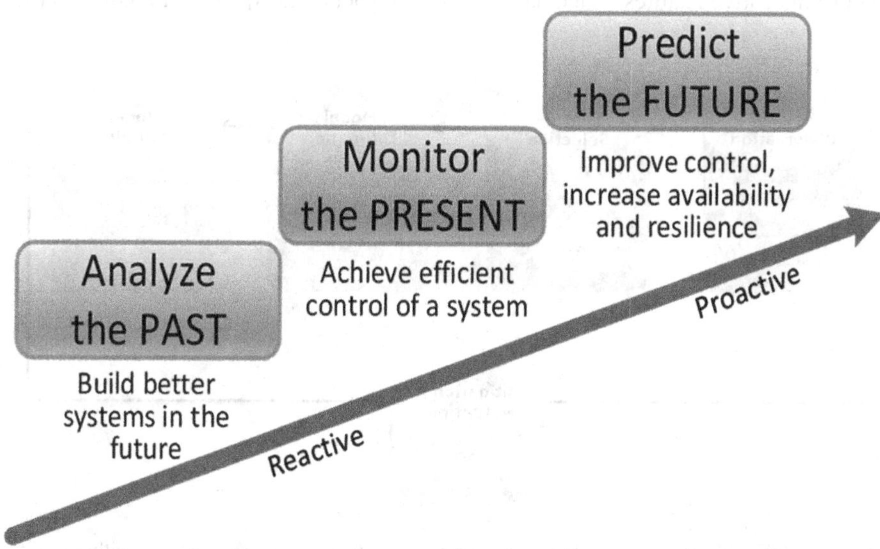

Fig. 1. The paradigm shift.

This leads us to Proactive Fault Management which uses algorithms and methods of failure prediction in order to avoid a failure (e.g., by failover) or minimize its impact [1, 2]. The area is maturing and has already entered the industrial practice, especially in the area of preventive maintenance. It seems to be already evident that the Industry 4.0 will use it as a major design paradigm. The potential of such approach is immense as it may improve a system availability by an order of magnitude or more.

This philosophy requires a change of the mindset: don't wait for a failure, anticipate and avoid it or at least minimize the potential damage. I call it a shortcut to dependable computing as we do not wait for a failure, we act on it before its occurrence.

3 Modelling for Prediction in a Nutshell

"The sciences do not try to explain, they hardly even try to interpret, they mainly make models. By a model is meant a mathematical construct which, with the addition of certain verbal interpretations, describes observed phenomena. The justification of such a mathematical construct is solely and precisely that it is expected to work."

John von Neumann (1903 - 1957)

The key to good predictive capabilities is a development of an appropriate model and selection of the most indicative features (also called variables, events or parameters by different research communities). Unfortunately, models are just an approximate reflection of reality and their distance to reality varies. Since, obviously, it is a challenge to capture all properties of such a complex system as, for example, computer cloud, the typical approach has been to focus on specific properties or functionalities of a system. In Fig. 2 we show the methodology of model development and its application. The interesting part is that the choice of model is not as important as selection of the most indicative features which have decisive impact on the quality of prediction [3].

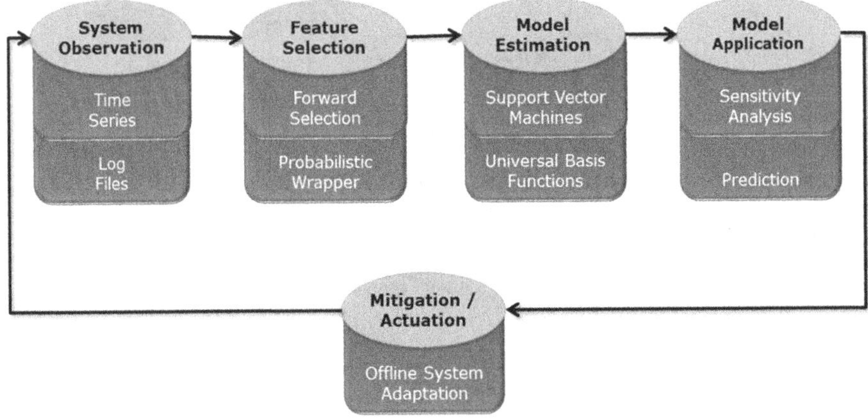

Fig. 2. Building blocks for modelling and failure prediction in complex systems either during runtime or during off-line preparation and testing. System observations include numerical time series data and/or categorical log files. The feature selection process is frequently handled implicitly by system expert's ad-hoc methods or gut feeling, rigorous procedures are applied infrequently. In recent studies attention has been focused on the model estimation process. Univariate and multivariate linear regression techniques have been used but currently nonlinear regression techniques such as universal basis functions or support vector machines are applied as well. While prediction has received a substantial amount of attention, sensitivity analysis of system models has been largely marginalized. Closing the control loop is still a challenge. Choosing the right mitigation/actuation scheme as a function of quality of service and cost is nontrivial [2, 6].

4 Predictive Analytics and Its Applications

Predictive analytics applies a set of methods/algorithms or classifiers that use historical and current data to forecast future activity, behaviour and trends.

Predictive analytics involves creating predictive models and applying statistical analysis, function approximation, machine learning and other methods to determine the likelihood of a particular event taking place.

In two case studies, we demonstrate the power of prediction or early detection to:

(1) Failure prediction in computer servers
(2) Early detection of malware under Android operating system.

The approaches are general and are applicable to other domains such as disturbance prediction in smart grids [4] and predictive maintenance [5].

5 Dependability Economics

Dependability economics concerns the risk and cost/benefit analysis of IT infrastructure investments in an enterprise caused by planned or unplanned downtime as a result of scheduled maintenance, upgrades, updates, failures, disasters and cyber attacks. Research community shied away from this question with only a few notable exceptions (e.g. D. Patterson, UC-Berkeley), yet from industrial perspective the problem is fundamental. Providers and users want to know what will be the Return-On-Investment (ROI) when they invest in dependability improvement.

Furthermore, we are able to assess what benefits, with respect to dependability, we can get by improving the prediction quality measured in terms of precision and recall [6].

6 Failure Prediction Methodology

The goal of online failure prediction is to identify, at runtime, whether a failure will occur in the near future based on an assessment of the monitored current system state and the analysis of past events. The output of a failure predictor is the probability of a failure imminence in the near future. A failure predictor should predict as many failures as possible while minimizing the number of false alarms. Numerous prediction methods are already successfully used for the enterprise computer systems for online, short-term prediction of failures [1]. The prediction quality is identified as a critical part of the entire predict-mitigate approach.

A design of a failure predictor should be conducted in three phases depicted in Fig. 3 [4]. In the first phase a model of the system should be conceived. The model should clearly identify parts of the system where, based on historical records, failures are most frequent and establish a relation between system parts in terms of fault and error propagation.

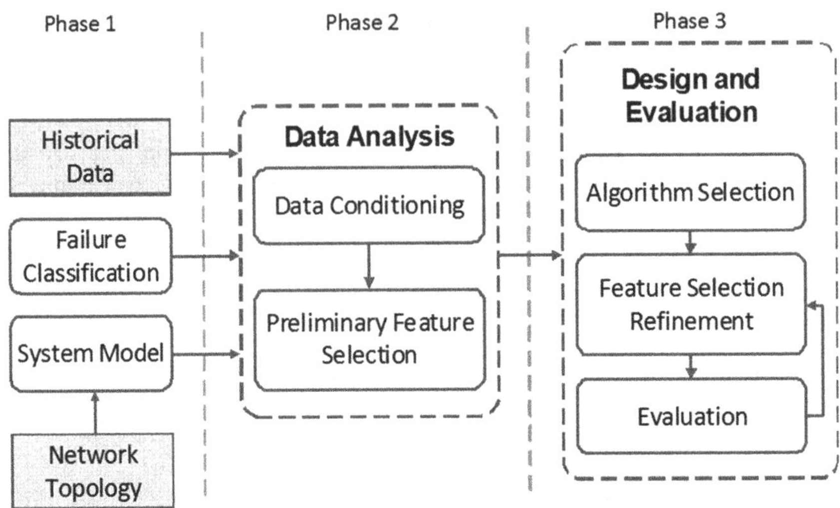

Fig. 3. Failure predictor design stages.

The main usage of the model is in preliminary selection of the most indicative features. Historical data, that are necessary to train and evaluate a predictor, may be obtained from measurement logs.

In the second phase, the obtained dataset should be analyzed. Data conditioning includes extraction of the features and structuring the data in a form that may be used as input for the prediction algorithm. In particular, each data set in the stream, that describes one system state, should be associated with a failure type or marked as failure-free. A preliminary feature selection should be conducted while taking into account system model. Feature selection is the process of selecting the most relevant features (and examples for algorithm training) and combining them in order to maximize predictors' performance; discard redundant and noisy data; obtain faster and more cost-effective algorithm training and online prediction; and better interpret the data relations (data simplification for better human understanding). Feature selection methods may be classified as filters, wrappers and embedded methods. A widely used filter method is Principal Component Analysis (PCA). PCA converts a set of correlated features into a set of linearly uncorrelated features (principal components) using orthogonal transformation. The procedure is independent with respect to the type of the prediction algorithm that will be used and thus very appropriate for preliminary selection of features. Numerous software packages are available for feature selection, including those that are a part of popular tools for statistical analysis (e.g. Matlab/Octave, Python and R). A good overview of feature selection methods is given in [7, 8].

In the final stage, the predictor is adapted and evaluated. In fact, an ensemble of predictors may be used to improve quality of prediction. Having in mind a large number of existing failure prediction algorithms, the most viable solution is to select and to adopt one of them. A comprehensive survey of failure prediction algorithms is given in [1]. Three main approaches used for prediction are: failure tracking, symptom monitoring and detected error reporting. Failure tracking draws conclusions about upcoming failures from the occurrence of the previous ones. These methods either aim at predicting the time of the next occurrence of a failure or at estimating the probability of failures co-occurrence. Symptoms are defined as side effects of looming faults that not necessarily manifest themselves as errors. Symptom-monitoring based predictions analyze the system features in order to identify those that indicate an upcoming failure. Several methodologies for the estimation were proposed in the past, including function approximation, machine-learning techniques, system models, graph models, and time series analysis. Finally, the methods based on detected error reporting, such as the rule-based, the co-concurrence-based and the pattern recognition methods, analyze the error reports to predict if a new failure is about to happen.

In order to speed up the prediction, the set of selected features should be refined by extracting the most indicative ones. To facilitate the process, heuristics (such as the ones presented in [7, 8]) may be employed. After each iteration, the quality of prediction has to be evaluated. The process terminates when a sufficient quality of prediction is reached so that resilience and availability are improved.

7 Failure Mitigation

Once the prediction mechanisms anticipate a failure, corrective actions that will mitigate it should be scheduled and activated. The mitigation is composed of three phases [4]: diagnosis, decision on countermeasures and implementation of countermeasures. In the diagnosis phase, the output of the prediction is analyzed. Additional algorithms may be employed to better identify the location of the anticipated failure. In the second phase of mitigation, a decision on a countermeasure is taken. This decision should take into account the probability of a failure (provided by the predictor), the cost of the measure (e.g. maintenance cost or the cost in terms of the number of customers affected), the probability of a successful mitigation and the overall effect on resilience (for example the effect on steady-state availability). Finally, the implementation of the countermeasure has to be performed.

The ultimate goal is to fully avoid the failure (e.g. by failing over an application to another server). If that is not possible, then the effect of a failure should be minimized or confined (e.g. by preventive load shedding) or a preparation of repair actions may be triggered to minimize the repair time (e.g. by checkpointing or saving critical files). Some of these techniques can lead to a system performance degradation. For example, if a failure predictor was wrong, unnecessary preventive load shedding may be conducted affecting a subset of customers. The entire process may be implemented as fully automated or it may require the involvement of an operator for decision-making. This may depend on the type of mitigation and its cost. When more than one failure is anticipated, a coordinated management of mitigation is required.

8 Case Study 1: Telecommunication System

The system we consider is an industrial telecommunication platform which handles mobile originated calls (MOC) and value adding services such as short message services (SMS) and multimedia messaging services (MMS) [3]. It operates with the Global System for Mobile Communication (GSM) and General Packet Radio Service (GPRS). The system architecture follows strict design guidelines considering reliability, fault tolerance, performance, efficiency and compatibility issues. We focus on one specific system which, at the time we took our measurements, consisted of somewhat more than 1.6 million lines of code, approximately 200 components[2] and 2000 classes[3]. It is designed to be operated distributed over two to eight nodes for performance and fault tolerance reasons. We focused on modeling and predicting system events (i.e. calls) which take longer time to be processed than some guaranteed threshold value. We call these events failures or target events (see Fig. 4).

The data we used to build and verify our models consists of

a. equidistant-time-triggered continuous features and
b. time-stamped, event-driven log file entries.

We gathered numeric values of 46 system features once per minute and per node. This yields 92 features in a time series describing the evolution of the internal states of the system. In a 24-hour period we collected a total of 132.480 readings. In total we collected roughly 1.3 million system variable observations.

Please note that in special purpose systems such as telecommunication systems probability of correctly predicting a failure is much higher than in a general purpose system when an arbitrary application may be invoked at any time.

When making predictions about the system's future state we must take into account true positive (TP), false positive (FP), true negative (TN) and false negative (FN) classifications. Focusing on TP alone may substantially bias a model. A metric which takes all four prediction outcomes into account is precision P and recall R.

$$P = \frac{TP}{TP + FN} \tag{1}$$

$$R = \frac{FP}{FP + FN} \tag{2}$$

Using a combination of forward selection and backward elimination we have identified two most indicative features, namely the number of semaphores (exceptions) per second and the growth rate in kernel memory. These two features were expressed as a linear combination of nonlinear kernel functions (Gauss/sigmoid) supported by

[2] A system element offering a predefined service and able to communicate with other components.

[3] Classes are used to group related features and functions.

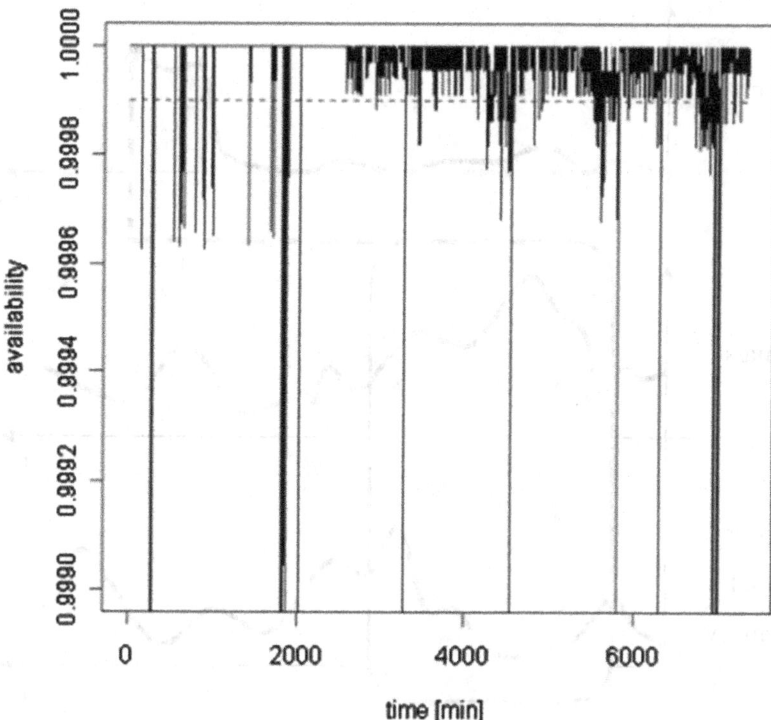

Fig. 4. The target is the system's interval call availability (A) of 0.9999. The dotted line indicates a 0.9999 availability limit. Any drop below that threshold is defined as a failure. Our objective is to model and predict the timely appearance of these failures. The system's interval call availability is reported in consecutive five minute intervals and is calculated as the number of successful calls over the total number of calls in this interval.

training with evolutionary algorithm formed, what we called, a Universal Basis Function (UBF) which gave us excellent results of P = 0.83 and R = 0.78, outperforming all other methods.

An example of correlating the two features and devising the UBF is given in Fig. 5.

Failure prediction quality deteriorates with increase of a lead time of the prediction. Figure 6 shows the prediction quality measure for the UBF Universal Basis Function, the Area Under Curve (AUC), deteriorates over extended lead time in comparison to methods based on Radial Basis Functions and Multivariate Linear models, including non-linear variations of UBF and RBF.

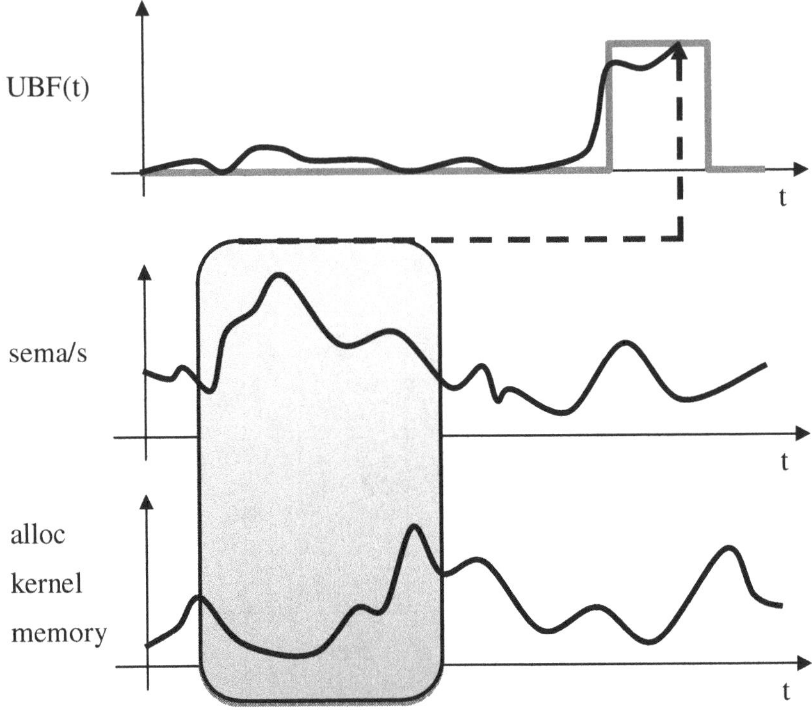

Fig. 5. Time series of the two features and the UBF

9 Case Study 2: Early Malware Detection

With an ever-increasing and ever more aggressive proliferation of malware, its detection is of utmost importance. However, due to the fact that IoT devices are resource-constrained, it is difficult to provide effective solutions.

The main goal of this case study is to demonstrate how prediction methodology can help in finding lightweight techniques for dynamic malware detection. For this purpose, we identify an optimized set of features to be monitored at runtime on mobile devices as well as detection algorithms that are suitable for battery-operated environments. We propose to use a minimal set of most indicative memory and CPU features reflecting malicious behavior.

To enable efficient dynamic detection of mobile malware, we propose the following approach to identify the most indicative features related to memory and CPU to be monitored on mobile devices and the most appropriate classification algorithms to be used afterwards [9]:

1. Collection of malicious samples, representing different families, and of benign samples
2. Execution of samples and collection of the execution traces
3. Extraction of features, from the execution traces, related to memory and CPU

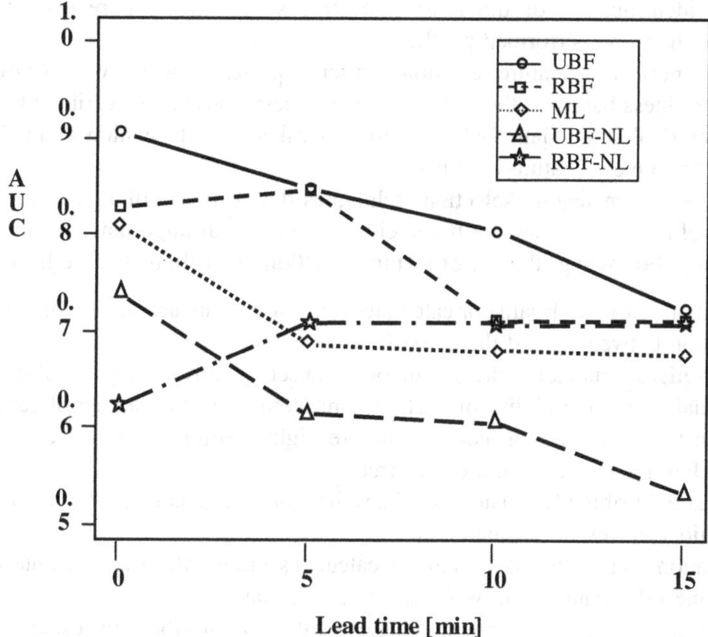

Fig. 6. Failure prediction results: the UBF model (AUC = 0.9024) outperforms the RBF (AUC = 0.8257) and ML (AUC = 0.807) approach with respect to 1, 5, 10 and 15-minutes lead time.

4. Selection of the most indicative features
5. Selection of the most appropriate classification algorithms
6. Quantitative evaluation of the selected features and algorithms

The first step defines the dataset to be used in the remaining parts of the methodology. Namely, it is important to use malicious samples coming from different malware families, so that the diverse behavior of malware is covered to as large extent as possible.

Furthermore, it is needed to set up the execution environment to run malicious samples, so that malicious behavior can be triggered. Additionally, such environment should provide the possibility to execute large number of malicious samples, within reasonable time, so that the obtained results have statistical significance. We have achieved these requirements, first, by using a variety of malware families with broad scope of behavior, second by triggering different events while executing malicious applications and, third, by using an emulation environment that enabled us to execute applications quickly. Since our goal is to discriminate between malicious and benign execution records, we have taken into account also benign samples, and executed them in same conditions used for malicious applications. While usage of an emulator enables us to execute statistically significant number of applications on one hand, on the other hand it is our belief that its usage instead of a real device has a limited or no effect on results, due to the nature of features observed. However, we are aware of the fact that the use of an emulator may prevent the activation of certain sophisticated malicious samples.

Before identification of the most indicative symptoms, feature extraction and selection needs to be performed [7, 8].

We have performed feature selection as a separate step, in which we have evaluated features usefulness based on the following techniques: Correlation Attribute Evaluator, CFS Subset Evaluator, Gain Ratio Attribute Evaluator, Information Gain Attribute Evaluator, and OneR Feature Evaluator.

We have chosen feature selection techniques due to their difference in observing usefulness of features as they are based either on statistical importance or information gain measure. Following, the list of feature selection algorithms that we have used:

- Correlation Attribute Evaluator calculates the worth of an attribute by measuring the correlation between it and the class.
- CfsSubsetEval calculates the worth of a subset of attributes by considering the individual predictive ability of each feature along with the degree of redundancy between them. Subsets of features that are highly correlated with the class while having low intercorrelation are preferred.
- Gain Ratio Attribute Evaluator calculates the worth of an attribute by measuring the gain ratio with respect to the class.
- Information Gain Attribute Evaluator calculates the worth of an attribute by measuring the information gain with respect to the class.
- OneR Feature Evaluation calculates the worth of an attribute by using the OneR classifier, which uses the minimum-error attribute for prediction.

In order to validate the usefulness of selected features we have used the following detection algorithms having different approach to detection: Naive Bayes, Logistic Regression, and J48 Decision Tree. While most of the steps of the proposed approach are executed offline (i.e., on machines equipped with extensive computational resources), the

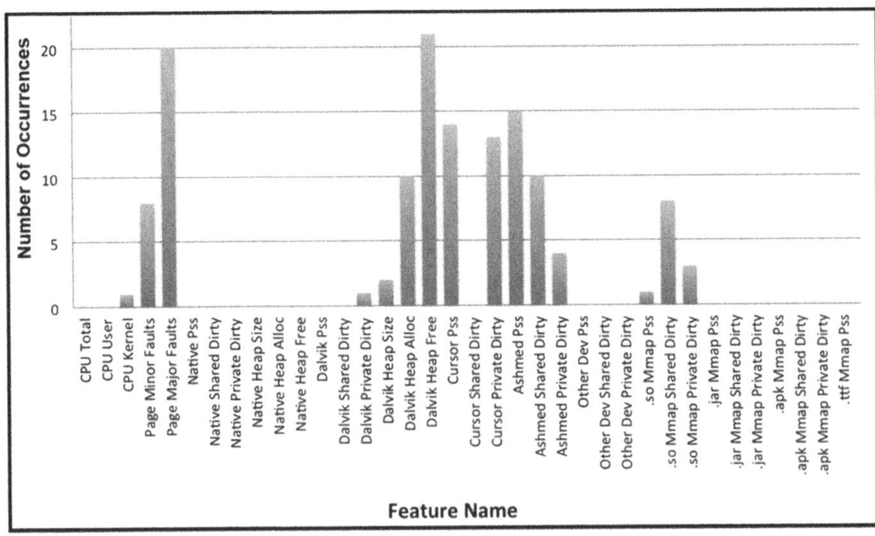

Fig. 7. Frequency of occurrence of features among top 5 of the most indicative features.

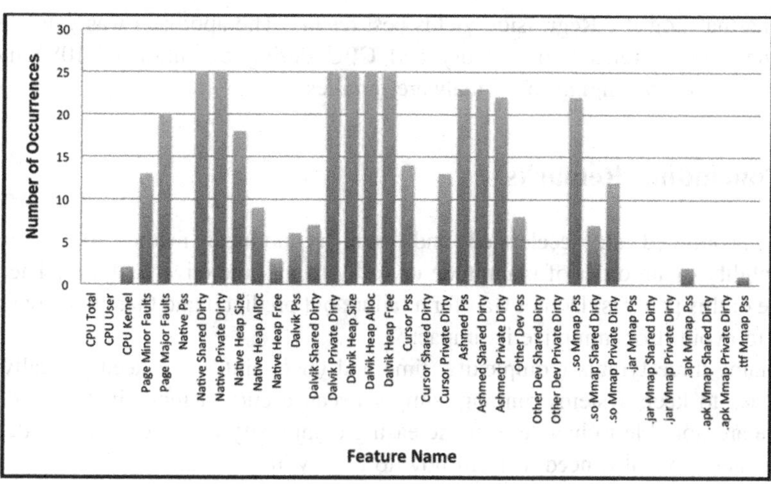

Fig. 8. Frequency of occurrence of features among top 15 of the most indicative features.

classification algorithm will be executed on the mobile devices; thus, it needs to be compatible with their limited resources. This is the reason why we also take into account the complexity of algorithms, and use the ones with low complexity.

Feature selection results are illustrated in Figs. 7 and 8 where the number of occurrences in top 5 or 15 of most indicative features is shown, respectively [10].

Based on these results, we have selected seven features out of 53 that practically give equal or higher probability of malware detection in terms of precision, recall and F-measure (harmonic mean of precision and recall) than the entire set of features (see Table 1). Furthermore, effectiveness of three different classifiers has been compared

Table 1. Performance of the classifiers when different number of features are considered.

		Model		
		Initial	**Max. F-measure**	**Optimized**
Naive Bayes	Precision	0.79	0.84	0.84
	Recall	0.76	0.83	0.83
	F-measure	0.77	0.83	0.83
	No. of features	53	7	7
Logistic Regression	Precision	0.84	0.86	0.84
	Recall	0.84	0.86	0.84
	F-measure	0.83	0.86	0.84
	No. of features	53	38	7
J48 Decision Tree	Precision	–	–	0.83
	Recall	–		0.83
	F-measure	–	–	0.82
	No. of features	–	–	6

indicating that Logistic Regression yields best results. The approach was validated by using the features related to memory and CPU during execution of 1080 mobile malware samples belonging to 25 malware families.

10 Concluding Remarks

We have outlined an accelerated and more economical method of improving dependability by an order of magnitude or so by using predictive analytics. The main message of this paper is: Do not wait for a failure but predict it and then you have better chance to avoid it or minimize its impact.

To tame three tyrants (complexity, time and uncertainty), we need radically new approaches to keep systems running, simply because current modeling methods and software are not able to handle ever-increasing complexity and ever-growing demand for timeliness. We also need to learn how to cope with uncertainty.

The proposed methodology based on predictive analytics provides an effective, efficient and economical approach to improve dependability, real time performance and security, highly needed, especially in the IoT environments where massive redundancy is usually too expensive and impractical.

With big data and machine learning, predictive analytics is charting a new paradigm shift where application of prediction methods will turn out to be successful in all aspects of computer and communication systems operation, be it performance, security, dependability, real time and others.

In addition to failure prediction and mitigation methodology, we have also presented two case studies on: (1) failure prediction in computer servers and (2) early malware detection where effectiveness of prediction methods has been demonstrated.

In the nutshell, applying the **AMP** principle: **A**nalyze the past, **M**onitor and control the present and **P**redict the future may significantly enhance dependability and other system properties.

Acknowledgement. I would like to acknowledge valuable contributions of my students Günther Hoffmann, Igor Kaitovic and Felix Salfner to the methodology and the case study on failure prediction. Alberto Ferrante and Jelena Milosevic contributed to the malware detection methodology and experiments.

References

1. Salfner, F., Lenk, M., Malek, M.: A survey of online failure prediction methods. ACM Comput. Surv. (CSUR) **42**, 10:1–10:42 (2010)
2. Hoffmann, G.A., Trivedi, K.S., Malek, M.: The best practice guide to resource forecasting for computing systems. IEEE Trans. Reliab. **56**(4), 615–628 (2007)
3. Hoffmann, G.A., Malek, M.: Call availability prediction in a telecommunication system: a data driven empirical approach, In: 25th IEEE Symposium on Reliable Distributed Systems (SRDS 2006), Leeds, UK (2006)

4. Kaitovic, I., Lukovic, S., Malek, M.: Proactive failure management in smart grids for improved resilience: a methodology for failure prediction and mitigation. In: IEEE GLOBECOM Workshops (SmartGrid Workshop), San Diego, USA, pp. 1–6 (2015)
5. Garcia, M.C., Sanz-Bobi, M.A., del Pico, J.: SIMAP: Intelligent System for Predictive Maintenance: Application to the health condition monitoring of a windturbine gearbox. Comput. Ind. **57**, 552–568 (2006)
6. Kaitovic, I., Malek, M.: Optimizing failure prediction to maximize availability, In: 13th International Conference on Autonomic Computing, Würzburg, Germany (2016)
7. Guyon, I., Elisseeff, A.: An introduction to variable and feature selection. ACM J. Mach. Learn. Res. **3**, 1157–1182 (2003)
8. Liu, H., Yu, L.: Toward integrating feature selection algorithms. IEEE Trans. Knowl. Data Eng. **17**(4), 491–502 (2005)
9. Milosevic, J., Malek, M., Ferrante, A.: A friend or a foe? detecting malware using memory and CPU features. In: 13th International Conference on Security and Cryptography (SECRYPT 2016), Lisbon, Portugal, pp. 73–84 (2016)
10. Milosevic, J., Ferrante, A., Malek, M., What Does the Memory Say? Towards the most indicative features for efficient malware detection, In: 13th Annual IEEE Consumer Communications and Networking Conference (CCNC 2016), Las Vegas, NV, USA. IEEE Communication Society (2016)

Modelling and Specification

Modeling and Monitoring of Hierarchical State Machines in Scala

Klaus Havelund and Rajeev Joshi(✉)

Jet Propulsion Laboratory, California Institute of Technology, Pasadena, USA
{klaus.havelund,rajeev.joshi}@jpl.nasa.gov

Abstract. Hierarchical State Machines (HSMs) are widely used in the design and implementation of spacecraft flight software. However, the traditional approach to using HSMs involves graphical languages (such as UML statecharts) from which implementation code is generated (e.g. in C or C^{++}). This is driven by the fact that state transitions in an HSM can result in execution of action code, with associated side-effects, which is implemented by code in the target implementation language. Due to this indirection, early analysis of designs becomes difficult. We propose an internal Scala DSL for writing HSMs, which makes them short, readable and easy to work with during the design phase. Writing the HSM models in Scala also allows us to use an expressive monitoring framework (also in Scala) for checking temporal properties over the HSM behaviors. We show how our approach admits writing *reactive monitors* that send messages to the HSM when certain sequences of events have been observed, e.g., to inject faults under certain conditions, in order to check that the system continues to operate correctly. This work is part of a larger project exploring the use of a modern high-level programming language (Scala) for modeling and verification.

1 Introduction

Hierarchical State Machines (HSMs) [13] are used extensively in the flight software that runs on spacecraft developed by NASA's Jet Propulsion Laboratory (JPL). The current practice is (depending on programmer taste) either to work textually and directly write low-level implementation code in C (which is hard to write and read), or work graphically and automatically synthesize C code from graphical HSM diagrams. In both cases it becomes difficult to prototype and execute (test) design choices during early development because the use of C forces introduction of low-level implementation details, hampering comprehension and analysis. Graphical formalisms are specifically not well suited for mixing control states and non-trivial code to be executed as part of transition actions for example. In this paper, we propose a method that allows HSMs to be

The research performed was carried out at Jet Propulsion Laboratory, California Institute of Technology, under a contract with the National Aeronautics and Space Administration.

A. Romanovsky and E.A. Troubitsyna (Eds.): SERENE 2017, LNCS 10479, pp. 21–36, 2017.
DOI: 10.1007/978-3-319-65948-0_2

implemented as an internal Domain-Specific Language (iDSL) in the high-level Scala programming language. Using an internal DSL allows us to express the HSM control state model and the code used in transitions all within the same language, which makes it easier to explore different design choices. We use Scala because it offers features that allow iDSLs to be implemented elegantly, including implicit functions, partial functions, call-by-name arguments, and dot-free method calls. We show how our iDSL for HSMs can be used with Daut (Data automata) [14], a library for writing monitors, thus allowing us to check temporal properties over the executions of an HSM. Daut offers a combination of flat state machines and a form of temporal logic, and furthermore allows monitoring of data parameterized events. An interesting feature of our approach is the ability to write *reactive monitors*, which allow the injection of specific events to the HSM when certain temporal properties are satisfied. This work is part of a long-term project exploring the use of a modern high-level programming language for writing models and properties, as well as programs.

The focus of this paper is the modeling and analysis of a single HSM, a situation typically facing a programmer responsible for a single module in a larger system. The modeling and analysis of multiple HSMs executing in parallel and communicating asynchronously via message passing over prioritized queues is described in [16]. Other topics not touched upon (and not used at JPL) are orthogonal regions, history states, and do-activities. The contributions of the paper are as follows. (1) We provide an elegant implementation of an internal Scala DSL for HSMs. (2) We show how single HSMs can be tested with the internal Daut monitoring DSL, which supports data parameterized monitors. This illustrates two forms of state machine DSLs, useful for different purposes. Each DSL is implemented in less than 200 lines of code. (3) We show how Daut monitors can be used to write reactive monitors that allow test scenarios to be described more conveniently. In [16], we extend the framework developed here to model multi-threaded systems with multiple HSMs, define a DSL for writing constraint-based test scenarios, and apply our approach to a real-life case study.

The paper is organized as follows. Section 2 describes related work. Section 3 introduces an example at an informal high level, and presents part of the implementation as an HSM in the Scala HSM iDSL. Section 4 outlines how the HSM is tested through monitoring with the Daut iDSL. Section 5 outlines how the HSM iDSL is implemented. Section 6 outlines how the Daut iDSL is implemented. Finally, Sect. 7 concludes the paper.

2 Related Work

The state pattern [11] is commonly used for modeling state machines in object-oriented programming languages. A state machine is implemented by defining each individual state as a derived class of the state pattern interface, and implementing state transitions as methods. The state pattern does not support hierarchical state machines. A variant of the state pattern to cover HSMs for C and C^{++} is described in [21]. This is a very comprehensive implementation compared to our less than 200 lines of code. The Akka framework provides features for concurrent programming and fault protection for the JVM, and in particular it includes a library for writing non-hierarchical finite state machines (FSM) in Scala [1]. The Daut iDSL for monitoring event sequences is related to numerous runtime verification frameworks, including [3,4,6,7,12,15,19]. An approach to use state charts for monitoring is described in [10]. The Umple framework [2] advocates, as we do, an approach to unifying modeling and programming, although it differs by having the modeling language being distinct from the programming language. The system is interesting because it allows updates to the model and the program in the same environment, while supporting visualization of the textual models. In contrast our DSLs are internal, completely eliminating the distinction between modeling language and programming language. Other internal Scala monitoring DSLs have been developed [5,15]. Daut itself is a simplification of the earlier TraceContract monitoring framework in Scala [5].

A standard way of formally verifying state machines is to encode them in the input language for, say, a model checker. However, this creates a gap between the modeling language and the implementation language. Model checkers have been developed for programming languages, for example Java PathFinder [17]. $P^{\#}$ [8] is an extension of $C^{\#}$ with concurrently executing non-hierarchical state machines, communicating asynchronously using message passing. It is inspired by the P external DSL [9] for modeling and programming in the same language, translated to C. $P^{\#}$ supports specification of environment and monitors as state machines. However, such monitors do not support the temporal logic notation or data parameterized event monitoring that Daut does.

3 Hierarchical State Machines in Scala

Example. In this section, we illustrate our ideas with an example. The example is based on a simple HSM for taking images with a camera. In our example, the HSM can receive a TAKE_IMAGE(d) request, where d denotes the exposure duration. It responds to this request by sending a command to power on the camera, and waiting until the camera is ready. It then opens the shutter for the specified exposure duration (using a timer service which generates a timeout event after a specified period). Following this, it optionally takes a dark exposure[1] with the shutter closed (but only if the ambient temperature is above a specified threshold). Finally, it saves the image data, and powers off the camera. Although this is a toy example, it serves to illustrate the key ideas in our approach. In a related paper [16], we describe the application of our approach to a real-life case study (a module that manages communication between the Curiosity rover and Earth).

HSM as a Diagram. Figure 1 shows a graphical view of the HSM that implements our simple imaging example. Following standard HSM notation, the filled out black circles indicate the initial substate that is entered whenever a parent

[1] A dark exposure allows determination of the noise from camera electronics, so that this can be subtracted from the acquired image.

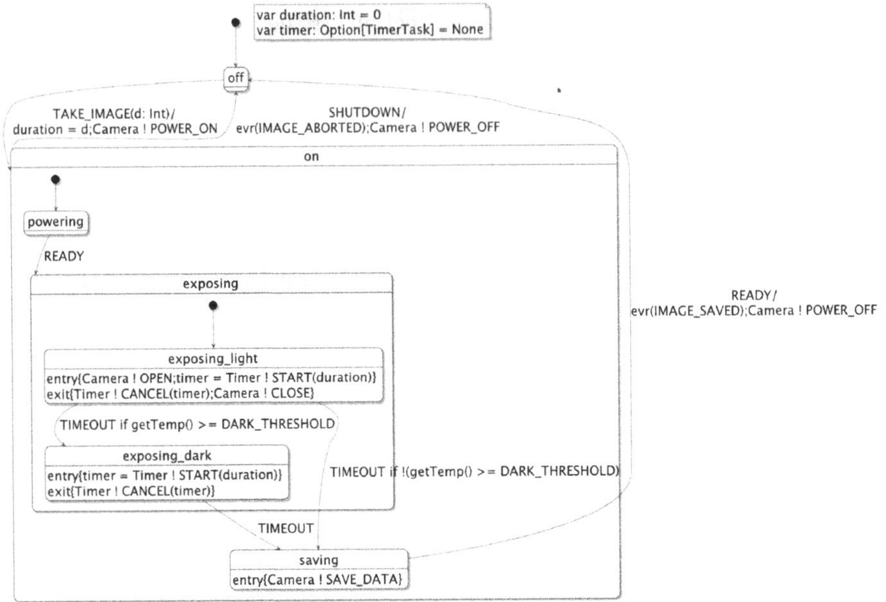

Fig. 1. HSM for imaging example

state is entered. (Thus, for instance, a transition to the on state ends with the HSM in the powering state.) Associated with each state are also two optional code fragments, called the *entry* and *exit* actions. The *entry* action is executed whenever the HSM transitions into a state, whereas the *exit* action is executed whenever the HSM transitions out of a state. Finally, the labeled arrows between states show the transitions that are caused in response to events received by the HSM. A label has the form EVENT/code, which denotes that the transition is triggered when the HSM receives the specified EVENT. In response, the HSM transitions to the target state, and executes the specified code fragment (which is optional). As an example, suppose the HSM is in state exposing_dark, and it receives the event SHUTDOWN (for which a transition is defined in the parent on state). This would cause the HSM to perform the following actions (in order): (1) the *exit* action for the state exposing_light, (2) the *exit* action for the state on, (3) the actions associated with the event handler evr(IMAGE_ABORTED) ; Camera ! POWER_OFF, and the (4) the *entry* action for the state off.

For our imaging example, the HSM works as follows. As shown in the figure, the HSM is associated with two variables: an integer-valued variable duration, which denotes the duration of the exposure when an imaging request is made, and the variable timer, of type Option[TimerTask]), which denotes whether there is an outstanding timer for which the HSM is waiting. The system starts off in the off state (marked initial). In the off state, the system responds only to a TAKE_IMAGE(d) event (where d is an integer). On receipt of this event, the system saves the requested exposure duration d in the state variable

```
trait Event
case class TAKE_IMAGE(duration: Int) extends Event
case object SAVE_DATA extends Event
...
class ImagingHsm extends SimpleMslHsm {
  var duration: Int = 0
  var timer: Option[TimerTask] = None

  initial(off)

  object off extends state() {
    when {
      case TAKE_IMAGE(d: Int) => on exec {
       duration = d ; Camera ! POWER_ON
      }
    }
  }

  object on extends state() {
    when {
      case SHUTDOWN => off exec {
       evr(IMAGE_ABORTED)
       Camera ! POWER_OFF
      }
    }
  }

  object powering extends state(on, true) {
    when { case READY => exposing }
  }

  object exposing extends state(on) {}

  object exposing_light extends state(exposing, true) {
    entry { Camera ! OPEN
            timer = Timer ! START(duration) }
    exit { Timer ! STOP(timer) ; Camera ! CLOSE }
    when {
      case TIMEOUT => {
        if (getTemp() >= DARK_THRESHOLD)
          exposing_dark
        else saving
      }
    }
  }

  object exposing_dark extends state(exposing) {
    entry { timer = Timer ! START(duration) }
    exit { Timer ! STOP(timer) }
    when {
      case TIMEOUT => saving
    }
  }

  object saving extends state(on) {
    entry { Camera ! SAVE_DATA }
    when {
      case READY => off exec {
        evr(IMAGE_SAVED) ; Camera ! POWER_OFF
      }
    }
  }
}
```

Fig. 2. The HSM for the imaging example in our internal DSL

duration, sends a request to the camera to power on (indicated by the action Camera!POWER_ON), and then transitions to the on state, which is a superstate, so the HSM ends up in the powering state. Here it waits until it gets a READY event from the camera, upon which it enters the exposing superstate, which in turn causes it to enter the initial exposing_light substate. The entry action for this state sends a request to the camera to OPEN the shutter, and then starts a timer for the specified duration (which was saved on receipt of the command). When the timer expires, the HSM receives a TIMEOUT event, which causes it to either transition to the exposing_dark state (if the ambient temperature is at least the DARK_THRESHOLD), or the saving state (if temperature is below the DARK_THRESHOLD). Whenever it is in a substate of the on state, the HSM can respond to a SHUTDOWN request, which causes it to power off the camera and transition back to the off state.

HSM in Scala. Figure 2 shows the formalization, in our internal Scala DSL, of the HSM in Fig. 1. The model first defines the Event type, denoting the set of events that trigger transitions in the HSM. The state machine itself is defined as the class ImagingHsm extending SimpleMslHsm which in turn extends the HSM trait defined by our iDSL, which is parameterized by the type of events sent to the HSM. The local state variable duration records the duration when an imaging request is received; this duration is used for both the light exposure (with shutter open) and the (optional) dark exposure (with shutter closed). The variable timer records the value of any timer for which the HSM is waiting (the value is None if there is no timer currently in progress). In the off state, the event handler for the TAKE_IMAGE(d) event causes the HSM to execute the action code which records the value d in variable duration and sends a POWER_ON request to the camera. The HSM then transitions to the on superstate, and in turn to its initial substate, the powering state. (In our iDSL, initial substates are denoted by the keyword true as the second argument to the extends state(..) declaration.) In the powering state, receipt of the READY event causes a transition to the exposing state, and in turn to the exposing_light substate, where the entry actions result in a request to OPEN the shutter and start a timer for the specified duration. The rest of the example is similar. Since graphical formalisms are useful for human comprehension, we have developed a tool based on Scalameta (see http://scalameta.org) that generates a visual representation from the HSM description in our Scala iDSL. This tool generated Fig. 1 directly from the code in Fig. 2.

During execution, the HSM generates a *log* that contains *event reports*, generated for monitoring purposes. Our HSM framework contains special calls of the form evr(E) which generates the event E, which can be used in monitors. For instance, as shown in Fig. 2, when a SHUTDOWN request is received in state on, the HSM generates the IMAGE_ABORTED log event. Similarly, the Timer service generates events when a timer is started, is fired or is stopped. (These timer events are used in the monitors described in the following section.) Fig. 3 shows a sample log of the HSM corresponding to a test scenario is which a TAKE_IMAGE(7) is requested at time 101, and completes normally, followed by a TAKE_IMAGE(10) requested at time 200, which is terminated by sending a SHUTDOWN request at time 205. This log can be checked by the Daut monitoring engine to verify that the HSM execution obeys given temporal properties.

```
101:RECEIVED_REQUEST(TAKE_IMAGE(7))
104:POWERING_ON
104:SHUTTER_IS_OPENED
104:TIMER_STARTED
111:TIMER_FIRED
111:TIMER_CANCELED
111:SHUTTER_IS_CLOSED
111:TIMER_STARTED
118:TIMER_FIRED
118:TIMER_CANCELED
120:SAVING_STARTED
120:IMAGE_SAVED
120:POWERING_OFF
```

```
200:RECEIVED_REQUEST(TAKE_IMAGE(10))
203:POWERING_ON
203:SHUTTER_IS_OPENED
203:TIMER_STARTED
205:SHUTDOWN_REQUESTED
205:TIMER_CANCELED
205:SHUTTER_IS_CLOSED
205:IMAGE_ABORTED
205:POWERING_OFF
```

Fig. 3. Sample event log for imaging example

HSM Execution. As mentioned in the introduction, the focus of this presentation is the modeling and analysis of single HSMs. The modeling and analysis of multiple HSMs executing in parallel is described in [16], where we model the full complexity of the implementation, such as message priorities, queue enabling and disabling, test scenario specifications, and analysis of timing properties. The HSM is composed with an *environment*, which *submits* events to, and receives requests from, the HSM as explained in the following. The environment contains a mutable set of events, which are waiting to be submitted to the state machine. This set can be augmented with new events from a test script and the HSM. In each iteration, the environment picks a random event from the set and submits it to the state machine. The state machine executes as far as it can, possibly sending new requests back to the environment, simulating communication with other state machines. The environment in addition keeps a mapping from requests it can receive to operations on the event set. For example, if the environment receives a timer!START(d) request, it adds a TIMEOUT event to the event set. This TIMEOUT event will then eventually be submitted back to the state machine after d seconds have elapsed. The notation recv ! E in the HSM denotes the sending of a request E to the receiver recv (via the environment). In our example, the receiver Camera denotes the camera hardware, whereas the receiver Timer denotes the timer service.

4 Monitoring with Daut

Daut (Data Automata) [14] is a simple internal Scala DSL for writing monitors on event streams. Daut, like many runtime verification systems, offers two major capabilities that HSMs do not: (i) the ability to track the state behavior for multiple instances of some data (spawning automata), and (ii) a convenient temporal logic formalism on top of a state machine formalism. In this section, we show how to use the Daut monitoring library to specify and monitor that certain temporal properties are satisfied by the executing HSM. We also show how one can use the monitoring framework to build *reactive monitors*, which allow us to inject events into the HSM when certain temporal patterns are met.

Figure 4 shows four temporal property monitors, representing requirements that the imaging HSM must satisfy. Each property is modeled as a class extending the MSLMonitor class, which itself is defined as an extension of the Daut Monitor class, which is parameterized with the type EventReport of event reports being monitored. The Monitor class defines the features of Daut. The MSLMonitor class defines additional functions that simplify writing monitors for our example. The monitors receive event reports as they are generated by the HSM and update their internal state accordingly, reporting any observed violations.

The first property, TimerUse, checks that once a timer is started, it should either fire or be canceled before another timer is started. The body of the class is an always-formula. The function always takes as argument a partial function from events to monitor states. In this case, whenever a TIMER_STARTED is observed, the monitor moves to a watch state, in which it is waiting for either a TIMER_FIRED or TIMER_CANCELED event – another TIMER_STARTED event is an error if observed before then.

The second property, TimerState, checks that if a timer is currently running (has been started but has not yet fired or been canceled), then the HSM must be

```
class MSLMonitor extends Monitor[EventReport] {
  def inState(name: String) = during(EnterState(name))(ExitState(name))
  ...
}

class TimerUse extends MSLMonitor {
  always {
    case TIMER_STARTED ⇒ watch {
      case TIMER_FIRED | TIMER_CANCELED ⇒ ok
      case TIMER_STARTED ⇒ error("Timer started before previous cancelation")
    }
  }
}

class TimerState extends MSLMonitor {
  val timerOn = during(TIMER_STARTED)(TIMER_FIRED, TIMER_CANCELED)
  val inExposing = inState("exposing")

  invariant("TimerState") {
    timerOn ==⇒ inExposing
  }
}

class ImageRequest extends MSLMonitor {
  always {
    case RECEIVED_REQUEST(TAKE_IMAGE(d)) ⇒ hot {
      case IMAGE_SAVED | IMAGE_ABORTED ⇒ ok
      case RECEIVED_REQUEST(TAKE_IMAGE(_)) ⇒ error("Image was not saved or aborted")
    }
  }
}

class ImgReactiveMonitor extends MSLMonitor {
  always {
    case POWERING_ON ⇒ watch {
      case SHUTTER_IS_OPENED ⇒ perhaps { Env.delayEvent(2, SHUTDOWN) }
    }
  }
}
```

Fig. 4. Monitors for the imaging example

in the exposing state, meaning in any of its substates. The Boolean expression occurring as argument to the invariant function gets evaluated in each new state the HSM enters. The notation p ==> q denotes implication and is interpreted as !p || q. The property uses the during construct to define the period during which the timer is active, namely in between an observed TIMER_STARTED, and either a TIMER_FIRED or TIMER_CANCELED event report is observed. Also the inState function defined in class MSLMonitor is defined using the during function, here tracking the event reports indicating respectively entering and subsequently exiting a state.

The third property, ImageRequest, is similar to the TimerUse property in form, and checks that once an image request has been received, then eventually the image must be saved or the imaging must be aborted. It is an error if another image request is received before then. The hot operator causes Daut to check that the image saving or image abortion is seen before the end of the execution (Daut reports an error if there are any hot states active at the end of the trace).

We have just discussed how we can use Daut to specify and monitor temporal properties. Since Daut is a Scala library, we can write Daut monitors to also take actions during a run, such as causing new events to be sent to the HSM, thus affecting the resulting behavior. We refer to such Daut monitors as *reactive monitors*. The last monitor, ImgReactiveMonitor, in Fig. 4 is an example of a reactive monitor, in this case randomly sending a SHUTDOWN event to the HSM whenever the monitor sees a POWERING_ON event followed by a SHUTTER_IS_OPENED event report. The perhaps function takes a code fragment (call-by-name) and randomly decides whether or not to execute it. In our example, this monitor results in a SHUTDOWN event being sent to the HSM 2 s after the SHUTTER_IS_OPENED event is seen. In the example execution trace shown in Fig. 3, there are two occurrences where the monitor sees a POWERING_ON followed by an SHUTTER_IS_OPENED event report. The perhaps function decided to execute the action after the second instance of the SHUTTER_IS_OPENED event report (which occurs at time 203), issuing a SHUTDOWN at time 205.

5 HSM Implementation

The concept of a hierarchical state machine is implemented as the Scala trait HSM (a trait is similar to an interface in Java), which a user-defined HSM must extend, and which is parameterized with the type Event of events that can be submitted to it:

```
trait HSM[Event] {...}
```

The HSM trait defines the following types and values used throughout:

```
type Code = Unit ⇒ Unit
type Target = (state, Code)
type Transitions = PartialFunction[Event, Target]
val noTransitions: Transitions = {case _ if false ⇒ null}
val skip: Code = (x: Unit) ⇒ {}
```

Code represents code fragments (with no arguments and returning no result), that are to be executed on event transitions, and in entry and exit blocks. A Target represents the target state and the code to be executed when a transition is taken. Transitions represents the transitions leading out of a state, encoded as partial functions from events to targets. Applied to an event a transition function will either be undefined on that event (corresponding to the transition not being enabled), or it will return a target. The default transition function from a state is represented by noTransitions which is undefined for any event. Finally, skip represents the code with no effect.

We can now present the state class encoding the states in a state machine. The contents of this class can be divided into the *DSL "syntax"*, permitting a user to create a state, and the DSL *implementation*. The DSL syntax, including its update on internal variables, can be presented as follows:

```
case class state(parent: state = null, init: Boolean = false) {
  var entryCode: Code = skip
  var exitCode: Code = skip
  var transitions: Transitions = noTransitions
  ...
  def entry(code: ⇒ Unit): Unit = {entryCode = (x: Unit) ⇒ code}
  def exit(code: ⇒ Unit): Unit = {exitCode = (x: Unit) ⇒ code}
  def when(ts: Transitions): Unit = {transitions = ts}

  implicit def state2Target(s: state): Target = (s, skip)
  implicit def state2Exec(s: state) = new {
    def exec(code: ⇒ Unit) = (s, (x: Unit) ⇒ code) }
}
```

The class is parameterized with the parent state (if it is a sub-state), and whether it is an initial state of the parent state (false by default). The class declares three variables, holding respectively the entry code (to be executed when entering the state), the exit code (to be executed when leaving the state), and the transition function, all initialized to default values. Three methods for updating these are furthermore defined. The code parameters to the first two functions entry and exit are declared as "call by name", meaning that at call time a code argument will not be evaluated, and will instead just be stored as functions in the appropriate variables. Since a method application $f(e)$ in Scala can be written using curly brackets: $f\{e\}$, we achieve the convenient code-block syntax for writing calls of these methods, making these methods appear as added syntax to Scala.

Finally two implicit functions are defined. An implicit function f will be applied to any expression e by the compiler if e occurs in a context $C[e]$ which does not type check, but $C[f(e)]$ does type check. Implicit functions are useful for defining elegant DSLs. In this case, the implicit function state2Target lifts a state to a target, allowing us to just write states as targets on transitions (and no code), and the function state2Exec lifts a state to an anonymous object, defining an exec method, allowing transition right-hand sides like: top exec {table.insert(w)}. The above definitions show the HSM syntax and how it is used to define states and transitions. In addition, the function initial is used for identifying the initial state in the HSM:

```
def initial(s: state): Unit = {current = s.getInnerMostState}
```

The function getInnerMostState is defined in the class state as follows, along with a method for finding the super states of a state (needed for executing HSMs):

```
var initialState: state = null
if (parent != null && init) {parent.initialState = this}


def getInnerMostState: state =
  if (initialState == null) this else initialState.getInnerMostState
```

```
def getSuperStates: List[state] =
  (if (parent == null) Nil else parent.getSuperStates) ++ List(this)
```

When a state is created, if it is an initial state, the initialState variable of the parent is initialized with the just created state (this). When a state is the target of execution, the innermost initial state of that state is the one becoming active.

An HSM is at any point in time in a current state, and will potentially change state when an event is *submitted* to it from the environment. Current state and the event submission method are defined as follows.

```
var current: state = null

def submit(event: Event): Unit = {
  findTriggerHappyState(current, event) match {
    case None ⇒
    case Some(triggerState) ⇒
      val (transitionState,transitionCode) = triggerState.transitions(event)
      val targetState = transitionState.getInnerMostState
      val (exitStates, enterStates) = getExitEnter(current, targetState)
      for (s <− exitStates) s.exitCode()
      transitionCode()
      for (s <− enterStates) s.entryCode()
      current = targetState
  }}
```

When executed from the current state, and given the submitted event, the function call findTriggerHappyState(current, event) finds the innermost state containing (or being equal to) current, which is ready to transition on the event. The result is Option[state], where None represents that no such state exists. In case such a state exists, its transition function is applied to the event, obtaining a target (target state, and code to execute), then the innermost initial state of the target state is computed, and based on current and target state, we compute the list of states to exit and the list of states to enter via the call getExitEnter(current, targetState), whose implementation is straightforward and not shown. It computes the super states (listed top down) for respectively the from-state and the to-state, and then strips off the common prefix of the two lists. The remaining lists are the lists of states to exit and enter respectively. Now we can execute exit codes, the transition code itself, and entry codes. Note that requests sent by the state machine in these code fragments will go back to the *environment*, which then in later iterations will submit corresponding events back to the state machine, as explained earlier. For performance reasons, we want to avoid repeated computation of innermost state for a state, and the list of exit and entry states. Thus our implementation caches these so they are only computed once (this is done with an additional 20 lines of code, not shown here due to space limitations). We can now define the function for finding the innermost enclosing state of the current state, containing a transition function enabled for an event:

```
def findTriggerHappyState(s: state, event: Event): Option[state] =
  if (s.transitions.isDefinedAt(event)) Some(s) else
  if (s.parent == null) None else findTriggerHappyState(s.parent, event)
```

The function calls itself recursively up the parent chain until it finds a state whose transition function is defined on the event. For verification purposes, a function is defined for determining which state (by name, including super states) an HSM is in, matching against a regular expression:

```
def inState(regexp: String): Boolean = {
  current.getSuperStates.exists(_.name.matches(regexp))
}
```

The presented code is the implementation in its entirety, except for the following concepts (30 lines of code): (i) computing exit/enter state chains; (ii) caching of computations of innermost states and exit/enter state chains; (iii) the ability for the user to announce call-back functions to be called whenever a state is entered, exited, or the monitor reaches a quiescent state.

6 Daut Implementation

The general idea behind the implementation of Daut is described in [14] (although the version used in this work differs in minor ways), summarized here with the addition of temporal invariants (during and invariant). The class Monitor contains a variable holding at any point during monitoring the set (logic conjunction) of active monitor states[2]:

```
class Monitor[E <: AnyRef] {
  type Transitions = PartialFunction[E, Set[state]]
  var states: Set[state] = Set()
  ...
}
```

A state is an instance of the following class, which contains a variable holding the transitions out of the state, as well as a variable indicating whether it is an acceptance state (acc = true) or not (by default a state is an acceptance state).

```
trait state {
  var transitions: Transitions = noTransitions
  var acc: Boolean = true
  if (first) {states += this;first = false}

  def apply(event:E): Option[Set[state]] =
    if (transitions.isDefinedAt(event)) Some(transitions(event)) else None
```

[2] Note that there is some terminology overlap between the HSM DSL and the Daut DSL, e.g. the concepts of states and transitions, with similar meanings although not necessarily in the details. This works out due to a clear separation of name spaces in that HSMs and Daut monitors extend different classes (HSM and Monitor).

```
  def watch(ts:Transitions) {transitions = ts}
  def always(ts:Transitions) {transitions = ts andThen (_ + this)}
  def hot(ts:Transitions) {transitions = ts; acc = false}
  def next(ts:Transitions) {transitions = ts orElse {case _ ⇒ error}; acc=false}
}
```

The first state created in a monitor becomes the initial state, e.g. the always-state in our monitors. A state is applied (the apply method) to an event to return an optional set of results, and None if the state does not contain transitions defined for the event. In addition a collection of temporal methods are defined: watch, always, hot, and next. Other methods are defined in the actual system, including weaknext, until, and weakuntil, known from temporal logic. These methods take as argument a transition function and store it or a modification of it in the transitions variable of the state, and also set the acc variable for non-acceptance states. The Monitor class in addition defines a method for each of the temporal methods defined inside the state class for creating states of the corresponding temporality. We show one of these, the rest follow the same pattern:

```
def always(ts: Transitions) = new state { always(ts) }
```

The during[3] class is defined as a particular form of state. It contains a Boolean variable on, true when one of the e1 events has been observed but an e2 event has not yet been observed.

```
case class during(e1: E*)(e2: E*) extends state {
  states += this
  val begin = e1.toSet
  val end = e2.toSet
  var on: Boolean = false

  def startsTrue: during = {on = true; this} // allows interval initially true

  always {
    case e ⇒ if (begin.contains(e)) {on = true} else
             if (end.contains(e)) {on = false}
  }
}
```

We have seen how an object of class during can be used as a Boolean (e.g. timerOn in Fig. 4). This is made possible with the following implicit function:

```
implicit def liftInterval(iv: during): Boolean = iv.on
```

We finally illustrate how invariants are realized. A variable contains all declared invariants (as pairs of an error message, and the predicate itself). An invariant is declared with invariant(txt)(p) (where p is a call-by-name argument not evaluated before invariant is called), checked initially and after each event processing.

[3] The *during(P)(Q)* operator is inspired by the $[P, Q)$ operator in MaC [18].

```
var invariants: List[(String, Unit ⇒ Boolean)] = Nil

def invariant(e: String)(inv: ⇒ Boolean): Unit = {
    invariants \newcolon= (e, ((x: Unit) ⇒ inv))
    check(inv, e)
  }

def check(b: Boolean, e: String) : Unit = {if (!b) printErrorMessage(e)}
```

We finally show how event reports are issued with the verify method, and how monitoring is ended (given a finite trace) with the end method. Note how invariants are evaluated after each processed event.

```
def verify(event: E) {
  for (sourceState <− states) {
    sourceState(event) match {
      case None ⇒
      case Some(targetStates) ⇒
        statesToRemove += sourceState
        for (targetState <− targetStates) {
          targetState match {
            case 'error' ⇒ printErrorMessage()
            case 'ok' ⇒
            case _ ⇒ statesToAdd += targetState
          }}}}
  states −−= statesToRemove; states ++= statesToAdd
  statesToRemove = Set(); statesToAdd = Set()
  invariants foreach { case (e, inv) ⇒ check(inv(), e) }
}

def end() {
  val hotStates = states filter (!_.acc)
  if (!hotStates.isEmpty) {printErrorMessage();...}
}
```

7 Conclusion and Future Work

We have shown how HSMs can be elegantly modeled in an internal DSL in the Scala programming language. The iDSL has been illustrated with a simple example of an HSM used for taking images with a camera. We have additionally illustrated how an existing internal Scala DSL for monitoring was extended and applied to testing the HSM. In particular, our approach allows the definition of reactive monitors, which can send events to the HSM when certain temporal properties are satisfied, which makes it easier to write complex test cases. The code for each of these iDSLs is less than 200 lines, which makes it easier to validate their semantics. A more comprehensive validation would be to model an existing HSM (written in C) in our iDSL (as done in [16]), and compare execution logs on the same inputs. We have also developed a capability for generating graphical representations (used to generate Fig. 1) directly from the HSM description in our iDSL. The work illustrates how a high-level programming language can be used for modeling as well as programming, as part of a model-based engineering approach. We plan to support refinement of high-level models into low-level programs which can directly be translated into C code. We are working on extending our approach to support automated test-case generation (using an SMT solver) and formal verification of Scala programs using the Viper framework [20].

References

1. Akka FSMs. http://doc.akka.io/docs/akka/current/scala/fsm.html
2. Umple - Model-Oriented Programming. http://cruise.site.uottawa.ca/umple. Accessed 26 May 2017
3. Barringer, H., Falcone, Y., Havelund, K., Reger, G., Rydeheard, D.: Quantified event automata: towards expressive and efficient runtime monitors. In: Giannakopoulou, D., Méry, D. (eds.) FM 2012. LNCS, vol. 7436, pp. 68–84. Springer, Heidelberg (2012). doi:10.1007/978-3-642-32759-9_9
4. Barringer, H., Goldberg, A., Havelund, K., Sen, K.: Rule-based runtime verification. In: Steffen, B., Levi, G. (eds.) VMCAI 2004. LNCS, vol. 2937, pp. 44–57. Springer, Heidelberg (2004). doi:10.1007/978-3-540-24622-0_5
5. Barringer, H., Havelund, K.: TRACECONTRACT: a scala DSL for trace analysis. In: Butler, M., Schulte, W. (eds.) FM 2011. LNCS, vol. 6664, pp. 57–72. Springer, Heidelberg (2011). doi:10.1007/978-3-642-21437-0_7
6. Barringer, H., Rydeheard, D., Havelund, K.: Rule systems for run-time monitoring: from EAGLE to RuleR. J. Logic Comput. **20**(3), 675–706 (2010)
7. Basin, D., Klaedtke, F., Marinovic, S., Zălinescu, E.: Monitoring of temporal first-order properties with aggregations. Formal Methods Syst. Des. **46**(3), 262–285 (2015)
8. Deligiannis, P., Donaldson, A.F., Ketema, J., Lal, A., Thomson, P.: Asynchronous programming, analysis and testing with state machines. In: Proceedings of the 36th ACM SIGPLAN Conference on Programming Language Design and Implementation, PLDI 2015, pp. 154–164. ACM, New York (2015)
9. A. Desai, V. Gupta, E. Jackson, S. Qadeer, S. Rajamani, and D. Zufferey. P: Safe asynchronous event-driven programming. In Proceedings of PLDI '13, pages 321–332, 2013
10. Drusinsky, D.: Modeling and Verification using UML Statecharts, p. 400. Elsevier, Amsterdam (2006). ISBN-13: 978-0-7506-7949-7
11. Gamma, E., Helm, R., Johnson, R., Vlissides, J.: Design Patterns: Elements of Reusable Object-Oriented Software. Addison-Wesley, Boston (1995)
12. Hallé, S., Villemaire, R.: Runtime enforcement of web service message contracts with data. IEEE Trans. Serv. Comput. **5**(2), 192–206 (2012)
13. Harel, D.: Statecharts: A visual formalism for complex systems. Sci. Comput. Program. **8**(3), 231–274 (1987)
14. Havelund, K.: Data automata in Scala. In: Proceeding of the 8th International Symposium on Theoretical Aspects of Software Engineering (TASE 2014) (2014)

15. Havelund, K.: Rule-based runtime verification revisited. Int. J. Softw. Tools Technol. Transfer **17**(2), 143–170 (2015)
16. Havelund, K., Joshi, R.: Modeling rover communication using hierarchical state machines with Scala. In: TIPS 2017, May 2017. Accepted for publication
17. Havelund, K., Visser, W.: Program model checking as a new trend. STTT **4**(1), 8–20 (2002)
18. Kim, M., Viswanathan, M., Kannan, S., Lee, I., Sokolsky, O.: Java-MaC: a runtime assurance approach for Java programs. Formal Methods Syst. Des. **24**(2), 129–155 (2004)
19. Meredith, P., Jin, D., Griffith, D., Chen, F., Roşu, G.: An overview of the MOP runtime verification framework. STTT, pp. 1–41 (2011)
20. Müller, P., Schwerhoff, M., Summers, A.J.: Viper: a verification infrastructure for permission-based reasoning. In: Jobstmann, B., Leino, K.R.M. (eds.) VMCAI 2016. LNCS, vol. 9583, pp. 41–62. Springer, Heidelberg (2016). doi:10.1007/978-3-662-49122-5_2
21. Samek, M.: Practical UML statecharts in C/C++. In: Event-Driven Programming for Embedded Systems, 2nd edn. Newnes, MA, USA (2009)

Stochastic Activity Networks for the Verification of Knowledge Bases

Luke Martin(✉) and Alexander Romanovsky

Centre for Software Reliability, Newcastle University, Newcastle upon Tyne, UK
{luke.burton,alexander.romanovsky}@ncl.ac.uk

Abstract. There has been much focus on applying graphical techniques to analyse various kinds of structural errors in knowledge bases as a method of verification and reliability estimation. The most commonly applied technique has been Petri nets, or variations thereof, in achieving this objective with much success. However, although this approach has been considerably useful for verifying rules in earlier generations of knowledge-based systems, it is unclear if this approach can continue to be as useful, or indeed accessible, for verifying current or later generations of KBS, which have significantly larger, more complex, probabilistic rule sets. It has recently been argued that stochastic Petri nets can be successfully applied to continue with knowledge base verification, although, this method has required extensive and complex modifications that has led into proposals for fuzzy Petri nets. It is the view of this paper that the stochastic activity network formalism can provide a potentially useful alternative for the verification of fuzzy rule sets and can be more efficient and effective than complex derivatives of Petri nets. We present a high-level discussion of how this approach could be applied and used to analyse knowledge bases in ensuring that there are free of structural errors.

1 Introduction

Knowledge-based systems (KBSs) have been widely used in many real-world applications and are fast emerging as the latest generation of embedded and real-time systems. A KBS is often defined as an expert system that emulates human reasoning capabilities for making decisions for a range of complex problems within specific domain areas [1]. The core component of a KBS is the knowledge base (or rule base), which lists a range of domain specific knowledge as inference rules. Typically, these rules are built into the knowledge base gradually over an extensive period of time resulting in an incremental and evolutionary style of development for this component. It is due, in part, to this construction process and also as a result of conflicting information from experts and varying perspectives from knowledge engineers that a knowledge base can contain several structural errors.

As addressed in [11, 13], structural errors can be classified as: redundancy (repeated rules), inconsistency (rules which conflict), incompleteness (rules that are missing) and circularity (infinite inference). Each of these clearly has adverse consequences for reliability and a method for detecting these errors is required for ensuring integrity. Researchers have been proposing the use of Petri nets and their extensions to model

A. Romanovsky and E.A. Troubitsyna (Eds.): SERENE 2017, LNCS 10479, pp. 37–44, 2017.
DOI: 10.1007/978-3-319-65948-0_3

non-fuzzy rule-based systems for earlier generations of KBSs [8, 10, 14]. While these were useful at the time, knowledge bases have since become more probabilistic and require formal representations that can capture this. This has in fact led to stochastic variations of Petri-nets being applied [12] and while these provide various advantages, it begs the question as to why stochastic activity networks (SANs), as stochastic extensions of Petri nets, have not been considered when they could, in principle, potentially provide a much more efficient and scalable alternative. This question has motivated the work of this paper to explore the application of SANs for this purpose. As the scope of this paper is limited to developing a an approach, a high level description of the method is given with preliminary results, with future work focusing on expanding the approach and deriving a more complete set of results.

The remainder of the paper is organized as follows: Sect. 2 discusses related work of rule base verification and fuzzy rule reasoning with high-level Petri nets and provides a brief overview of the SANs formalism. Section 3 presents types of structural errors in a rule base and the issues of rule base verification and reliability estimation. Section 4 addresses our SANs-based approach and the phases of rule normalization, rule transformation, and rule verification. We conclude the paper with our future research in Sect. 5.

2 Related Work

As addressed in [11], structural errors in a KBS could be classified as redundancy, conflict, and incompleteness. Each of these affects the reliability of a KBS and must be addressed and repaired. In the case of redundancy, it includes redundancy in pairs of rules, subsumed in pairs of rules, redundancy in chains of inference, and subsumed in chains of inference. In the case of conflict, it includes conflict with initial facts, conflict between the deduced facts, and circularity. In the case of incompleteness, it includes unnecessary inputs, dead-ends, unreachable goals, and missing facts. Besides various mechanisms of rule base verification, there are many researches targeted to using the graphical and mathematical natures of Petri nets (PN) for fuzzy rule reasoning. Researchers have been proposing the extension of Petri nets to fuzzy Petri nets (FPN) and using FPN to model and reasoning fuzzy rule-based systems. We will briefly summarise some of these mechanisms in this section.

2.1 Rule Verification

Nguyen et al. [13] describes potential problems about a knowledge base and introduces their tool, CHECK, detecting errors on the Lockheed Expert System (LES). The LES is a rule-based building tool, which represents factual data in its frame database and heuristic and control knowledge in its production rule. The LES allows knowledge engineers to use both data-driven and goal-driven rules. In the knowledge base, consistency and completeness must be insured. There are five steps to implement the rule checking. At the first three steps, CHECK finds the relationship of clauses and records the information in 2D table of interclause relationship. The some problems can be detected by using the table to deduce rule relationships, SAME (redundant), CONFLICT, SUBSET (subsumption), SUPERSET (subsumption), UNNECESSARY CLAUSE, or DIFFERENT. Then, find the properties of unreachable conclusions, dead-end goals, and dead-end IF conditions in the 2D table. The 2D table also can generate the dependency chart for detecting the circularity. At last, this paper figures out how certainty factors affect the checking. Zhang and In [10], it was noted that Nazareth proposed an approach based on Petri nets to verify a rule-based system. His approach adds new arcs backward to all the input places and a new input place to ensure every transition will fire at most once and ensure the conditions will hold even if the transition has fired. He compares the difference of marking before and after firing any sequence of transitions. If a place has no token before firing any firing sequence and the place has two tokens after firing two individual sequences of transitions, then the system has redundancy or conflict. If a place has one token before firing a sequence of transitions and has two tokens after firing a sequence of transitions, then the system has circularity. If a place has no token before all transitions are fired and still has no token after all transitions are fired, then it has a dead end or unreachable goal.

2.2 Stochastic Activity Networks

Stochastic activity networks (SANs) are stochastic extensions to Petri nets and to the best of the author's knowledge have not been applied for verifying rules of KBSs. SANs have the modelling power of Petri nets and allow a compact representation of systems. They consist of: places, activities, input gates and output gates. - Places can be seen as a state of the modelled system. Each place of a SAN contains a certain number of tokens which represents the marking of the place. Places are represented graphically by circles. - Activities represent actions of the modelled system that could take some specified amount of time to complete. They are similar to transitions in ordinary Petri nets, and are of two types: timed and instantaneous. Timed activities have durations that impact the performance of the modelled system such as a packet transmission time. This duration can be stochastic. Instantaneous activities represent actions that complete or fire immediately when enabled in the system. Activities are graphically represented by thick lines for the timed ones, and thin lines for the instantaneous ones. Unlike autonomous Petri nets, SANs allow the use of uncertainties associated with the completion of an activity. It is called Case probabilities, and is represented graphically by small circles on the right side of an activity (see Fig. 2). Each case stands for a possible outcome, such as a routing choice in a network, or a failure mode in a faulty system. So each activity in the SAN can have a probability distribution associated with its cases. Moreover, this distribution can depend on the marking of the network at the moment of completion of an activity. This shows how SAN could be a high level modelling formalism.

3 Structural Errors in Rule-Based Systems

In this paper, we are concerned in finding structural errors and the set of rules causing these, which affects the reliability of the knowledge base. The reasons of structural errors may be due to rule conflicting, missing/mismatched condition, and conclusion. As pointed out in [7, 11–13], we have identified four kinds of rules, which may lead to structural errors. They are redundancy, inconsistency, incompleteness, and circularity rules. Inconsistency rules result in conflict, which is the direct source of incorrect rule derivation. Redundancy rules increase the size of rule base and cause non-necessary reasoning. Incompleteness rules prohibit rule bases from activating certain normal rule derivation. Circularity rules will force the rule base to run into an infinite loop of reasoning. Following, we describe those structural errors and give example to express.

Inconsistency. Inconsistency results in a conflict of facts and must be resolved for correct functioning of a KBS. This means a set of rules are conflicting if contradictory conclusions can be derived under a certain condition. An example of inconsistency rules is as follows:

```
R1 : -> P1
R2 : P1 -> P2
R3 : P1 -> P3
R4 : P2 -> P3
```

Incompleteness. Incompleteness occurs when there are missing rules in a rule base. Except the rules for representing facts and queries, a rule is called as a useless rule if the rule's condition (conclusion) cannot match other rules' conclusion (condition). The unmatched conditions are called dangling conditions, while the unmatched conclusions are called dead-end conclusions. Mostly, the reasons of useless rules are due to some missing rules. An example of incompleteness rules is as follows:

```
R1 : -> P1
R2 : P1 AND P3 -> P2
R3 : P1 -> P4
R4 : P4 -> .
```

Redundancy. Redundancy occurs when unnecessary rules exist in a rule base. Redundancy rules not only increase the size of the rule based but also may cause additional useless inferences. Redundancy is classified as being of two kinds: forms-redundant rule and subsumed. A rule is forms-redundant with respect to a conclusion if the conclusion can be reduced from other rules under the same conclusions. A rule is subsumed with respect to a conclusion if the conclusion can be reduced from both rules and the condition part of the former is included in the condition part of the latter. An example of redundancy rules is as follows:

```
R1 : P1 AND P3 -> P2
R2 : P1 AND P3 -> P2
R3 : P1 -> P2
R4 : P4 -> P5
R5 : P4 -> P5 AND P6
R6 : P2 -> P7
R7 : P1 -> P7
```

Circularity. Circularity occurs when several inference rules have circular dependency. Circularity rules can cause infinite reasoning and must be broken. If the cycle is formed within a rule itself, then we called such circular rule as self-circular rule. An example of circularity rules is as follows:

```
R1 : P1 -> P2
R2 : P2 -> P3
R3 : P3 -> P1
R4 : P1 AND P4 -> P4
R5 : P5 -> P5
```

4 Stochastic Activity Network Based Verification Approach

For the purpose of effective verification using SANs, it is essential that the KB be formulated in order to precisely represent the reasoning status of the rule set. Moreover, the errors must be detectable by means of this representation, i.e., the KB will be examined for unreachable goals caused by structural errors, which would allow us to identify these and correct them. Currently, the verification is limited to systems without uncertainty, since it contains some scope of errors. The verification system also hires definitional domain knowledge so as to improve the capability of error(s) detection. The formulation of a KBS as a SAN involves the representation of each rule or fact as a transition. Predicates are also relations among arguments. A predicate is applied to a specific number of arguments and has a value of either true or false when transitions fire. An arc label specifies a variable extension of a predicate to which the arc is connected. An element t $\in$T defines a logical implication between its input places (i.e., input predicates) and its output place (i.e., output predicate). This can be understood in the sense that the output predicate can produce some prescribed conclusion when the input predicates satisfy certain conditions. Figure 1 shows a very basic example of a predicate rule can be expressed using SAN formalism. Note that the place P1 and Pm are antecedents and Q1 and Qm are conclusions, with R being the logical connector. The input and output gates specify the conditions in which the rule is activated and concluded respectively.

Tokens are used to indicate validity or establishment of facts. However, some constraints are to be placed on the input and output functions for proper transformation. In its most primitive form, each rule will have all the antecedents as input places and the consequents as output places for the transition in question.

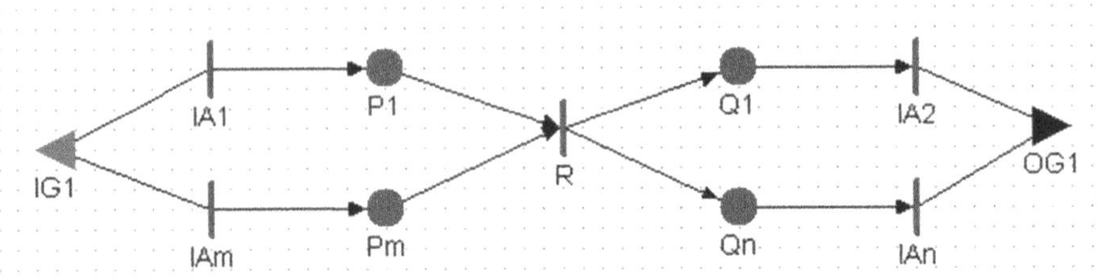

Fig. 1. Inference rule (clause) expressed as a simple stochastic activity network

This indicates that the firing of transition tl will add both Q to the set of known clauses. However, in its current state, transition tl cannot be fired as there are no tokens in its input places. However, information concerning the validity of P is lost as a result of the firing. This can be rectified by including A in the set of output places when tl is fired indicating A, B, and C as known facts. This represents an improvement, but is still problematic in that transition tl can be fired again, more so, at will, thus increasing the tokens in places A, B, and C ad infinitum. To counteract this, each transition will have associated with it, a special place with a single token in it. Additionally, the transition can be fired only once, indicating a persistent Petri net with no information loss. The use of definitional knowledge in a domain does pose some problems. Most KBSs will employ some such knowledge, since it is natural information as far as the experts are concerned. This knowledge may take the form of data abstraction or mutual exclusiveness.

Data abstraction rules cover qualitative abstraction, definitional abstraction and generalization [SI. Qualitative abstraction involves the transformation of a value on one dimension (usually quantitative) to an equivalent value on another dimension, as in "if the patient's temperature exceeds 104OF, then the patient's temperature is high." Definitional abstraction involves the use of related concepts to describe the same property of an object, as in "if the patient's blood count is low, then that patient is anaemic." Generalizations, on the other hand tend to relate concepts through hierarchical structuring, e.g., "if the patient is male, then the patient cannot be pregnant." Mutually exclusive knowledge relates different classes of a concept, as in "if the patient has infection X, then the patient cannot have infection Y." Knowledge of this sort is frequently employed by domain experts when reasoning, but may not be explicitly incorporated into the system. Any verification strategy that excludes this knowledge would be suspect in that it would ignore potential errors, and possibly indicate the possibility of error when none is present. Incorporating knowledge about abstraction in a verifier is relatively straightforward; the abstracted knowledge can be represented as rules and added to the current rule set. Mutually exclusive knowledge can be handled more elegantly through the use of a single place denoting inconsistency, as opposed to the use of several rules denoting combinations of incompatible clauses. Adopting a more formal notation, let the rule set R consist of k rules, with T; = R representing individual rules. In order to produce greater efficiency, error-detection procedures can be formulated as reachability or submarking reachability problems. For the purpose of maintaining the readability of this paper and meeting the requirements of paper length, the proofs for these propositions are described briefly. Proposition 1: Redundancy: In incidence matrix A, for every element of any pair of rows, ri and rj, if [ri] = [rj], then either ri or rj is redundant, where [ri] and [rj] denote the content of elements in ri and rj, respectively. Proof: Based on incidence matrix A, a specification clause Ci is said to be redundant if there exists another specification clause Cj such that Ci and Cj are the same. Example 2: Add one more clause C21 into the logic program, as shown in Example 1. C21 ancestor(x, y) ← ancestor(z, y), parent(x, z).

From Proposition 1, we can obviously understand that either t2 or t21 is redundant. Similarly, assume that a set of specification clauses is of the form (C1) P0(y, z) ← P1 (y, z), P2(y, z), P3(y, z) (C2) P0(y, z) ← P1(y, z), P3(y, z), P2(y, z). Since both clauses (C1) and (C2) are identical, either (C1) or (C2) is redundant. Proposition 2: Subsumption: In incidence matrix A, for every element of any pair of rows, ri and rj, if {[ri]} ⊆ {[rj]}, then rj is subsumed by ri, where {[ri]} and {[rj]} denote a set of elements in ri and rj, respectively. Proof: Based on incidence matrix A, a specification clause Ci is said to be subsumed by another clause Cj if Ci and Cj have the same conclusion predicate and Ci has more useless condition predicates than Cj.

By using the propositions and error-detection algorithm described in the previous section, the following errors can be detected. Redundancy: In A, by Proposition 1, since the content of elements in rows t1 and t2 is identical, either clause C1 or clause C2 is redundant.

5 Conclusion and Future Research

In the paper, we have briefly presented the preliminaries of normalizing and ordering rules of a KBS and explained the reasoning for this. Once the rules have been transformed into high-level SANs, the approach should (in theory) be able to answer queries over the net structure and compute the degree of truth to answers, however, further technical investigation is required for evaluating this. In future work, our focus will be to apply the method presented to an example case study of a KBS, where an ongoing PhD research project is focused on developing an advisory system for use in railway traffic planning. The knowledge base of the advisory system has been designed and developed, but not yet fully evaluated, where it is hoped that this presented mechanism can evaluate and verify the knowledge base. We also plan to integrate the approach into a reliability estimation method that can help in motivating and justifying design decisions at each iterative stage of development. We also aim to concentrate on formalizing and automating the transformation between rules and SANs with certainty factors. Furthermore, we have addressed types of structural errors in a KBS and proposed a SANs formalism for verifying these structural errors. By following the four phases as presented in this paper, we can automatically detect types and causes of error. We will further integrate the modeling and reasoning strength of SANs and fuzzy set theory to extend the usage of our approach to real-world applications such as multimedia synchronization, telecommunication, reuse, and maintenance. We have applied Mobius, which allows the drawing, execution, and reasoning of SANs.

Acknowledgements. The authors would like to thank Siemens and EPSRC for their support in this PhD project and for the support of Newcastle University.

References

1. Agarwal, R., Tanniru, M.: A petri-net based approach for verifying the integrity of production systems. Int. J. Man-Mach. Stud. **36**(3), 447–468 (1992)
2. Ahson, S.: Petri net models of fuzzy neural networks. IEEE Trans. Syst. Man Cybern. **25**(6), 926–932 (1995)
3. Bugarin, A.J., Barro, S.: Fuzzy reasoning supported by petri nets. IEEE Trans. Fuzzy Syst. **2**(2), 135–149 (1994)
4. Cao, T., Sanderson, A.C.: Task sequence planning using fuzzy petri nets. IEEE Trans. Syst. Man Cybern. **25**(5), 755–768 (1995)
5. Chen, S.M., Ke, J.S., Chang, J.F.: Knowledge representation using fuzzy petri nets. IEEE Trans. Knowl. Data Eng. **2**(3), 311–319 (1990)
6. Hammer, P.L., Kogan, A.: Essential and redundant rules in horn knowledge bases. In: IEEE Proceeding of 28th Hawaii International Conference System Sciences, pp. 209–218 (1995)
7. Wu, C.H., Lee, S.J.: A token-flow paradigm for verification of rule-based expert systems. IEEE Trans. Knowl. Data Eng. **30**(4), 616–624 (2000)
8. Nguyen, T.A., Perkins, W.A., Laffey, T.J., Pecora, D.: Knowledge base verification. AI Mag. **49**, 69–75 (1987)
9. Jensen, K.: Coloured petri nets: a high level language for system design and analysis. In: Jensen, K., Rozenberg, G. (eds.): High-Level Petri Nets, pp. 44–122 (1991)
10. Konar, A., Mandal, A.K.: Uncertainty management in expert systems using fuzzy petri nets. IEEE Trans. Knowl. Data Eng. **8**(1), 96–105 (1996)
11. Laffey, T.J., Perkins, W.A., Nguyen, T.A.: Reasoning about fault diagnosis with LES. Proc. IEEE **1**(1), 13–20 (1986)
12. Lin, C., Chaudhury, A., Whinston, A.B., Marinescu, D.C.: Logical inference of horn clauses in petri net models. IEEE Trans. Knowl. Data Eng. **5**(3), 416–425 (1993)
13. Liu, N.K., Dillon, T.: An approach towards the verification of expert systems using numerical petri nets. Int. J. Intell. Syst. **6**, 255–276 (1991)
14. Looney, C.G., Alfize, A.R.: Logical control via Boolean rule matrix transformation. IEEE Trans Syst. Man Cybern. **17**(6), 1077–1082 (1987)
15. Looney, C.G.: Fuzzy petri nets for rule-based decisionmarking. IEEE Trans. Syst. Man Cybern. **18**(1), 178–183 (1988)

A Generated Property Specification Language for Resilient Multirobot Missions

Swaib Dragule[1,4], Bart Meyers[2,3], and Patrizio Pelliccione[1(✉)]

[1] Department of Computer Science and Engineering, Chalmers University of Technology, University of Gothenburg, Göteborg, Sweden
dragule@chalmers.se, patrizio.pelliccione@gu.se

[2] Antwerp Systems and Software Modelling, University of Antwerp, Antwerpen, Belgium
bart.meyers@uantwerpen.be

[3] Flanders Make vzw, Lommel, Belgium

[4] Makerere University, Kampala, Uganda

Abstract. The use of robots is gaining considerable traction in several domains, since they are capable of assisting and replacing humans for everyday tasks. To harvest the full potential of robots, it must be possible to define missions for robots that are domain-specific, resilient, and collaborative. Currently, robot vendors provide low-level APIs to program such missions, making mission definition a task-specific and error-prone activity. There is a need for quick definition of new missions, by users that lack programming expertise, such as farmers and emergency workers. In this paper, we extend the existing FLYAQ platform to support the high-level specification of adaptive and highly-resilient missions. We present an extensible specification language that allows users to declaratively specify domain-specific constraints as properties of missions, thus complementing the existing FLYAQ mission language. This permits to move at runtime, the actual generation of low-level operations to satisfy the declaratively specified mission. We show how this specification language can be automatically generated from a domain-specific FLYAQ mission language by using the generative ProMoBox approach. Next, we show how mission goals are achieved taking mission properties into account, and how missions may change due to unexpected circumstances.

Keywords: Domain-specific languages · Robotics · Model-driven engineering · Resilient systems · Cyber-physical systems

1 Introduction

The use of multirobot systems in civilian missions requires high variability due to the diversity of domains [4,21]. Moreover, robotic systems are defined through a craftsmanship instead of established engineering processes. Programming missions for robots requires high knowledge of robotic programming and robot mechatronics. While domain users are experts in their domains (e.g., emergency,

A. Romanovsky and E.A. Troubitsyna (Eds.): SERENE 2017, LNCS 10479, pp. 45–61, 2017.
DOI: 10.1007/978-3-319-65948-0_4

commercial and agriculture) they are not trained to program missions for multirobot execution in their domains using the low-level APIs provided by robot vendors. Not much has been done to enable domain experts to easily use robots to execute missions in the respective domains.

To address this problem, Di Ruscio et al. introduced FLYAQ [3,7]. FLYAQ is a platform designed to enable non-expert domain users to program missions for a team of multicopters. The platform has been then generalized to different types of robots in [4,6]. The platform is extensible, so that domain-specific robots and missions can be defined. Unfortunately, this platform can only define missions at design time. This is unrealistic since most missions will be faced by unforeseeable and emergent situations during mission execution, and, consequently, robots should be resilient to these unforeseeable and emergent situations. For example, one robot may malfunction calling for re-planning so that another robot can take the roles this robot was executing. This need for run-time adaptation is clearly described in the Robotics Multi-Annual Roadmap 2020 [21]. In this context, the document describes the degree in which models can be used in robotics in three steps ([21] Sect. 5.2). Step 1 assumes that models are used to define missions by people at design time. Step 2 requires robots to use models at run-time to interact and explain what they are doing. Step 3 means that robots adapt and improve models to redefine what they are doing based on artificial intelligence.

The FLYAQ platform uses models according to step 1. In this line of research, we intend to improve FLYAQ to support self-adaptive robots at the mission level, thus achieving step 3. This means that robots can change their behaviour to successfully carry out missions under unforeseen circumstances. We achieve this by introducing a declarative language for describing mission goals and constraints. In this research we exclusively focus on the high-level strategic, domain-specific, collaborative aspects of self-adaptation. To this end, we specify mission objectives in a declarative way, as properties, using a language we call the Mission Specification Language (MSL). We present a technique that allows the generation of such a MSL for a specific FLYAQ extension (e.g., emergency, commercial, agriculture). As MSL is declarative, it does not specify *how* the mission is planned for a team of robots, but instead specifies what goals must be achieved and what constraints cannot be violated. This way, missions become fully specified only at run-time and they can be re-planned at run-time.

Paper structure: Sect. 2 discusses the background of this research. Section 3 introduces the property specification language. Section 4 evaluates the approach by showing an implementation of the property specification language. Section 5 discusses related work. Section 6 concludes the paper with opportunities for future works.

2 Background

In this section, we briefly explain domain-specific modelling, and the FLYAQ platform, on which we build our research.

Domain Specific Modelling. In Domain-Specific Modelling (DSM) [14], a methodology in model-driven software engineering, the general goal is to provide means for domain users to model systems in their problem domain. Model-driven techniques such as metamodelling and model transformation enable the creation of Domain-Specific Modelling Languages (DSMLs). These DSMLs can be used by domain experts, to specify, for example, missions for a team of robots. Current DSM techniques allow domain users to model at the domain level and simulate, optimise, and transform the model to other formalisms, synthesise code, generate documentation, etc.

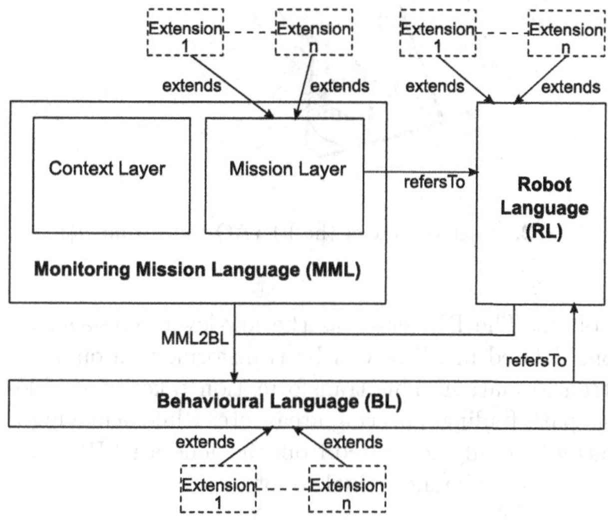

Fig. 1. The family of FLYAQ DSMLs (adapted from [6]).

FLYAQ Platform. The FLYAQ platform [3,4,7] employs domain-specific modelling to take care of the various domains involved in mission definition and specification. The approach proposes a family of DSMLs for the specification of missions of multirobot systems (MMRSs), as shown in Fig. 1:

- Monitoring Mission Language (MML): this DSML consists of the context layer and mission layer. This DSML is meant to be used by domain users, to model missions. Missions are represented in the mission layer as sequences of tasks on a map, as shown in Fig. 2. The context layer provides additional constrains over the mission area, such as obstacles and no-fly zones;
- Robot Language (RL): using this DSML, types of robots or individual robots can be defined by a robot engineer, mapping out their capabilities and characteristics;
- Behaviour Language (BL): this language allows the definition of sequential atomic movements and actions of each robot that are used to instruct the

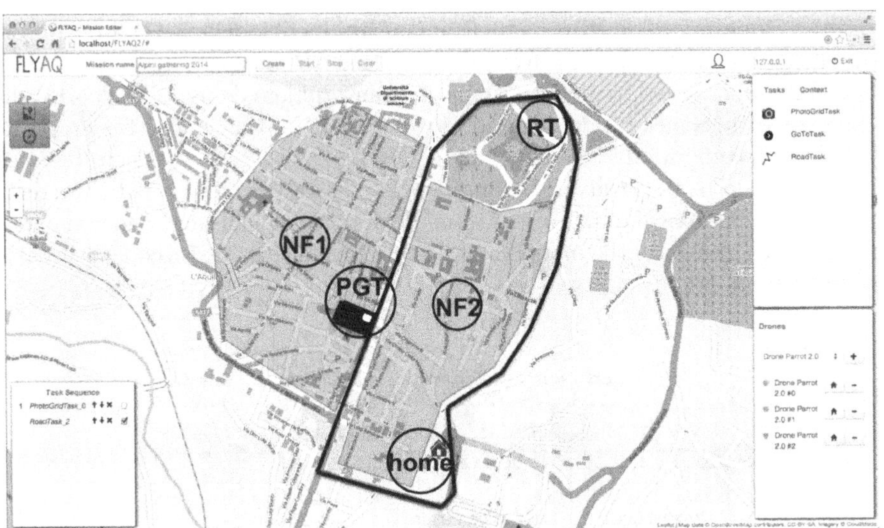

Fig. 2. A screenshot of the FLYAQ tool (from [7]).

individual robots. The BL serves as the low-level language, to which high-level missions defined in MML can be transformed automatically using the MML2BL transformation. This transformation takes care of low-level planning, such as path finding, covering areas, etc. while achieving the high-level goals. Code can be easily generated from the generated BL models, and then it can be uploaded to the individual robots.

Mission goals, robot characteristics, and actions should be customised to the application domains. Therefore, extensions can be defined on MML, RL and BL, as shown in Fig. 1. In case of MML, extensions may define a task to "scan an area by taking pictures". Example extensions to RL may include domain-specific notions like "number of propellers", "launch type" (horizontal or vertical take-off), "maximum altitude", etc. BL may be extended with movements like "take off" and "land", and a "go to strategy" (move first over the horizontal or vertical axis, or move diagonally?), "take a picture", "start recording a video", etc.

For example, it is possible to define extensions in FLYAQ to allow flying robots to take pictures of areas. Using this extension, one can specify missions to e.g., survey an area where a public event is being held. Another example is in the domain of agriculture. One multicopter is able to detect pests by taking pictures and using image recognition techniques. If a pest is detected, another multicopter that is able to spray insecticide must spray the infected plants. It should only spray plants that are infected. We use these examples throughout the paper.

Despite its extension mechanism, FLYAQ does not support (a) advanced temporal constraints (other than order, fork or join) over various tasks or robots in MML, e.g., a certain task can only start if another robot is surveying the task area (for safety reasons), or video recording can only start after clearance (for privacy reasons); and (b) run-time adaptation of a mission due to some information at run-time, e.g., taking pictures of areas where high temperature was detected by another robot, or reacting to a loss of signal of a robot. The research presented in this paper addresses these shortcomings.

3 Mission Specification Language

Our approach extends the FLYAQ platform as shown in Fig. 3. The mission layer of MML is annotated, and as a consequence a *Mission Specification Language* (MSL) can be generated automatically from MML and a *Property Template* to better match the platform extensions of MML. MSL extends MML with language constructs to define temporal properties for robot missions. Our approach ensures that, when an extension is defined as done in FLYAQ, no additional effort is required to generate MSL.

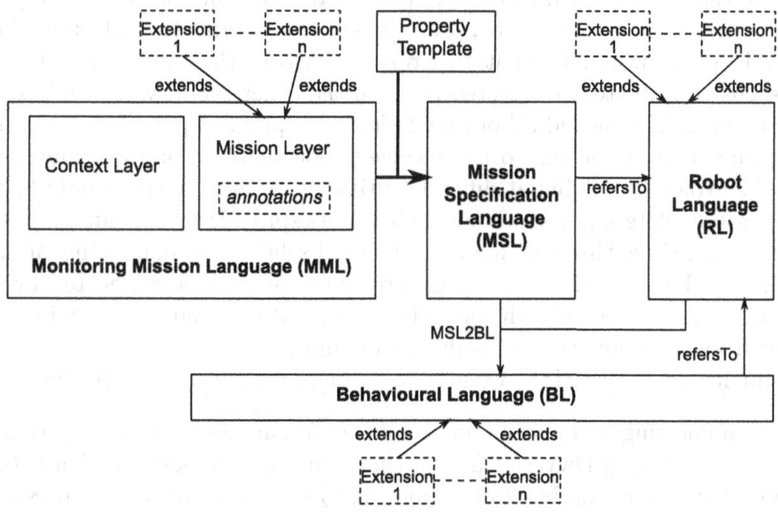

Fig. 3. Overview of the approach as an extension of the FLYAQ platform.

3.1 Mission Specification Language

The mission specification language (MSL) is intended to specify properties of a mission that allows users to define temporal mission constraints in a highly declarative way. This complements MML, where areas are selected, and specific tasks, obstacles and no-fly zones are plotted on the map. MSL replaces the order, fork and join of MML, supporting more expressive constraints. We use a number of temporal patterns, taken from Dwyer et al. [8] and Autili et al. [1], as a basis for the Property Template from which MSL is generated. According to this work, properties consist of a *temporal pattern* in a *scope*, over some propositions P, Q, R and S (i.e., occurrences of something, e.g., spraying, entering an area, etc.). Temporal patterns can be *absence* (something should never occur), *universality* (something should always occur), *existence* (something should eventually occur), *bounded existence* (something should occur at most n times), *precedence* (an occurrence of P must be preceded by an occurrence of Q), or *response* (an occurrence of P must be followed by an occurrence of Q). Scopes can be *globally*, *after* the occurrence of R, *before* the occurrence of S, *between* occurrences of R and S, or after an occurrence of R until an occurrence of S (*after until*).

The declarative constraint specification shields the user from the actual planning. For example, if pests are detected, the corresponding areas are sprayed. This is an example of a response pattern with global scope. The user may use a precedence pattern to say that a pest needs to be detected at a location before this point is sprayed. This constraint can be met in a number of equally valid ways. A first option would be that one robot first detects all locations, then returns to the base where its data is downloaded and locations of infected plants are uploaded to a second robot, who goes out to spray the infected plants. A second option would be that two robots perform the task in parallel: one robot sends coordinates of detected pests to the other robot, which only sprays infected points. The second robot may follow a preplanned path, or may plan its path at run-time, according to the received coordinates. Collisions may occur, or may be avoided by flying at different altitudes. A third option would be that multiple robots detect pests, and multiple robots spray. If robots can adapt their mission at run-time, this may involve advanced scheduling, employing run-time monitors [5]. This shows that a declarative language can be supported by very simple to very advanced algorithms. The goal of MSL is that the domain user is shielded from such advanced planning algorithms.

To further illustrate MSL, we give some more examples of properties.

- Between entering and exiting an area, a robot can never exceed a given altitude. According to Dwyer et al. [8], this is an absence pattern with between scope. Note that this between scope may be more intuitively expressed as "during" or "while".
- Between receiving a "stop" message and a "start" message, pictures cannot be taken.
- A robot can only start its activity if another robot is in a given position to monitor this activity.

3.2 Run-Time Adaptation of Multirobot Missions

In its current state, the MML platform generates robot missions at design time. This means that robot missions cannot be adapted at run-time. We intend to support the run-time recalculation of BL models (i.e., robot commands) from a declarative mission description; this is needed in case information at run-time prompts the robots to change the mission. Our approach is applicable to various implementation techniques: for example, the mission recalculation may be achieved by the robot or by the ground station, and may be specified off-line or at run-time, or a mix of these.

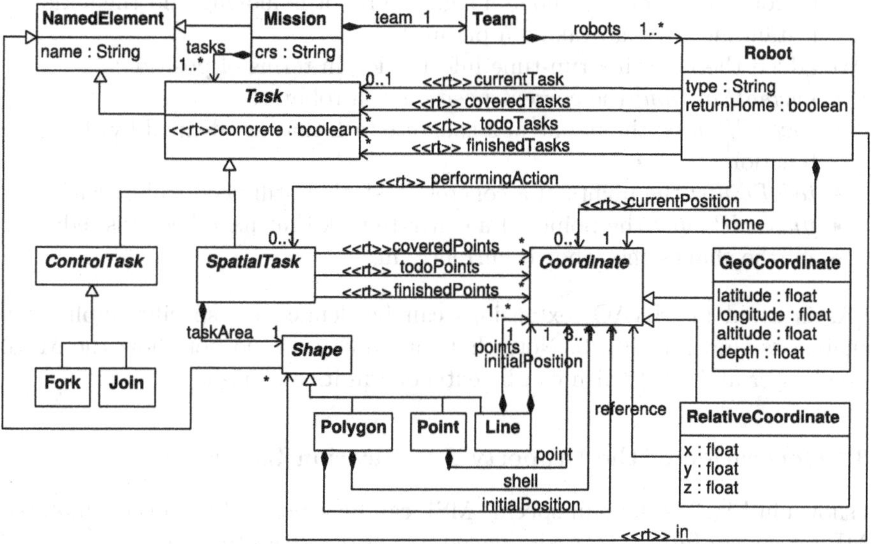

Fig. 4. The annotated class diagram of the MML mission layer (context layer remains unchanged and is not shown).

In order to allow run-time information in a mission specification in MSL, we altered the existing MML mission layer from [4], as shown in Fig. 4. We have changed the metamodel in several ways:

- We have extracted a Shape class (and Polygon, Point, Line subclasses) from the original PolygonTask, LineTask, and PointTask. In particular, the new Polygon class serves now as superclass of Area in the context layer of MML in [6]. This new Shape class will allow users to specify new shapes on the map that may trigger rules like: do not record within a specific area.
- The meaning of Task has been extended. At mission specification time, a task may be addressed by multiple robots. After mission generation, tasks are split up into multiple concrete tasks, each for one robot.

- TaskDependency has been removed from MML and its functionality will be subsumed by the specification language.
- We added run-time language constructs (annotated with *rt*), so that specifications can be defined in terms of the current state of the mission in terms of tasks and position. We added the following run-time information in terms of tasks:
  - *currentTask:* the task a robot is currently working on;
  - *coveredTasks:* the concrete tasks that are planned for a robot;
  - *todoTasks:* the concrete tasks that a robot still needs to perform;
  - *finishedTasks:* the concrete tasks that a robot has done;
  - *performingAction:* the action (defined in the task) a robot is currently performing. It may be none if e.g., the robot is moving and the action is instantaneous (e.g., taking a picture).

  We added the following run-time information in terms of position:
  - *currentPosition:* the current position of a robot;
  - *coveredPoints:* the points of a concrete task that are defined by the cover function;
  - *todoPoints:* the points of a concrete task that still need to be visited;
  - *finishedPoints:* the points of a concrete task that have been visited;
  - *in*: the shapes the robot is currently in.

As is usual in FLYAQ, extensions can be defined for specific application domains, as shown in Fig. 3. Note that for brevity, we do not show the MML context layer and RL (which can be extended in its own right).

3.3 Generation of the Property Specification Language

As shown in Fig. 3, a domain-specific MSL can be generated from the annotated MML (as shown in Fig. 3), with defined extensions (e.g., to enable detection of pests in an area, and spraying certain plants). This means that extensions have to be defined only once, and can be used for specifying missions in the original MML as well as in MSL. The metamodel of MSL, which results from the language generation process without an extension, is shown in Fig. 5. It consists of three parts:

- Mission layer: the upper part (unshaded) represents our variant to the original MML mission layer, which allows the user to define missions at design-time like in the original MML. For example, "pictures should be taken in an area, with a distance of x from each other". Additionally, shapes can be defined, that can be used in MSL properties. In case of an MML extension, extensions will also appear in this part.
- Temporal pattern layer: the middle part (shaded) represents the temporal patterns, which allow the user to define temporal constraints based on the patterns by Dwyer et al. [8]. For example, "after *R* happens, *P* must be followed by *Q*".

– Proposition layer: the bottom part (unshaded) represents the language fragment to define propositions P, Q, R, and S of temporal patterns. More specifically, it allows the user to specify a condition on the state of a mission (i.e., a structural pattern). For example, "a robot is in a specific area", or "a task is completed". In case of an MML extension, pattern versions of extensions will also appear in this part.

With MSL, a mission can be specified by plotting an area on the map, and defining a DetectPest and Spray task in this area, using the MSL mission layer, which is extended with language concepts from agriculture. With the MSL temporal pattern and MSL proposition layer, a property can be specified that states that detecting a pest at a location must result in spraying that location.

The MSL metamodel of Fig. 5 is generated fully automatically from an annotated (and possibly extended) MML metamodel (Fig. 4) and the generic property template (shaded part of Fig. 5). Why do we need to automatically generate an MSL metamodel? Please note that, if there was no generative approach, each of the domain-specific language constructs (e.g., spraying a pest, maximum altitude of a robot, etc.) would have had to be modelled a second time in MSL. With our approach, the extension mechanisms of FLYAQ can be reused as described in [4], and a domain-specific MSL is generated without any additional effort.

We use techniques from the ProMoBox framework [17,18] to achieve this. First, the MSL mission layer is generated by taking the annotated MML metamodel and removing all run-time language constructs, which are annotated with *rt*, thus creating the unshaded upper part of Fig. 5. Next, the property template is merged into this model by adding an association called *specification* from Mission to Specification. Finally, the annotated MML metamodel is taken for a second time, and the run-time language constructs are kept (by removing the annotation). This time, the metamodel is converted into a structural pattern language by using the RAMification process [16]: relaxing all lower multiplicities, making all abstract classes concrete, and changing all attribute types to Condition, as can be seen in the proposition layer of Fig. 5. This RAMified metamodel is merged into MSL by generating inheritance links from all top-level classes to PropertyElement.

3.4 Transforming MSL to BL

Transforming MSL to BL (see MSL2BL in Fig. 3) can be done according to several stategies. Given the tight relation between MSL and MML, the transformation algorithms of MML2BL [7] (i.e., path finding, covering areas) can be reused. Moreover, various implementation strategies as mentioned in Sect. 3.1 can be covered by MSL2BL: mission recalculation may be achieved by a mix of the robot or the ground station, off-line or at run-time. These strategies may requiring enhancement of BL to e.g., explicitly support data communication or monitoring. As this paper focuses on the definition and generation of MSL, this is left as future work.

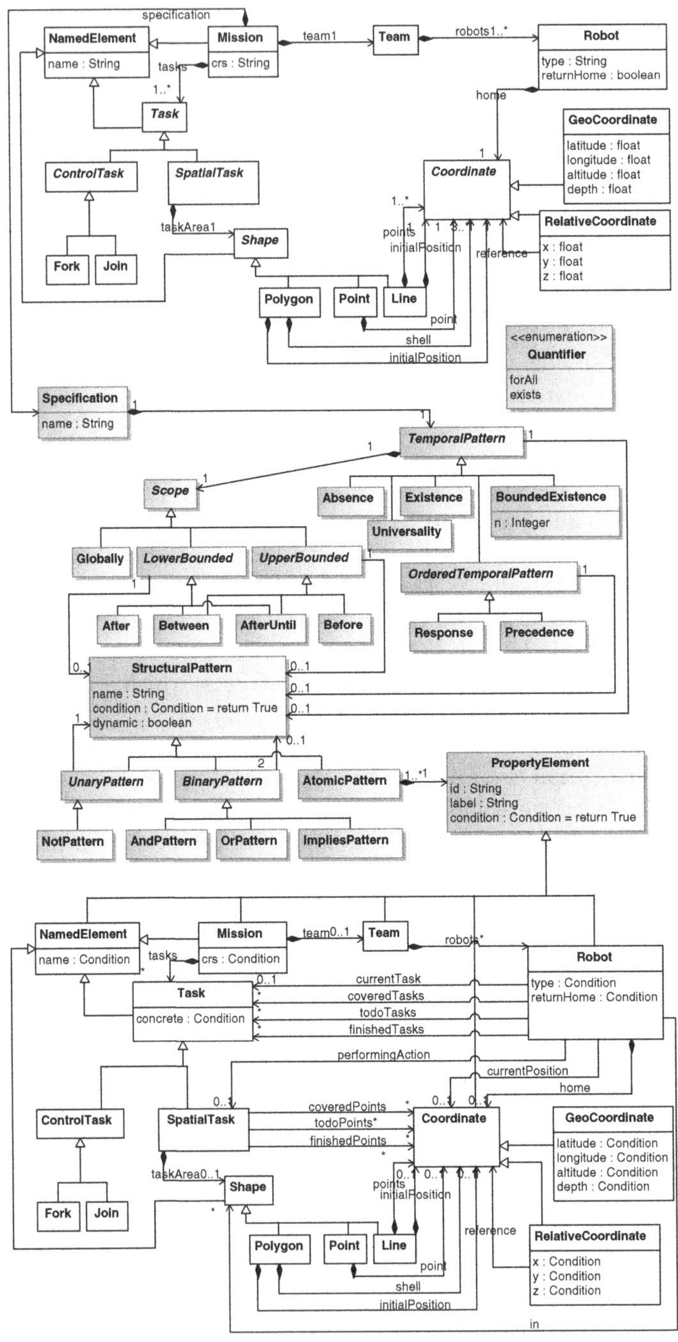

Fig. 5. The generated metamodel of MSL without extensions.

4 Evaluation: Implementation of MSL as Textual DSL

In this section, we evaluate the MSL by introducing an implementation as a textual language in Xtext [9], and show how missions can be expressed in this language.

4.1 A Concrete Syntax for MSL

According to what described in [1], temporal properties (the shaded part of Fig. 5) might be profitably described using a structured English grammar. For instance, we can devise a textual syntax for the MSL proposition layer (the bottom part of Fig. 5), where each of the associations can form a subsentence with the two attached instances. For example, "*a Robot currently on a GeoCoordinate*" denotes the presence of an instance of Robot and an instance of GeoCoordinate, with a currentPosition link in between. More intricate, "*a Robot r currently on a GeoCoordinate with latitude lower than 100*" denotes additional conditions on the robot, etc. A structured English grammar to represent a subsentence for one association is defined as follows (id, Label, Value, Attribute, Class, Association are terminals):

```
Proposition ::= Proposition (and also Proposition)+
| Proposition (or Proposition)+
| Proposition (implies Proposition)+ | AtomicProposition
AtomicProposition ::= Expression [Association Expression]
Expression ::= Instance [InstanceCondition]
InstanceCondition ::= with (ValueCondition | BooleanCondition (and ValueCondition | BooleanCondition)*)
ValueCondition ::= {Attribute} (as | less than | greater than) {Value}
BooleanCondition ::= [not] {Attribute}
Instance ::= {id} | {Label} | a {Class} [{Label}]
Association ::= (that is a task of | that is a team of | that is in | [currently] doing | that has scheduled |
that has planned in the future | that has finished | [currently] performing | in | [currently] on | with as
home | with task area | which visits | which will visit in the future | which has visited | with points |
with initial position | which references | {Association})
```

The above grammar is combined with the grammar for temporal properties presented in [1] so that temporal properties can be described in standard LTL or CTL. This might enable the use of model checking approaches, like UPPAAL[1]. With this grammar, temporal patterns involving multiple links can be expressed with AndPatterns. MML extensions can be used by instantiating classes defined by the extension. This is illustrated below in the examples.

Our current implementation in Xtext includes variable name resolution, parse error visualisation, auto-completion and syntax highlighting[2]. A screenshot of the MSL editor is shown in Fig. 6. Since both the FLYAQ platform and MSL are implemented on top of the Ecore platform, they can be easily merged at the EMF layer [19].

---

1 http://www.uppaal.org/.

2 An implementation of this grammar can be found at http://msdl.cs.mcgill.ca/people/bart/flyaq/flyaq.html.

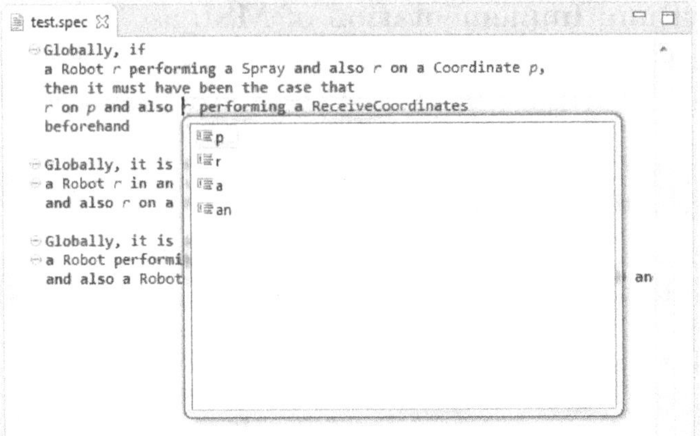

Fig. 6. Screenshot of the MSL in Xtext.

4.2 Examples of MSL

This section presents examples of temporal properties defined in MSL, while illustrating the relation between the grammar presented above and the MSL metamodel presented in Fig. 5. For these examples, we define a MML extension in the agricultural domain as shown in Fig. 7, with:

- DetectPest: scanning for a pest in an area and in case of detection, send some coordinates;
- Spray: spraying pesticides at a point;
- ReceiveCoordinates: receiving coordinates where a pest has been detected, with the "at" association referring to the received coordinates.

Note that, after generation of MSL, these additional language constructs will occur twice in MSL, namely in the MSL mission layer and in the MSL proposition layer.

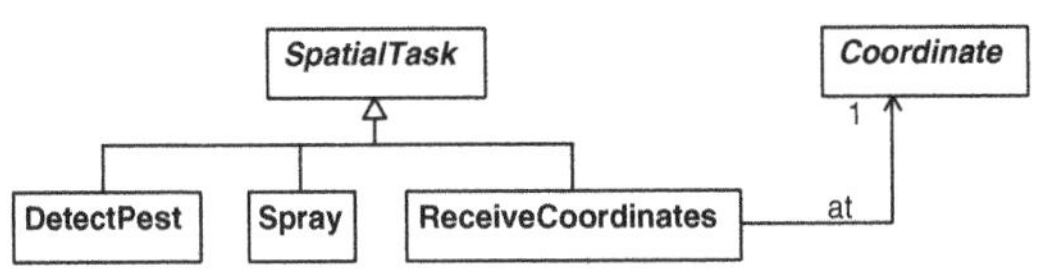

Fig. 7. The MML extension.

The example of Fig. 8 (top) shows the abstract syntax of the MSL property "a robot only sprays at a location if it has received these coordinates to spray at that location" as an object diagram. The Specification consists of a Precedence pattern. The left AtomicPattern states the condition Q, saying that a Receive-Coordinates task is executed at a coordinate **p**. Note how the "at" association

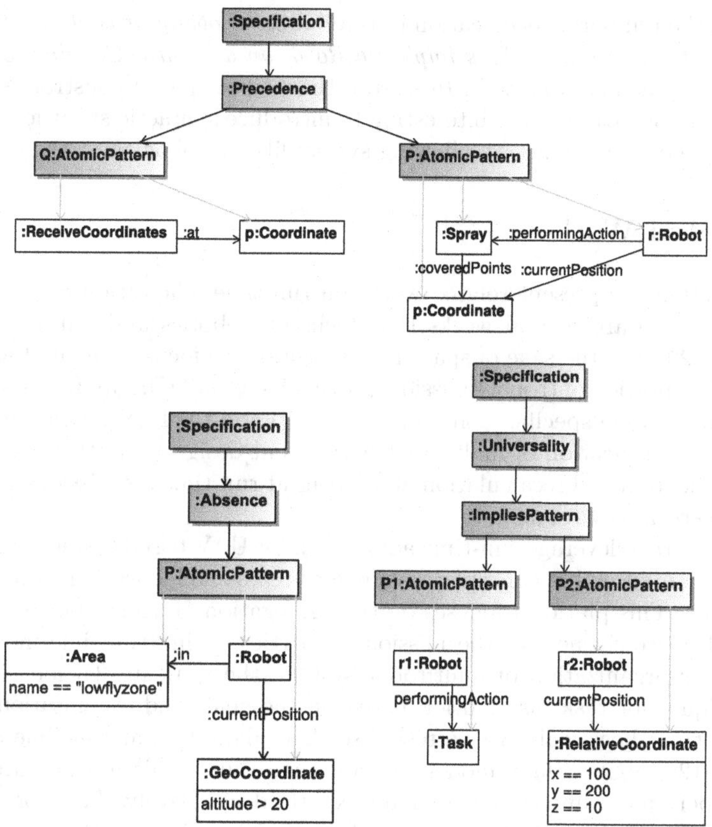

Fig. 8. Three examples of temporal specifications as instances of MSL.

is used. The right AtomicPattern P describes a robot **r**, spraying at aforementioned point **p**. Note that the coveredPoints link is superfluous, because if the robot is currently performing an action of a task, it must be inside the task area. In structured English grammar, the temporal specification is as follows (leaving out the superfluous quantification and coveredPoints link): "*Globally, if a SprayRobot* ***r*** *performing a Spray and* ***r*** *on a Coordinate* ***p****, then it must have been the case that a ReceiveCoordinates* ***at p*** *beforehand*". Note how "at" is automatically resolved to an instance of the "at" association.

The example of Fig. 8 (bottom left) represents "in a certain area, a robot can never exceed a given altitude". Note that the Area class (now a subclass of Polygon) is part of the MML context layer and is not shown in Fig. 5. In structured English grammar, the temporal specification is as follows: "*Globally, it is never the case that a Robot* ***r*** *in an Area with name as "lowflyzone" and also* ***r*** *on a GeoCoordinate with altitude more than 20*".

The example of Fig. 8 (bottom right) represents "a robot can only perform a certain task if another robot is at a certain position". In structured English grammar, the temporal specification is as follows: "*Globally, it is always the case that a Robot performing a Task implies a Robot on a RelativeCoordinate with **x** as 100 and **y** as 200 and **z** as 10*". Note that, since spatial constraints are at the very core of FLYAQ, it is interesting to introduce syntactic sugar for a robot being at a coordinate, e.g., by allowing syntax like "a robot on (100, 200, 10)".

5 Related Work

In this section, we present related works on run-time adaptation of multirobot missions. There are several works that focus on robotics and self-adaptation, like [10,11,20]. For the sake of space in this section we focus on related works in run-time adaptation of (robot) missions, with a focus on MDE approaches. While most of the mission specification tools (e.g., [23]) and the FLYAQ platform [3,6] provide for specification of multirobot missions at design time, there is need to have specification and recalculation of missions at run-time for missions executed under uncertain environments.

In an effort to leverage run-time adaptation for UAV based systems, the work in [2] uses an ensemble concept to aggregate teams collaborating in a mission at run-time. This platform focuses on the aggregation of agents but on not the high-level expressiveness of the mission properties. Using run-time models for automatic reorganization of multirobot system, the work in [24] focuses more on techniques for task distribution based on the goals and organisation of the teams, but not how goals are expressed so that adaptation at run-time is made easy. In [12] robots adapt models at run time, but configurations are made by an expert programmer, not domain experts declaratively. The work in [15] focuses on the behavioural model and how it auto-validates at run-time, yet we employ a generative approach. The work in [22] focuses on design-time to run-time explication of models, however this work does not really deal with adaptation triggered by run-time uncertainties. The work in [13] proposes an approach that uses models at design-time and run-time for collaboration. The proposed approach is specific to a particular domain without a clear path to adapt it for working in other domains.

6 Conclusion and Future Work

In this paper, we extended the FLYAQ platform with MSL, a highly declarative language that allows users to describe robot missions with temporal properties as constraints. The declarative nature of MSL allows run-time adaptation of these missions in case of unforeseen circumstances. We showed how MSL can be automatically tailored with domain-specific extensions by a generative approach. Additionally we presented a structured English grammar for MSL.

Future work will mainly focus on the mapping from MSL to BL (a language for describing individual robot movements and actions), allowing run-time adaptation and exploring different execution strategies. We intend to model communication between robots and/or the ground station explicitly in BL to achieve this. Furthermore, we are planning to incorporate real-time constraints in missions. Moreover, since our approach for enabling run-time adaptation of missions is model-driven and relies on code generation, we intend to analyse the feasibility of generating code in real-time.

Acknowledgement. This research is partially supported by Flanders Make vzw. This research is also partially funded by the COST action IC1404 "MPM4CPS". This work has been carried out within the framework of the MBSE4Mechatronics project (grant nr.130013) of the agency for Innovation by Science and Technology in Flanders (IWT-Vlaanderen). More support for this work was from the SIDA Bright 317 project. Finally, this work is partially supported from the EU H2020 Research and Innovation Programme under GA No. 731869 (Co4Robots).

References

1. Autili, M., Grunske, L., Lumpe, M., Pelliccione, P., Tang, A.: Aligning qualitative, real-time, and probabilistic property specification patterns using a structured english grammar. IEEE Trans. Softw. Eng. **41**(7), 620–638 (2015). http://dx.doi.org/10.1109/TSE.2015.2398877
2. Bozhinoski, D., Bucchiarone, A., Malavolta, I., Marconi, A., Pelliccione, P.: Leveraging collective run-time adaptation for UAV-based systems. In: 2016 42nd Euromicro Conference on Software Engineering and Advanced Applications (SEAA), pp. 214–221 (2016). http://ieeexplore.ieee.org/document/7592799/
3. Bozhinoski, D., Di Ruscio, D., Malavolta, I., Pelliccione, P., Tivoli, M.: FLYAQ: enabling non-expert users to specify and generate missions of autonomous multicopters. In: Proceedings - 2015 30th IEEE/ACM International Conference on Automated Software Engineering, ASE 2015, pp. 801–806 (2015)
4. Ciccozzi, F., Di Ruscio, D., Malavolta, I., Pelliccione, P.: Adopting MDE for specifying and executing civilian missions of mobile multi-robot systems. IEEE Access **3536**(c), 1 (2016). http://ieeexplore.ieee.org/document/7576686/
5. Cohen, D., Feather, M.S., Narayanaswamy, K., Fickas, S.: Automatic monitoring of software requirements. In: Adrion, W.R., Fuggetta, A., Taylor, R.N., Wasserman, A.I. (eds.) Pulling Together, Proceedings of the 19th International Conference on Software Engineering, Boston, Massachusetts, USA, 17–23 May 1997, pp. 602–603. ACM (1997). http://doi.acm.org/10.1145/253228.253493
6. Di Ruscio, D., Malavolta, I., Pelliccione, P.: A family of domain-specific languages for specifying civilian missions of multi-robot systems. In: CEUR Workshop Proceedings, vol. 1319, pp. 16–29 (2014)
7. Di Ruscio, D., Malavolta, I., Pelliccione, P., Tivoli, M.: Automatic generation of detailed flight plans from high-level mission descriptions. In: Proceedings of the ACM/IEEE 19th International Conference on Model Driven Engineering Languages and Systems - MODELS 2016, pp. 45–55. ACM Press, New York (2016). http://dl.acm.org/citation.cfm?doid=2976767.2976794
8. Dwyer, M.B., Avrunin, G.S., Corbett, J.C.: Patterns in property specifications for finite-state verification. In: Boehm, B.W., Garlan, D., Kramer, J. (eds.) Proceedings of the 1999 International Conference on Software Engineering, ICSE 1999, Los Angeles, CA, USA, 16–22 May 1999, pp. 411–420. ACM (1999). http://portal.acm.org/citation.cfm?id=302405.302672

9. Eysholdt, M., Behrens, H.: Xtext: implement your language faster than the quick and dirty way. In: Cook, W.R., Clarke, S., Rinard, M.C. (eds.) Companion to the 25th Annual ACM SIGPLAN Conference on Object-Oriented Programming, Systems, Languages, and Applications, SPLASH/OOPSLA 17–21, 2010, Reno/Tahoe, Nevada, USA, pp. 307–309. ACM (2010). http://doi.acm.org/10.1145/1869542.1869625
10. Filieri, A., Tamburrelli, G., Ghezzi, C.: Supporting self-adaptation via quantitative verification and sensitivity analysis at run time. IEEE Trans. Softw. Eng. **42**(1), 75–99 (2016)
11. Franco, J.M., Correia, F., Barbosa, R., Zenha-Rela, M., Schmerl, B., Garlan, D.: Improving self-adaptation planning through software architecture-based stochastic modeling. J. Syst. Softw. **115**, 42–60 (2016). http://www.sciencedirect.com/science/article/pii/S0164121216000212
12. Gherardi, L., Hochgeschwender, N.: RRA: Models and tools for robotics run-time adaptation. In: IEEE International Conference on Intelligent Robots and Systems 2015, pp. 1777–1784, December 2015
13. Götz, S., Leuthäuser, M., Reimann, J., Schroeter, J., Wende, C., Wilke, C., Aßmann, U.: A role-based language for collaborative robot applications. In: Hähnle, R., Knoop, J., Margaria, T., Schreiner, D., Steffen, B. (eds.) ISoLA 2011. CCIS, pp. 1–15. Springer, Heidelberg (2012). doi:10.1007/978-3-642-34781-8_1
14. Gray, J., Neema, S., Tolvanen, J., Gokhale, A.S., Kelly, S., Sprinkle, J.: Domain-specific modeling. In: Fishwick, P.A. (ed.) Handbook of Dynamic System Modeling. Chapman and Hall/CRC (2007). http://dx.doi.org/10.1201/9781420010855.pt2
15. Kim, Y., Jung, J.W., Gallagher, J.C., Matson, E.T.: An adaptive goal-based model for autonomous multi-robot using HARMS and NuSMV. Int. J. Fuzzy Logic Intell. Syst. **16**(2), 95–103 (2016). http://www.ijfis.org/journal/view.html?doi=10.5391/IJFIS.2016.16.2.95
16. Kühne, T., Mezei, G., Syriani, E., Vangheluwe, H., Wimmer, M.: Explicit transformation modeling. In: Ghosh, S. (ed.) MODELS 2009. LNCS, vol. 6002, pp. 240–255. Springer, Heidelberg (2010). doi:10.1007/978-3-642-12261-3_23
17. Meyers, B., Denil, J., Dávid, I., Vangheluwe, H.: Automated testing support for reactive domain-specific modelling languages. In: Proceedings of the 2016 ACM SIGPLAN International Conference on Software Language Engineering - SLE 2016, pp. 181–194. ACM Press, New York (2016). http://dl.acm.org/citation.cfm?doid=2997364.2997367
18. Meyers, B., Deshayes, R., Lucio, L., Syriani, E., Vangheluwe, H., Wimmer, M.: ProMoBox: a framework for generating domain-specific property languages. In: Combemale, B., Pearce, D.J., Barais, O., Vinju, J.J. (eds.) SLE 2014. LNCS, vol. 8706, pp. 1–20. Springer, Cham (2014). doi:10.1007/978-3-319-11245-9_1
19. Schätz, B.: Formalization and rule-based transformation of EMF ecore-based models. In: Gašević, D., Lämmel, R., Wyk, E. (eds.) SLE 2008. LNCS, vol. 5452, pp. 227–244. Springer, Heidelberg (2009). doi:10.1007/978-3-642-00434-6_15
20. Shevtsov, S., Weyns, D.: Keep it simplex: Satisfying multiple goals with guarantees in control-based self-adaptive systems. In: Proceedings of the 2016 24th ACM SIGSOFT International Symposium on Foundations of Software Engineering, FSE 2016, pp. 229–241. ACM, New York (2016). http://doi.acm.org/10.1145/2950290.2950301
21. SPARC: Robotics 2020 Multi-Annual Roadmap. 2016, 325 (2015)

22. Steck, A., Lotz, A., Schlegel, C.: Model-driven engineering and run-time model-usage in service robotics. In: Proceedings of the 10th ACM International Conference on Generative Programming and Component Engineering - GPCE 2011, p. 73 (2011). http://dl.acm.org/citation.cfm?doid=2047862.2047875
23. Ulam, P., Endo, Y., Wagner, A., Arkin, R.: Integrated mission specification and task allocation for robot teams - Design and implementation. In: Proceedings - IEEE International Conference on Robotics and Automation, pp. 4428–4435 (2007)
24. Zhong, C., DeLoach, S.A.: Runtime models for automatic reorganization of multi-robot systems. In: Proceeding of the 6th International Symposium on Software Engineering for Adaptive and Self-Managing Systems - SEAMS 2011, p. 20. ACM, New York (2011). http://portal.acm.org/citation.cfm?doid=1988008.1988012

Safety and Security

Towards a Model-Driven Security Assurance of Open Source Components

Irum Rauf(✉) and Elena Troubitsyna

Åbo Akademi University, Turku, Finland
{irum.rauf,Elena.Troubitsyna}@abo.fi

Abstract. Open Source software is increasingly used in a wide spectrum of applications. While the benefits of the open source components are unquestionable now, there is a great concern over security assurance provided by such components. Often open source software is a subject of frequent updates. The updates might introduce or remove a diverse range of features and hence violate security properties of the previous releases. Obviously, a manual inspection of security would be prohibitively slow and inefficient. Therefore, there is a great demand for the techniques that would allow the developers to automate the process of security assurance in the presence of frequent releases. The problem of security assurance is especially challenging because to ensure scalability, such main open source initiatives, as OpenStack adopt RESTful architecture. This requires new security assurance techniques to cater to stateless nature of the system. In this paper, we propose a model-driven framework that would allow the designers to model the security concerns and facilitate verification and validation of them in an automated manner. It enables a regular monitoring of the security features even in the presence of frequent updates. We exemplify our approach with the Keystone component of OpenStack.

1 Introduction

The adoption of open source technology has increased tremendously in the last decade. Today most of the modern enterprises are centered around open source technology. The source code of open source software is distributed publicly and it is often developed in a collaborative manner.

The open source feature provides diverse design perspectives to the software. However, the open source software are subject to frequent updates by unknown users. This raises security concerns as the code can be used and manipulated in ways that were not initially intended by the organization.

In this work we present model-driven methodology to handle the security concerns of open-source software from design to implementation level. This work becomes more challenging when open source software are combined with REST architectural style. The adoption of REST architecture provides additional benefits of scalability and extensibility to the software encouraging providers to offer their services to a wider audience and add more features with more convenience.

A. Romanovsky and E.A. Troubitsyna (Eds.): SERENE 2017, LNCS 10479, pp. 65–80, 2017.
DOI: 10.1007/978-3-319-65948-0_5

The use of REST APIs require usage of design methodologies and security mechanisms that can handle stateless protocol for stateful applications.

Our approach to handle security concerns for REST compliant open-source software builds upon the use of *Design by Contract* strategy [18]. Contracts use preconditions and postconditions for the methods of a class to identify correctness of the program. They are capable of detecting change in the state of the program, identify when a certain piece of code violates the pre-defined conditions and can be used for fault localization. We used contracts with models to provide Security and Rest compliant UML Models (SecReUM). By using model-based test generation approach, we can generate test cases from SecReUM that can validate the behavior of the software. In addition, SecReUM can be used to provide an online/offline monitoring mechanism for KeyStone.

We exemplify our approach with the Keystone component of OpenStack. OpenStack is an open-source software platform for cloud computing that offers REST interfaces to provide IaaS (Infrastructure as a Service). The main characteristics of OpenStack include scalability, flexibility, compatibility, and openness [27]. The open source nature of OpenStack and encouragement of its partners has made it one of the most prominent cloud computing paradigm. It is deployed in various companies worldwide that have data volumes measured in petabytes and are scalable up to 60 million virtual machines and billions of stored objects [21]. Keystone offers identity service in OpenStack for authentication and authorization. This makes it a critical component of OpenStack as it serves as a gateway to all its assets.

The objective of our work is to provide an engineering solution to security experts to periodically monitor their open-source software and identify any security loopholes that may arise due to frequent updates to code in a collaborative and open environment. The use of model-driven approach facilitates an automated approach to validate the open-source components.

The paper is organized as follow: Sect. 2 briefly explains Keystone and its interface. Section 3 presents an overview of our overall approach. Section 4 presents our overall approach and Sect. 5 shows generation of contracts with security features. Section 6 presents the related work and Sect. 7 concludes the paper.

2 Keystone Open Stack

Keystone is the centralized identity service of OpenStack that offers authentication and authorization. KeyStone authenticates a user by generating a token. Token can either be scoped or unscoped depending on client's request and the configured policy of KeyStone. An unscoped token identifies a user without identifying any project scope, roles etc., whereas a scoped token provides authorization information of user for particular projects or domains. Figure 1 shows how KeyStone authentication and authorization mechanism is used with OpenStack. The client sends the authentication request to KeyStone and is sent back an *Identity Token*. This token is used by the client to request services from other OpenStack components. These services validate the identity of the client by sending the message directly to KeyStone.

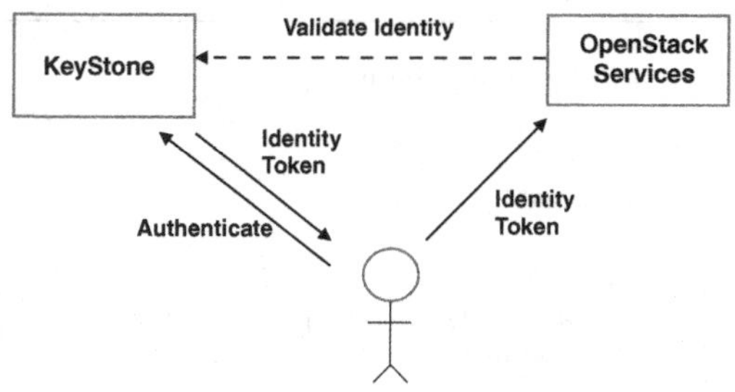

Fig. 1. KeyStone overview [4]

KeyStone offers REST API in compliance with OpenStack policy. An important feature that distinguishes REST from its contemporary SOAP-based APIs is the concept of resources. REST services expose their functionality as resources and each resource has a unique URI that provides *addressability*. CRUD (create, retrieve, update and delete) operations can be performed on resources using standard HTTP methods. These HTTP methods are considered as application-level constructs that the programs can use to interact with another program over the network in a standard manner with well-defined semantics [29]. This implies that only HTTP request methods (GET, PUT, POST, DELETE) can be invoked on KeyStone resources. In order to offer scalability, the *statelessness* feature of REST is ensured by treating every request independently. This means that every request from the client should contain all the information that is required to process it and the server is not responsible of keeping any context information with it. Each resource, when invoked via a URI and standard HTTP method, responses with response code and resource representation which contains data about resource attributes and links to other resources. The HTTP response code is a numeric code that tells the clients whether the request went successful or not. HTTP has a list of status codes that reveal how the request went [11], for example, 200 means the request was successful, 404 means the resource was not found and 403 implies that it is forbidden to make this request on this resource. The client machine interpret these response codes to know how their request went. The links in resource representation connect resources to each other and the service client gets an experience of *connectivity* between resources, i.e., moving from one resource to another.

The features of *connectivity* and *uniform interface* allows use of existing tools and infrastructure like web crawlers, curl, caches etc. The addressability requirement (specially when using hierarchical addresses) helps to provide extensibility and the statelessness requirement simplify the development of systems that can handle many service requests simultaneously facilitating scalability [25].

Listing 1.1 below shows an excerpt of POST method on *tokens* resource in KeyStone using *curl* [2] for authentication. This method is called to authenticate a user with his *name* and *password*. The payload contains JSON data that provide the required information.

```
curl -i \
  -H "Content-Type: application/json" \
  -d '
{ "auth": {
    "identity": {
      "methods": ["password"],
      "password": {
        "user": {
          "name": "admin",
          "domain": { "id": "default" },
          "password": "adminpwd"
}}}}
}' \
  http://localhost:5000/v3/auth/tokens ; echo
```

Listing 1.1. POST method for KeyStone [1]

The contemporary SOAP based services are operation centric and are based on WS-* protocol stack (SOAP, WSDL, etc.). They use different specifications built on top of each other to address different tasks. For example, WS-Resource Framework [6] and WS-Transfer [12] are commonly used to model state and WS-Security [10] is used for authentication. A common approach to invoke SOAP-based service is to call a POST method with a SOAP envelope as shown in Listing 1.2 where *curl* is used to invoke a POST method to an authentication service. All the information about the request parameters and method call are put inside the body of SOAP (*request.xml*). The server receives the request, opens the SOAP envelope and understands the message request. This means the SOAP messaging protocol is used to just transfer the messages and the semantics of the method call are determined by the message contents.

```
 curl --header "Content-Type: text/xml;charset=UTF-8" --header
      "SOAPAction:
      \"http://api.../IAuthenticationService/ClientLogin\"" \"--data
      @request.xml http://11.22.33.231:9080/AuthenticationService.svc
// Contents of request.xml
 <?xml version="1.0"encoding="utf-8"?>
<soap:Envelope xmlns:xsi="http://www.w3.org/2001/XMLSchema-instance"
xmlns:xsd="http://www.w3.org/2001/XMLSchema"
xmlns:soap="http://schemas.xmlsoap.org/soap/envelope/">
  <soap:Header>
    <Authentication xmlns="http://tempuri.org/">
      <Password>string</Password>
      <UserName>string</UserName>
    </Authentication>
  </soap:Header>
  <soap:Body>
    <HelloWorld xmlns="http://tempuri.org/"/>
  </soap:Body>
</soap:Envelope>
```

Listing 1.2. WS-Security Username Authentication [5]

Thus, the lightweight message handling mechanism and distinct features of REST architectural style make it a popular choice for adoption.

3 Overall Approach

Open-source software are open to changes and are updated frequently by different users. It becomes a challenge for in-house developers and service providers of the open-source software to validate periodically that the software continues to comply with its functional and security requirements. In a usual setting, the in-house software/security team manually look for changes and run different type of analysis techniques, ranging from manual code-inspections to running different testing tools, to identify errors. Our work provides model-driven security assurance framework for open-source software in an automatable manner. This enables the providers of open-source software to periodically verify and validate their software for the functional and security requirements it promises to deliver.

The framework is presented in Fig. 2. The framework consists of three main steps: (1) Designing (2) Generating Contracts (3) Testing. The specifications and implementation of the open source software, that are publicly available, are taken as input. The security requirements for the system are provided by security experts and also taken as an input. These three entities are marked as grey boxes in Fig. 2 to indicate their availability beforehand.

In the first step, our Security and REST compliant UML Models (SecReUM) are designed using our approach detailed in Sect. 4.

In the second step, we build upon the design by contract strategy and generate contracts from SecReUM that are implemented as code skeletons. These code skeletons are enriched with method contracts using our model-to-code transformation tool [24] and are then manually updated with security contracts and requirements, using information from SeCReUM, along with the method implementations. The code-skeletons are implemented as wrapper on top of the open-source software. A wrapper program is capable of invoking another program, perhaps with a larger body of code, by providing an interface to call. Implementation of a wrapper on top of the open-source software under test is an important component of our model-driven security assurance framework. This wrapper is maintained in-house and is updated as specifications of open source software are updated or in case of new security specifications.

The third step of our framework is *Testing* in which test cases are generated using different model-based test generation approaches from SecReUM. These test case are run against the wrapper program, generated above, to validate the implementation of open source software. Thus, by periodically running same test suites (in case the specifications are unchanged) or updated one (in case the specifications are changed), the implementation of open source software can be validated and errors can be identified using pass/fail results of the test cases.

The traceability of security requirements is also an important part of our approach. The security requirements are included as part of UML specifications and are used during validation to identify coverage level of our test cases. These requirements can be traced back to errors in the models and implementations in case of failure. This help the developers and security experts in better analysis of the system. In addition, the unfulfilled pre- and post-conditions help in localizing the faults in the implementation for both functional properties and the non-functional properties, e.g., security.

In addition to testing, the models along with implemented wrapper can also be used to provide verification of specifications and can also serve as a monitor to identify when a certain piece of updated code violates the functional or security requirements.

In this paper, we focus in detail on our designing and contract generation approach, presented in Sects. 4 and 5, respectively. The model-based test generation from SecReUM is out of scope of this paper and hence not addressed. However, for validation, we can not only benefit from our previous work for validating behavioral REST interfaces [26] but can also take advantage of large body of work done in generating test cases from behavioral contracts using UML as a familiar notation.

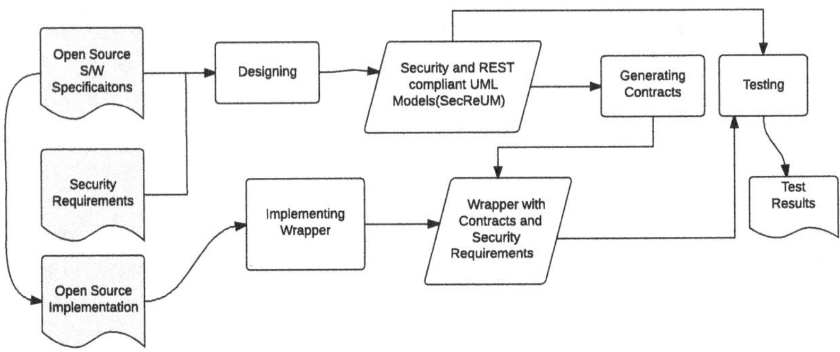

Fig. 2. Model-driven framework for security assurance

4 Modeling Approach for SecReUM

REST APIs use stateless protocol but they can be used to provide applications with complex behavior having stateful behavior. The stateful services require that a certain sequence of method invocations must be followed in order to fulfill the service goals. For example, in order to delete a user in KeyStone, the user must first authenticate herself in *admin* role and get a scoped token. The benefit of giving a stateful view to this behavior of KeyStone facilitates the understanding of KeyStone behavior and helps in validating the functional and non-functional behavior of KeyStone by defining conditions under which different methods can be invoked.

The UML standard provides different types of diagrams that can model the system from different viewpoints [28]. We model the static structure and behavioral interface of a REST service with a UML class diagram and a UML state machine, respectively. Both the diagrams are defined with additional constraints to represent REST features as explained in Sects. 4.1 and 4.2. Our previous work models stateful behavior of REST services [23]. In this work, we extend our modeling approach with technique to integrate security concerns in models. Figures 3 and 4 give an example of how we model the REST interface of KeyStone. We model the behavioral interface of KeyStone from the viewpoint of our wrapper program that will invoke the KeyStone and can constrain the user to invoke the service under right conditions and service provider to fulfill the functionality expected from it.

4.1 Resource Model

The static structure of the REST service is represented with a resource model. The resource model is a class diagram that describes the resources that constitute the service and the relationships between them. The information about allowed methods on the resources is inferred from the behavioral model. All the attributes are public since they are available on public APIs. Figure 3 shows an excerpt of the resource model for KeyStone with our wrapper program. It consists of five resource namely, *SecKS*, *Token*, *Project*, *User*, *Role*. *SecKS* represents our security KeyStone wrapper which is connected to KeyStone via *Token* resource.

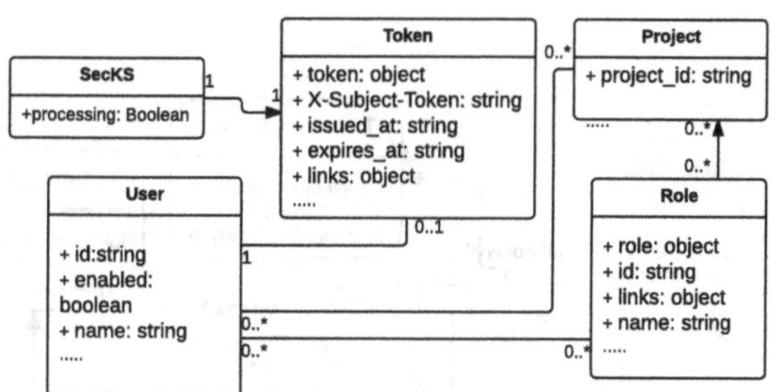

Fig. 3. Resource model for KS security wrapper (SecKS)

4.2 Behavioral Model

The purpose of the behavioral model is to describe the dynamic structure of behavioral interface of a REST service and is represented by a UML state-machine. Figure 4 shows an excerpt of behavioral interface of KeyStone and provides information on what methods a user can invoke on a resource and under what circumstances. Any client can invoke the service to request the token but only an *admin* user (shown as actor) can delete a user. If the client is valid, the token is generated, otherwise not.

A UML state-machine has transitions that are triggered by method calls and each state has a *state invariant*. State invariant is a boolean condition that is true when service is in that state and otherwise false.

In our work, we define invariant of a state as a boolean expression over addressable resources. In this way, the stateless nature of REST remains uncompromised since no hidden information about the state of the service is being kept between method calls. We have used OCL to define state invariants in behavioral models of REST services [20]. The UML specification proposes the use of OCL to define constraints in UML models, including state invariants. OCL is well supported by many modeling tools [13,14].

In Fig. 4, an OCL expression of $Token.token->size() = 0$ in state $Token\_Not\_Granted$ means that the response for invoking GET on token resource was not 200, meaning either the resource does not exist or is not reachable to infer anything about its state. Similarly, $Token.token->size() = 1$ implies the response for invoking GET on token resource was 200, meaning the resource exists. The state invariant $[self.processing = False\ and\ Token.token->size() = 1]$ for $Token\_Granted$ specify that whenever a token is requested, as a result KeyStone can generate a token and it should not be processing the request (token generation is an asynchronous call). Thus, in order to define state with stateless protocol REST, we define the state invariant as a predicate over resources.

In addition, we constrain our behavioral model to have only side-effect methods, i.e., PUT, POST and DELETE methods as method calls for a transition. This is because only these HTTP methods are capable of making any changes to resources.

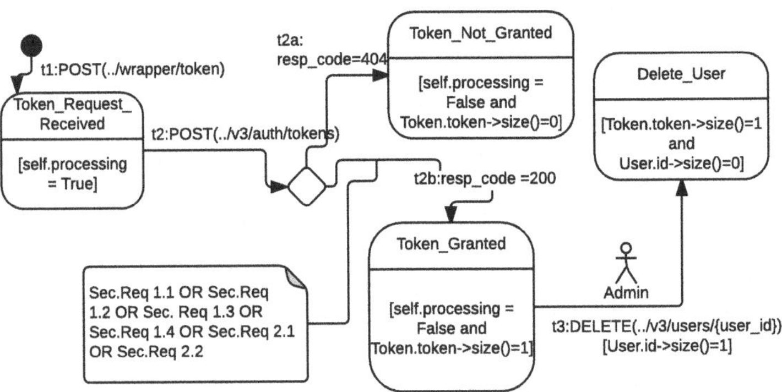

Fig. 4. Behavioral model for KS security wrapper (SecKS)

5 Generating Contracts from SecReUM

Stateful behavior of a software requires a certain order of method invocation or the conditions under which the methods can be invoked. These condition, i.e., the pre- and post-conditions of a method are called contracts. This information together with the expected effect of an operation become part of the behavioral interface of a service. Our design approach preserves the sequence of method invocations and contains behavioral information specifying the conditions under which these methods can be invoked.

5.1 Method Contract with Functional Requirements

The method contracts can be generated from the behavioral model. The precondition of a method should be true in order to fire the method in behavioral model as it defines the conditions under which a method is allowed to be invoked by the client. We say that if a method m triggers a transition t in a state machine, then the precondition for method m is true if the invariant of the source state of transition t and the guard on t is true. The post-condition constraints the implementation to provide the functionality expected from it as specified in its specification document. Thus, the post-condition states that if the precondition for invoking a method is true then its post-condition should also be true. We say, that the postcondition of method m is true if the conjunction of state invariant of target state of t and the effect on transition t are true provided its pre-condition is true. The implication principle encompasses the stateful behavior since same method can be fired from different states of the system and have different results. Thus, if the method is fired with certain pre-conditions then the corresponding post-condition for that method should be true.

The re-evaluation of the precondition of a method for evaluating the post-condition may not return the same values, i.e., before the method execution, since after the method execution values of some of the resources may change. This situation is kept safe by saving the resource values before method execution in local values in the wrapper. The values of these variables are later used to calculate the post-condition. We believe this is not computationally expensive as we do not need to save the copy of the whole resource/s but only the values that constitutes guards and invariants that are enabled. Usually, that only requires few bits of storage per method.

The method contract for method POST on *t2* can be written as under. This listing does not contain information about security requirements for invoking the method.

```
PreCondition(POST(../v3/auth/tokens)):
(self.processing = True)

PostCondition(POST(../v3/auth/tokens)):
[(self.processing = True)==>
(self.processing = False and token.token->size()=1) or
(self.processing = False and token.token->size()=0)]
```

Here, the post-condition implies that whenever a POST method is invoked on *tokens* resource from the SecKS(wrapper), SecKS is in processing state implying an asynchronous behavior. SecKS should eventually get a reply (the wrapper should not stay in processing state) and a token should either be created or not. The security requirements for generating a token and their inclusion in the contract of POST method on *tokens* are detailed in Sects. 5.2 and 5.3

A DELETE method on *User* resource will delete the user from the system and only an authorized user, i.e. an *admin*, can invoke this method. Sections 5.2 and 5.3 explain how authorization is handled in our approach. The method contract for method on *t3* can be written as under without any authorization information.

```
PreCondition(DELETE(../v3/users/{user_id})):
(self.processing = False and token.token->size()=1)

PostCondition(DELETE(../v3/users/{user_id})):
[(self.processing = False and token.token->size()=1) and
    user.id->size()=1==>
(token.token->size()=1 and user.id->size()=0]
```

For detailed description on how contracts are generated from state-machines under different scenarios, readers are referred to [22].

5.2 Security Requirements in OCL

The security requirements are usually specified by security experts. We expect these security requirements to be specified in tabular format for each method. These specifications of security requirements in a tabular format are then translated to OCL manually. These OCL-based security requirements become part of method contract during code transformation process as shown in Sect. 5.3.

The functional and security requirements for Keystone at the application level are not clearly separable. This is because the KeyStone functionality is to validate the identity of the user, his roles and access rights before generating scope or unscope token. The security requirements on KeyStone also impose the same semantics. We classify them under security requirements since the security experts expect these behaviors from KeyStone at the application level to assure its security. We explain our approach with two important security concerns, authentication and authorization. Authentication is explained with transition *t2* and authorization is explained with transition *t3*.

Authentication: Authentication is an important security concern that require that only the user with right credentials is able to enter the system. It is also considered as one of the top three security concerns addressed by existing model-driven security engineering approaches [19]. In Fig. 4, an authentication request to KeyStone triggers transition t2. The security requirements attached to t2 are listed in Table 1.

These security requirements are written in OCL. For example, the security requirement for scoped token is written as:

```
((user.credential->size()=1 or  token.token->size()=1)  and
(request.scope->size()=1 and  not  request.scope.oclIsInvalid()))
   ==> (token.token->size()=1) and token.catalog->size()=1)
```

Table 1. Requirements for authentication in KeyStone (excerpt)

No.	If	Then
1.1	User is valid and has not given scope information	An unscoped token should be generated
1.2	User is valid and has explicitly requested unscoped token	
1.3	Token is valid and has not given scope information	
1.4	Token is valid and has explicitly requested unscoped token	
2.1	User is valid and has valid scope information	A scoped token should be generated
2.2	Token is valid and has valid scope information	

In Table 1, the security requirements specify different conditions under which scoped and unscoped tokens are issued and are written in if-else format on resources and resource attributes. The security requirements can also be in a statement form enforcing some rule, for example, the authorization requirement explained in the next section.

Authorization. Authorization defines access rights of users by defining permissions on user, user roles and user groups. KeyStone determines whether a request from the user should be allowed or not based on policy rules defined in Role Based Access Control (RBAC). In Fig. 4, *t3* can only be fired by an *admin* user and not other wise. In addition, the guard value show that initially the user being deleted should exist in the system. The information of actors in the behavioral model can be realized in three ways.

(1) Developer can use this information to implement the access rights on resources and help users in understanding and writing correct authorization headers. Different authentication mechanisms can be implemented to control access to resources [3]. In case, Basic authentication mechanism is implemented, client sends the user name and password to the server in authorization header. The authentication information is in base-64 encoding. It should only be used with HTTPS, as the password can be easily captured and reused over HTTP.

In a typical setting, the authorization header is constructed by first combining *username* and *password* into a string "username:password" and then encoded in based64. A typical authorization header in Basic authentication is shown below:

```
DELETE /v3/users/22/ HTTP/1.1
Host:http://localhost:5000/v3/
Authorization: Basic aHR0cHdhdGNoOmY=
```

In case an anonymous requests for a protected resource, HTTP can enforce basic authentication by rejecting the request with a 401 (Access Denied) status code.

```
HTTP/1.1 401 Access Denied
WWW-Authenticate: Basic realm="User"
Content-Length: 0
```

For KeyStone, authorization to resources is check with *token*. A typical call from *curl* to access *User* resource using user's *token* is given as:

```
curl -s \ -H"X-Auth-Token:
    $OS_TOKEN"\"http://localhost:5000/v3/users"
```

(2) The security requirements can be attached as predicates of boolean variables to transitions and translated to code as such. All the boolean variables for security requirements are initialized to be false, e.g. $sreq1 = False$. Whenever, the postcondition of a requirement is true in the implementation, the boolean variable is set as True, $sreq1 = True$. The boolean values of these security requirements are displayed to the user after the system is tested with different test cases. This added feature gives clear information to security experts as to what security requirements are satisfied and in identifying the met and unmet security requirements by the system without looking into the implementation details.

(3) It becomes part of method contract. The security requirement for authorization is: *Only an admin user can delete a user.* In OCL, it is written as: $user.role = $ '*admin*'.

This can be specified in UML as notes (not shown in Fig. 4 due to space limitation). In the next section, we define rules on how they becomes part of the method contract.

5.3 Method Contracts with Functional and Security Requirements

The security requirements are merged with functional requirements during the translation process to code. In our example, the KeyStone service is invoked by POST method on the token resource ($POST(../v3/auth/tokens)$). We populate our definition of contracts with security requirements given above such that:

- The statement in *if* clause become part of the method pre-condition
- The statement in *else* clause become part of the method post-condition
- The statement/s that are not part of *if-else* clause become part of both the pre- and post-condition. By checking the rule in pre-condition, the user request is validated before processing the method and causing undesired changed in the system. By placing in the post-condition, the system is validated that it behaves as expected and does not do what it is not required to do. This serves as a double check on security requirements.

We, thus, require that in order for KeyStone to generate a token the following method contract must be met:

```
PreCondition(POST(../v3/auth/tokens)):

[(self.processing = True and (user.credential->size()=1 or
token.token->size()=1)
and
((request.scope->size()=1 and request.scope <> 'unscope' and not
     request.scope.oclIsInvalid())
or (request.scope->size()=0 or request.scope.oclIsInvalid() or
request.scope = 'unscope' ))]

PostCondition(POST(../v3/auth/tokens)):
[((user.credential->size()=1 or
token.token->size()=1) and
request.scope->size()=1 and request.scope <> 'unscope' and not
     request.scope.oclIsInvalid())==>
(self.processing = False and token.token->size()=1 and
     token.catalog->size()=1)
or (self.processing = True and request.scope->size()=0 or
     request.scope.oclIsInvalid() or
request.scope = 'unscope' ) ==> (self.processing = False and
     token.token->size()=1) and token.catalog->size()=0)
]
```

The preconditions in the listing above shows the boolean expression that should be true for invoking a POST on KeyStone for either scoped or unscoped token. The postcondition circumscribes different scenarios for scoped and unscoped token. In order to return an unscoped/scoped token, the previous values, i.e. the values before method invocation, are checked. If the previous values require an unscoped/scoped token then the response of method calls are checked to ensure if unscoped/scoped token is actually delivered. The previous values, i.e., the values before the method invocation are stored as local variables in the wrapper program.

Similarly, for authorization, the method contract for DELETE on user resources is given as:

```
PreCondition(DELETE(../v3/users/{user_id}))):

[self.processing = False and token.token->size()=1 and
user.id->size()=1 and user.role='admin']

PostCondition(DELETE(../v3/users/{user_id})):
[(self.processing = False and token.token->size()=1 and
user.id->size()=1  and user.role='admin') ==>
(token.token->size()=1 and user.role='admin' and
user.id->size()=0)]
```

In this listing, *user.role* = '*admin*' is checked before invoking DELETE method on $User$ resource to ensure that user with the right credentials is making the desired change in the system. Interestingly, *user.role* = '*admin*' is also a part of the post-condition, i.e., the credentials of the user are checked before and after the method execution to ensure that the system change is made by the right user. This double check of the security requirement for authorization provides added security and guards the system against malicious user during the communication.

6 Related Work

Research in using models to develop and analyze secure systems has been an active area of research for more than a decade. The work of Nguyen et al. [19] provides a comprehensive review of efforts done in the area of model-driven development of secure systems. Their work encompasses various modeling approaches like UML-based approaches, UML profiles, DSLs and aspect oriented approaches and analyzes them for their support for model-to-code and model-to-model transformations, verification, validation and different types of security concerns.

UML has been used much to model security concerns. Some approaches use only UML (e.g., [7], *MDSE@R* [9], *AOMSec* [15] etc.) and some use UML profiles(e.g., SECTET [8], *UMLsec* [16], etc.)

In [7], Abramov et al. present a model-driven approach to integrate access control policies on database development.

SECTET [8] provides a model-driven security approach for web services. They also use OCL to define constraints on UML to provide access control. The approach generates XACML policy files that provide a platform independent policy for enforcing the access control policy. The SECTET framework mainly addresses authorization and provides state-dependent permissions that are not applicable to REST interfaces. *UMLsec* [16,17] provides a comprehensive and consistently progressing approach to formally analyze the security properties. *MDSE@R* [9] provides a UML profile based approach that uses aspect-oriented programming to integrate security concerns at the runtime. *AOMSec* [15] also uses aspect-oriented approach to model security mechanism and attacks to the system. A detailed analysis of existing literature is out of scope of this paper. However, compared to previous work our work strongly relies on existing UML without the need of any new profiles. This gives the benefit of using many well-known and mature tools with a wide user base for our approach. Our work also caters well with the stateless nature of REST APIs.

7 Conclusions

Security experts are often looking out for ways to assure that their security expectations from a system are met. This becomes even more challenging in an open-source environment that encourages collaborative environment between developers that are working within a controlled environment and developers that are outside a controlled boundary. Our approach provides a security assurance framework that facilitates the security experts by providing a semi-automatable approach for validating the system under study for its behavior. We show how the security concerns can be integrated into the behavioral models of REST services and how method contracts can be generated from them that can be used to validate any security loopholes in the open source software in case of frequent updates. We address authentication and authorization of open source software using models and provide series of steps on how the security requirement can be combined with functional contracts. The approach is applied on the KeyStone component of OpenStack. In our future work, we plan to provide automation of security concerns to code and extend our work with other security concerns.

References

1. API Examples using Curl. https://docs.openstack.org/developer/keystone/devref/api_curl_examples.html. Accessed June 2017
2. cURL. http://curl.haxx.se/. Accessed 20 May 2017
3. HTTP Authentication. http://www.httpwatch.com/httpgallery/authentication/. Accessed 20 Aug 2013
4. KeyStone Security and Architecture Review. https://www.openstack.org/summit/openstack-summit-atlanta-2014/session-videos/presentation/keystone-security-and-architecture-review. Accessed June 2017
5. SOAP Request and CURL. http://dasunhegoda.com/make-soap-request-command-line-curl/596/. Accessed June 2017
6. Web services resources framework (wsrf 1.2). https://www.oasis-open.org/committees/tc_home.php?wg_abbrev=wsrf. Accessed 01 Nov 2013
7. Abramov, J., Anson, O., Dahan, M., Shoval, P., Sturm, A.: A methodology for integrating access control policies within database development. Comput. Secur. **31**(3), 299–314 (2012)
8. Alam, M.M., Breu, R., Breu, M.: Model driven security for web services (MDS4WS). In: Proceedings of INMIC 2004 - 8th International Multitopic Conference, pp. 498–505. IEEE (2004)
9. Almorsy, M., Grundy, J., Ibrahim, A.S.: Adaptable, model-driven security engineering for SaaS cloud-based applications. Autom. Softw. Eng. **21**(2), 187–224 (2014)
10. Atkinson, B., Della-Libera, G., Hada, S., Hondo, M., Hallam-Baker, P., Klein, J., LaMacchia, B., Leach, P., Manferdelli, J., Maruyama, H., et al.: Web services security (WS-Security). Specification, Microsoft Corporation (2002)
11. Berners-Lee, T., Fielding, R., Frystyk, H.: Hypertext transfer protocol-HTTP/1.0 (1996)
12. Davis, D., Malhotra, A., Warr, O.K., Chou, W.: Web services transfer (WS-Transfer). World Wide Web Consortium, Recommendation REC-ws-transfer-20111213 (2011)
13. Demuth, B., Wilke, C.: Model and object verification by using Dresden OCL. In: Proceedings of the Russian-German Workshop Innovation Information Technologies: Theory and Practice, pp. 81–89 (2009)
14. Garcia, M., Shidqie, A.J.: OCL compiler for EMF. In: Eclipse Modeling Symposium at Eclipse Summit Europe (2007)
15. Georg, G., Ray, I., Anastasakis, K., Bordbar, B., Toahchoodee, M., Houmb, S.H.: An aspect-oriented methodology for designing secure applications. Inf. Softw. Technol. **51**(5), 846–864 (2009)
16. Jürjens, J.: Towards development of secure systems using UMLsec. In: Hussmann, H. (ed.) FASE 2001. LNCS, vol. 2029, pp. 187–200. Springer, Heidelberg (2001). doi:10.1007/3-540-45314-8_14
17. Jürjens, J., Shabalin, P.: Tools for secure systems development with UML. Int. J. Softw. Tools Technol. Transf. **9**(5–6), 527–544 (2007)
18. Meyer, B.: Applying ‘design by contract’. Computer **25**(10), 40–51 (1992)

19. Nguyen, H.P., Kramer, M., Klein, J., Traon, Y.L.: An extensive systematic review on the model-driven development of secure systems. Inf. Softw. Technol. **68**, 62–81 (2015)
20. OMG: OCL, OMG Available Specification, Version 2.0 (2006)
21. Pepple, K.: Deploying OpenStack. O'Reilly Media Inc., Sebastopol (2011)
22. Porres, I., Rauf, I.: From nondeterministic UML protocol statemachines to class contracts. In: 2010 Third International Conference on Software Testing, Verification and Validation (ICST), pp. 107–116. IEEE (2010)
23. Porres, I., Rauf, I.: Modeling behavioral restful web service interfaces in UML. In: Proceedings of the 2011 ACM Symposium on Applied Computing, pp. 1598–1605. ACM (2011)
24. Rauf, I., Porres, I.: REST: from research to practice. In: Wilde, E., Pautasso, C. (eds.) Beyond CRUD, vol. 2029, pp. 117–135. Springer, New York (2011). doi:10.1007/978-1-4419-8303-9_5
25. Rauf, I., Ruokonen, A., Systa, T., Porres, I.: Modeling a composite restful web service with UML. In: Proceedings of the Fourth European Conference on Software Architecture: Companion Volume, pp. 253–260. ACM (2010)
26. Rauf, I., Siavashi, F., Truscan, D., Porres, I.: Scenario-based design and validation of REST web service compositions. In: Monfort, V., Krempels, K.-H. (eds.) WEBIST 2014. LNBIP, vol. 226, pp. 145–160. Springer, Cham (2015). doi:10.1007/978-3-319-27030-2_10
27. Sefraoui, O., Aissaoui, M., Eleuldj, M.: Openstack: toward an open-source solution for cloud computing. Int. J. Comput. Appl. **55**(3) (2012)
28. OMG Uml. 2.0 superstructure specification. OMG, Needham (2004)
29. Webber, J., Parastatidis, S., Robinson, I.: REST in Practice: Hypermedia and Systems Architecture. O'Reilly Media Inc., Sebastopol (2010)

A Cyber-Physical Space Operational Approach for Crowd Evacuation Handling

Henry Muccini(✉) and Mahyar Tourchi Moghaddam

DISIM Department, University of L'Aquila, Vetoio St. 1, L'Aquila, Italy
henry.muccini@univaq.it,
mahyar.tourchimoghaddam@graduate.univaq.it

Abstract. Crowded public venues are significantly under risks and uncertainties caused by fire and overcrowding hazards. For this purpose, Situational Awareness (SiA) -that is a mechanism to know what is going on around- can facilitate the automatic (or human involved) critical decision making and executing processes. Considering the dynamic and uncertain essence of crowd and hazard behavior in an emergency, executing the optimum *evacuation plan* is highly complex and needs strong models. In this paper, taking in input a model of the Cyber-Physical Space under SiA monitoring, we define an architectural-map-based Dynamic Bayesian Network (DBN) to describe and predict crowd and hazard behavior. Then, in order to minimize the total evacuation time, the authors present a quickest flow model for consecutive time intervals. Overall, the paper shows the importance of hazard quiddity, and crowd behavior on the evacuation efficiency in emergency situations. The approach is demonstrated through a small (but concrete) running example.

Keywords: Cyber-Physical Space (CPSpace) · CPSpace modeling architecture · Emergency evacuation handling · Situational Awareness (SiA) · IoT · Crowd monitoring · Dynamic Bayesian Network

1 Introduction

Situational Awareness (SiA) can be defined as what is going on around and the ability of dynamic situation prediction. Literally, SiA deals with the perception of the elements of environment within a volume of time and space, the comprehension of their meaning, and the projection of their status in the near future (Endsley 1995). Moreover, Internet of Things (IoT) opens exquisite views on SiA. IoT is a "heterogeneous network of objects that communicate with each other and their owners over the Internet" (Gendreau 2015). With growing the IoT technologies, the SiA management and monitoring will be a critical issue, qua according to an estimation, "by 2020, a trillion IP addresses (objects) will be connected to the Internet" (Pretz 2014). IoT serves Machine-to-Machine connectivity to provide a degree of automation in many fields like crowd critical monitoring.

Indeed, an ideal SiA system is one that can put aside human factor from the loop, but there is still a huge gap to achieve this point.

A. Romanovsky and E.A. Troubitsyna (Eds.): SERENE 2017, LNCS 10479, pp. 81–95, 2017.
DOI: 10.1007/978-3-319-65948-0_6

Therefore, human plays a key role in “Cyber Situational Awareness” (CSiA) alongside of physical and virtual sensors. Mainly “Cyberspace” referred to the Internet as a type of dimension in the space, however, in IoT it extended from Internet to the physical spaces between the objects and their owners.

The role of CSiA becomes more highlighted in critical conditions like earthquakes, fires or floods where the rapid situation understanding is essential for an optimal decision making and agile executing by the emergency bodies. The problems are more critical in the case of overcrowding in a closed area where people are severely occluded.

Recently, the scientists are trying to deal with crowd monitoring problems vastly, considering both related social and technical aspects. From social point of view, the models study crowd behavior anthropologically and based on psychology and sociology sciences. The technical view, instead, investigates on event detection and especial aspects deriving from computer vision based algorithms.

In this paper, on the one hand, the authors define an architectural-map-based Dynamic Bayesian Network (DBN) to describe and predict crowd and hazard behavior. On the other hand, for minimizing the total evacuation time, the authors present a quickest flow model. Overall, the paper shows the importance of hazard quiddity and crowd behavior on the evacuation efficiency in emergency situations.

Based on our objective, this paper is organized as follow. Section 2 mentions some related works. Section 3 focuses on backgrounds and deals with issues, controversies, and problems. In this section, we briefly recall the theoretical foundations of SiA, CSiA, processing loops, BN, DBN, CAPS, social-behavioral modeling and their cost functions. Then we discuss social behavior modeling for evacuation in Sect. 4. Section 5 explains the definition of quickest flow and its application to the problem. A case study is presented in Sect. 6, to help better understanding the solving method. Section 7 targeted on presenting conclusions and future work.

2 Related Works

Following a literature review, we studied some researches concerning the application of Situational Awareness in crowd monitoring and decision making. In this regard, Tadda et al. (2010) provided a chapter as an “overview of Cyber SiA”; the chapter defines the basics of SiA, the models and some processes to performance measuring of a SiA system. Gendreau (2015) investigated on SiA measurement enhanced for efficient monitoring in the Internet of Things. Naderpour et al. (2013) used the fuzzy Dynamic Bayesian Network-based SiA to support the operators in decision making process in hazardous situations. Radianti et al. (2015) have proposed a spatio-temporal probabilistic model of hazard and crowd dynamics in disasters (based on DBN), with the intent of supporting real-time evacuation planning by means of situation tracking and forecasting. Tashakori et al. (2015) have introduced an indoor/outdoor 3D spatial city model for indoor incidents, using SiA concepts. Muccini et al. (2017) introduced CAPS modeling that is an architecture-driven modeling framework for the development of Situational Aware Cyber-Physical Systems. He et al. (2015) discussed K-shortest-path-based evacuation routing with police resource allocation in city transportation networks that can be somehow related to our topic.

Taking advantage from all above mentioned literatures, this paper introduces a combination of DBN and Quickest flow models for emergency evacuation problems, taking into account a risk index that refers to each area's crowd density. Thus, we involved the real time crowd dynamic behavior in our model to choose the optimum evacuation path in each time slice.

3 Background

3.1 Situational Awareness (SiA) and Cyber-Situational Awareness (CSiA)

SiA is a type of context aware behavior that refers to "knowing what is going on" within an environment (Endsley 2000). SiA involves direct and indirect information acquiring about the environment, about who is doing what and where, and then interpreting this information for a particular goal. The formal definition of SiA breaks down into three separate levels: (1) perception (recognition) of the elements in the environment, (2) comprehension of the current situation, (3) projection of future status (Endsley et al. 1995). Perception level involves the sensory detection of the system and its environment. Comprehension phase includes data perceiving and situation understanding to achieve the specified goal. Projection means deducing information to see its future effect on the operative environment.

Considering CSiA as a subset of SiA, it can be defined as a section of SiA that deals with Cyber-Physical systems (CPSs). CPSs are a kind of system of system (SoS) that define as a network of individual systems coordinating each other to benefit from the joined operation as a whole. CPSs create the situational information, with formalizing sensors values to situation parameters. Therefore, such situation parameters "can be fed to a data fusion process or be interpreted directly by the decision maker" (Franke et al. 2014). Despite CSiA concept is using in various fields like Industrial Control Systems, Military, and Information Fusion, we call it notably for its "emergency management" application.

3.2 Processing Loops

To monitor large areas, a relatively large number of sensors are needed. In such a cases, due to so-called large number of sensors, a quality loss of produced data could be occurred, which makes the monitoring failed or inefficient. To solve the above-mentioned problem, processing loops are introduced. Processing loops are some feedback models that guide operators on the decision making process. A processing loop is a module that can receive sensors' data, process them, and find the dangerous or odd events under interaction with environment and human operator. Among different processing loops, OODA (observe, orient, decide, act), MAPE-K (monitoring, analysis, plan, executing, knowledge), and cognitive cycle (sensing, analysis, decision, action) are more often used in the related literature.

As it stands, despite there exist some differences between the processing loops, their applications are somehow the same. We take advantage from the concept of feedback loops to have a structured view on our monitoring and decision making steps.

3.3 CAPS

CAPS (an architecture-driven modeling framework for Situational Aware Cyber-Physical Systems) is a modeling languages used to describe (1) software architecture, (2) hardware configuration, and (3) physical space views for a situational aware CPS (SiA-CPS) proposed with one of the authors in previous work (Muccini et al. 2017). The framework is aimed at supporting the architecture description, reasoning, and design decision process.

According to the objective of this paper, we take advantage from the Physical Space View Modeling Language [SPML] CAPS viewpoint for our case. SPML describes the physical space involved in situation awareness. The SPML modeling language defines an area with its coordinates, as well as rooms with associated walls, ceiling, and floor.

The SPML language is about the site in the real world where the SiA-CPS equipment will be deployed. The central class in the SPML is the CyberPhysicalSpaces class. The CyberPhysicalSpace represents the overall environment in the 3D space in which the SiA-CPS nodes will be deployed. Any kind of SiA-CPS element (cyber element or physical element) can be placed in the environment. Each element is characterized by the name, the abscissa and the ordinate of the center of this element, dimensions (width, depth, height), elevation, fixed or movable, door or window, the angle, material type, and its attenuation coefficient of this material (Muccini et al. 2017). The attenuation coefficient is a decimal number ranging from zero to one.

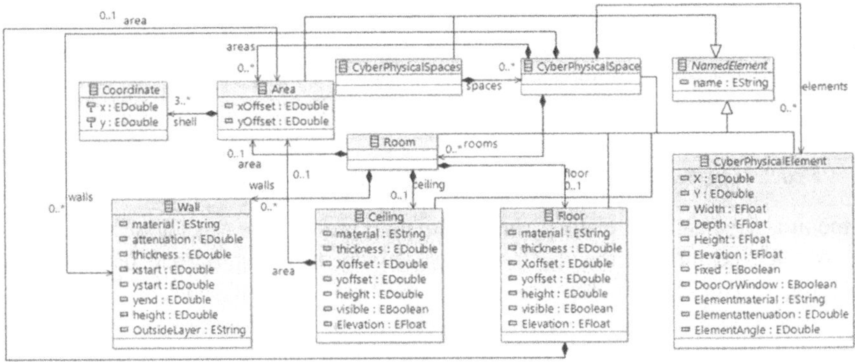

Fig. 1. SPML metamodel

In SPML an area identifies a portion of physical space in which element can be distributed. The shape of this area is given by its shell: a sequence of coordinates representing the perimeter of the area in the 2D space. A Wall is a class characterized by name of the material, attenuation coefficient, thickness, and the abscissa and the ordinate for the beginning and the end of this wall. To avoid unnecessary repetition of effort, we used existing extensible 3D modeling environments (and specifically, Sweet Home 3D) to represent the space model generated by CAPS. In other words, the model is realized using a customization of Sweet Home (Fig. 4) according to the SPML metamodel (Fig. 1). Sweet Home 3D supports the implementation of new plug-in files to develop new features.

3.4 Bayesian Network (BN) and Dynamic Bayesian Network (DBN)

A BN is a directed acyclic graphical model in which nodes correspond to random variables and arcs represent dependencies or causal relationships between these variables with conditional probabilities. The standard BN represents the static cause-effect relations among different objects in a situation. Thus, the BN is a compact graphical representation of the full joint probability distribution P(X) of discrete or continuous random variables $X = \{X_1, X_2, \ldots, X_n\}$, included in the distribution network as:

$$P(X) = \prod_{i=1}^{n} P(X_i where|Par(X_i)) \quad \text{Par } (X_i) = \text{ the parent set of } X_i \text{ for any } i = 1, \ldots, n \tag{1}$$

DBN is a BN by adding the temporal behavior to some system's variables. The dependency between random variables in a specific moment, capture their dynamic behavior. The random variables of BN (nodes) that in presence of time become temporal nodes, are assumed to have the first order Markov dependency on their values at the previous moment and each temporal node has an additional parent (a copy of the same node from the previous time slice) (Tolstikov et al. 2007). Thus, here X_t^i is i^{th} node at time frame t and random variables $par(X_t^i)$ are its parents, which can include variables from a preceding time step, repetitive.

$$P(X_t \middle| X_{t-1}) = \prod_{i=1}^{n} P(X_t^i|Par(X_t^i)) \tag{2}$$

The joint probability distribution for a sequence of length T is therefore given by unrolling the formula 2:

$$P(X_{1:T}) = \prod_{t=1}^{T}\prod_{i=1}^{n} P(X_t^i|Par(X_t^i)) \tag{3}$$

3.5 DBN-Based Hazard and Crowd Behavior Model

DBN can explain the dynamic behavior of a hazard. Let us consider occurring a hazard in a closed area with some rooms linked together (like a museum), assume that we realize a growing fire or overcrowded situation in time t = 1 in room 1. The hazard can spread time by time to neighbor locations with different possible behaviors (Radianti et al. 2015). In overcrowding hazard, we can consider each location's crowdedness as empty, some, full, or overcrowded. Although an empty location or a place in which located some people, can host more people from neighbor locations, a full location should be unloaded in order to accept more people. Whilst the overcrowded location considers as presence of a hazard that crowd evacuation should be perform to lead the flow to other places as fast as possible. The following figure is an example to illustrates the links between location situation and crowd behavior for two neighbor rooms.

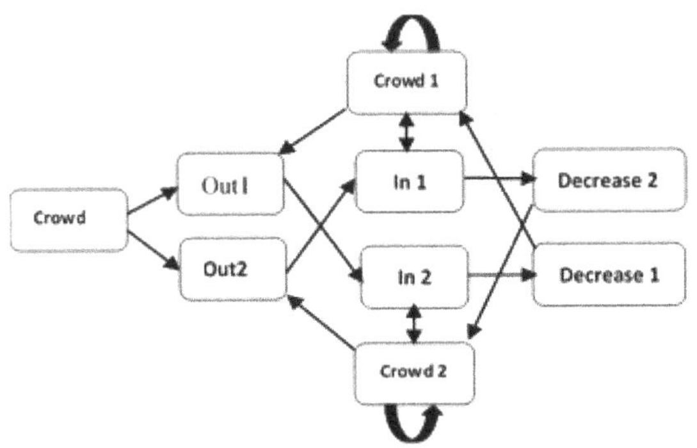

Fig. 2. DBN behavioral model

In both situations of overcrowding and other hazards (like fire and terrorist attacks), we can study the crowd flow with DBN. The model assesses the crowd direction who are leaving a hazardous area. Figure 2, models the crowd flow between two rooms in an indoor venue according to DBN. If the hazard happens in room 1 (or near to room 1), people will move from room 1 to room 2 that supposedly is the optimum next interval destination, and decreasing the number of persons located in area 1 impact crowdedness of both rooms. Here, 1 is a parent for in-1 and out-1 and people can move to 2 or stay in the same place.

Therefore, our following quickest flow model specifies what destination is selected for next interval and DBN calculates the remained crowd in location X based on its parents "in X" and "out X". In other words, the situation of each location depends on the neighbor locations that are directly linked to that. The structure of graff highly depends on the number of neighbors and parental situation.

In the same way, the hazard status (like fire) can be modeled with DBN. The hazard in time step t which can spread to neighbors considering the time delay. For the above example, in the next time step, room1 hazard can spread to room 2 or can have another state in the same room. Thus, the hazard1 can be a parent for hazard2 or hazard1 itself.

4 Social Behavior Modeling in Evacuation

In the special situation that a space gets increasingly crowded and evacuation is needed, flow of people cannot be smooth and they cannot follow a straight path. In this situation, some variables such as crowd confusion and velocity are important.

4.1 Confusion

In a Crowded area, confusion due to stress, anxiety, low visibility, and etc. can negatively impact the evacuation process (Radianti et al. 2015). When a person is confused, he is not able to take the optimal decision in the critical moment. Confusion depends on the number of human operators in evacuation procedure. It means that, in the presence of operators, the possibility of optimum path selection would be high and the confusion possibility would be trivial. The reason is that, the operators will have the optimum evacuation path provided by the DBN and quickest flow models. However, in our case, the confusion considered as a variable of Risk Index that is the number of persons located in each area divided by the capacity of that area, which highly impact on the crowd walking speed. In other words, a high density makes people more confused and slow.

4.2 Velocity

In the walking speed issue, the age of each person can determines his default walking speed. For example, the average walking speed of pedestrians age 65 or above is 0.889 to 1.083 m/s, while that of pedestrians aged below 65 is 1.042 to 1.508 m/s (Feng et al. (2016); TranSafety Inc. (1997)). However, the pedestrians' walking speed is highly depending on crowdedness rate, which is specified by Risk Index.

5 Optimal Crowd Evacuation Using Quickest Flow Model

The model performs the crowd evacuation optimization in emergency cases, with minimization of the total evacuation time. The idea has its roots in vehicle routing optimization in transportation problems, however it fixed with the human factors and crowded areas characteristics in a conceptual application. The indoor area that will be used as case study, consists of a set of rooms linked by a set of paths, and a number of entrances (as sources) and a number of emergency exits (as destinations). We assume that in an emergency, crowd will be evacuated from source to destination through the network taking into account the rooms and paths capacity and the crowd arrival rate in each area.

Considering the above discussed social behavioral aspects, we assume that more crowdedness situation leads to more confusion, less velocity, and obstacle.

The confusion is assumed to be dependent on the risk element calculated by the number of persons that are located in an area divided by the area's capacity for different time intervals. In other words, we assume that the confusion has a positive linear relation to the obstacle on the path. Indeed, the more crowd in the path, the more individual confusion. The risk value will be considered as a cost for our quickest flow network calculations. We also assume that the operators are located in the paths intersections in a proper specific number, thus, their role is to lead crowd's flow to the optimum path, without any additional cost.

To illustrate the implementation of the proposed approach in a real environment, the "Uffizi Gallery" is chosen as a running example. The museum is located in central Florence, Italy, and is one of the world's best known and most visited museums with almost 2.1 M visitors per year. The museum is spread out over three floors and the visit starts from second floor because of its grand staircase. To implement our model, we consider the following section of the second floor 2D map that is consist of seven different areas. Due to a non-disclosure agreement, the position of the emergency doors is fictitious.

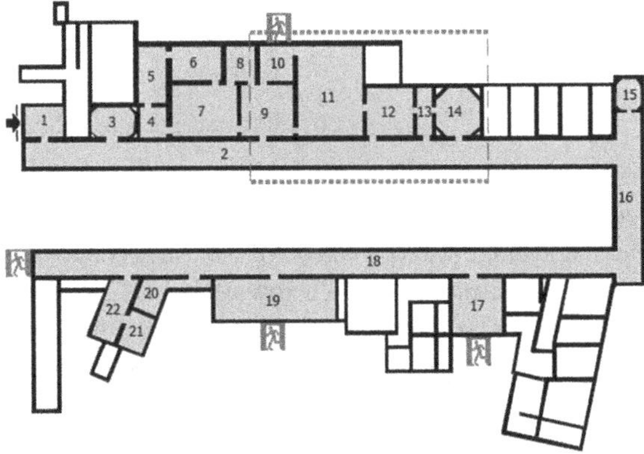

Fig. 3. 2D map of UFFIZI second floor

Our approach takes into account the following components:

- the OODA processing loop, as the reference control loop model;
- the CAPS modeling environment, to specify the area under monitoring;
- a risk index, to dynamically calculate the density of each area;
- the Dynamic Bayesian Network, to model the location network layout.

Based on those inputs, we then compute the quickest evacuation path. Section 6 provides a description of the steps above, whit their application to the running example.

6 Application of the Optimal Crowd Evacuation Approach to the Running Example

Considering our case as a situational aware IoT system, we apply our method to find the optimal evacuation path in a dynamic real time system. In other words, we mainly concentrate our investigations about situational aware IoT systems on indoor crowd management in emergency situations. This would provide us with some concrete real world experiences and a scenario to reason upon.

6.1 CSiA and Processing Loops

To monitor a large area such as the UFFIZI museum, a relatively large number of sensors are needed. In such a cases, due to so-called large number of sensors, a quality loss of produced data could be occurred, which makes the monitoring failed or inefficient. Software Engineering scientists tried to adopt novel processing loops (such as OODA loop, MAPE-K feedback loop, and cognitive cycle) to manage a process. Here we recall the OODA loop for UFFIZI case.

The OODA loop guide operators on the decision making process, and on using available information. This loop originally designed for military command and control system, anyhow it is compatible by other civil systems like our CSiA Model. The OODA process can be defined in four main steps: **Observe** (know what is happening), **Orient** (understand the meaning of what was observed), **Decide** (weighing the options available and picking one), and **Act** (carrying out the decision). The loop starts again from beginning, after a decision has been made and the related action has been taken.

Observe: the sensors (cameras and people counters) monitor the crowd situation and count the number of people in each area.

Orient: the data gathered refines in this phase to be ready for decision step. Information should be classified in consecutive time slices.

Decide: predefined rules for each area are set, for instance, the count of persons inside the room should be lower than the room capacity in normal situation, if not the overcrowding emergency situation is detected. In emergency case, the quickest flow should be chosen in accordance with the DBN risk element. If an emergency case is detected, a message will be send to the involved operators to execute evacuation, otherwise no action required by the system.

Act: The situation monitors by the human operators and in the emergency situation, they lead the crowd flow to the optimum path for evacuation.

6.2 Caps

Figure 4 shows the SPML model representing the physical environment of our UFFIZI scenario, the selected part of the second floor. It contains many kinds of obstacles that are concrete walls dividing the whole building into rooms and corridors, connector doors and an emergency door. The physical environment of our scenario contains many deployment areas. From the figure, we can see a number of SiA-CPS elements deployed in the environment (they are hypothetical because of an agreement). Here we used existing extensible 3D modeling environments (Sweet Home 3D) to represent the space model generated by CAPS. Sweet Home 3D supports the implementation of new plug-in files to develop new features (SWEETHOME-SWEET 2015).

Fig. 4. 3D map of selected area

6.3 Risk Index

A simulation performed for 7 selected areas that are monitored by the virtual sensors (counters) in accordance with the DBN model. The model (Chiappino et al. 2013) analyzes the risk level of each selected area by introducing a performance indicator that monitors each room's crowd based on its maximum capacity.

$$R_i = \frac{N_i}{N_i^{max}} \tag{5}$$

Where R_i is the risk index, N_i is the number of people located in an area in a specific time interval, and N_i^{max} is the maximum capacity of the related area. This index can show the crowd flows in a dynamic mode and let the decision makers to take best decision in overcrowding situations. As the index is a variable of confusion and velocity, it will be used in the following quickest flow model as a cost function to choose the optimum evacuation path at each time slice. The temporal window between each surveillance considered 20 s and the number of intervals are 4.

6.4 DBN

According to above mentioned Risk Index and DBN definitions, the structure layout is shown in Fig. 6. Nodes represent the different locations, node E represents the exit door, and arcs show the paths the people should be evacuated through. For example, a

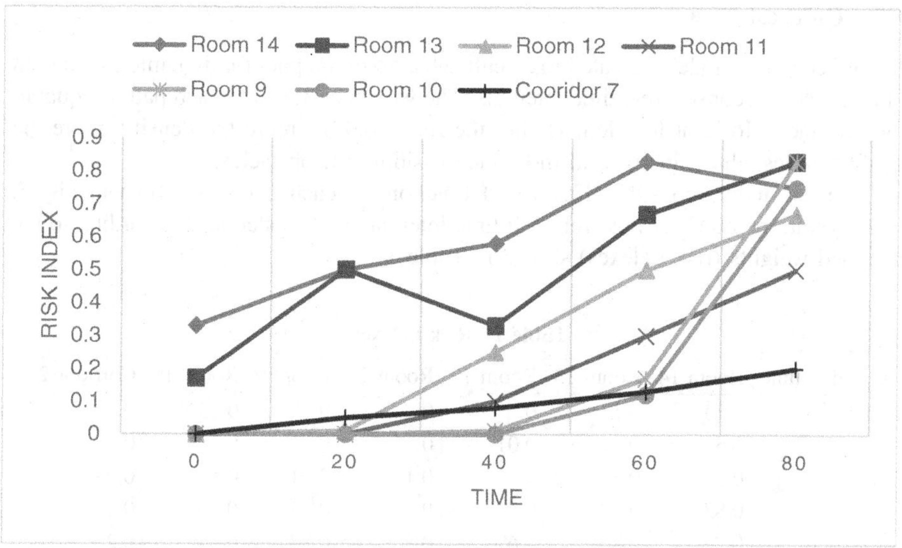

Fig. 5. Risk index

person located in the area 14, may pass to the area 13 or 2 (according to above 2D and 3D maps), or can stay in the same room in timespan between *t-1* to *t*. In case of overcrowding (or any other emergency case), the system shows to the operators the most efficient path for leading people toward emergency exit by considering the quickest flow, behavioral aspects (like confusion), and structural constraints (e.g., size of rooms and doors).

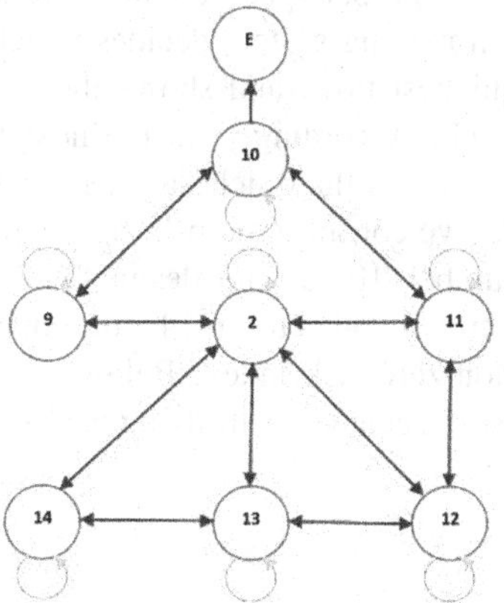

Fig. 6. Location network layout

6.5 Quickest Flow

In this section, a model is created to calculate the optimum path for dynamic evacuation in four selected consecutive time intervals. The weight assigned to each path is equal to the risk index for that location. Higher the risk index is, more the density, more the confusion, less the velocity, and more the possibility of obstacles.

The risk index, considered as a cost function for each node, is shown in Fig. 5. Based on it, the quickest flow for each time interval can be calculated according to the assigned weights (risk indexes) shown in Table 1.

Table 1. Risk indexes.

Location time	Room 14	Room 13	Room 12	Room 11	Room 9	Room 10	Corridor 2
0	0.33	0.17	0	0	0	0	0
20	0.5	0.5	0.01	0	0	0	0.05
40	0.58	0.33	0.25	0.1	0.01	0	0.08
60	0.83	0.67	0.5	0.3	0.17	0.12	0.13
80	0.75	0.83	0.67	0.5	0.83	0.75	0.2

The table shows the density of each place in each monitored time slice. The crowd is entering from the entrance and passing by room number 14 and so on. We suppose an emergency situation happens and crowd should be evacuated from the quickest path. According to Fig. 3, the emergency exit is located on the room 10, thus, all people should pass by that room to be evacuated. Therefore, the density of the room 10 becomes higher than other areas.

The model applies a real time optimum path selection that leads crowd to the low density neighbor location. According to our primary assumptions, human operators are located on the intersections in a proper specific number to lead crowd to the optimum path. Practically, the decision making system decides which neighbor node has lower risk index, calculates the quickest flow, and shows the corresponding operator what area people should go through. Accordingly, in the next timespans, the system calculates new risk indexes and shows the quickest emergency evacuation flows.

In the following example, we consider room 14 as the origin and room E (exit door that is located on room number 10) as the destination to perform a maneuver of emergency evacuation. The crowd enters room 14, consequently the other areas will be crowded and will have a non-zero risk index. Below we show graphically how the system displays the quickest evacuation path dynamically with assigning related risk index weights to each node:

T0:
14(0.33) → 2 (0) → 9 (0) or 11(0) → 10 (0) → E

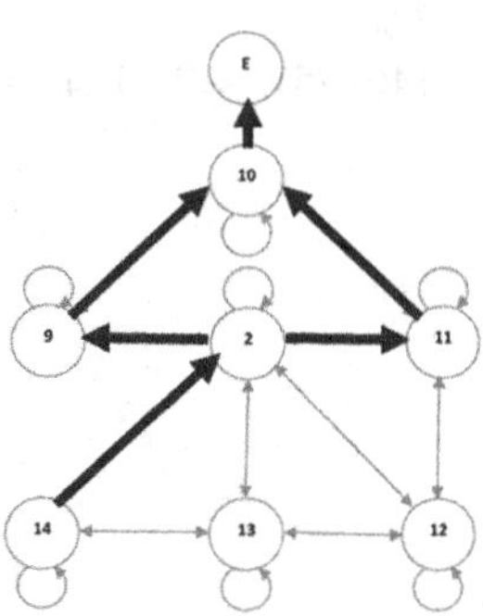

T20:
14(0.5) → 2 (0.05) → 9 (0) or 11(0) → 10 (0) → E

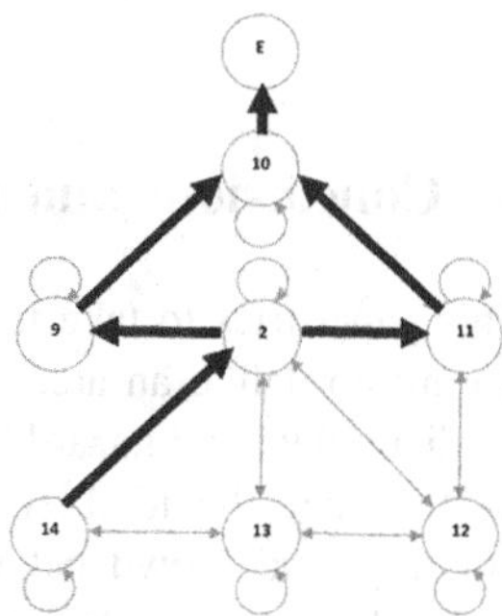

T40:
14(0.58) → 2 (0.08) → 9 (0.01) → 10 (0) → E

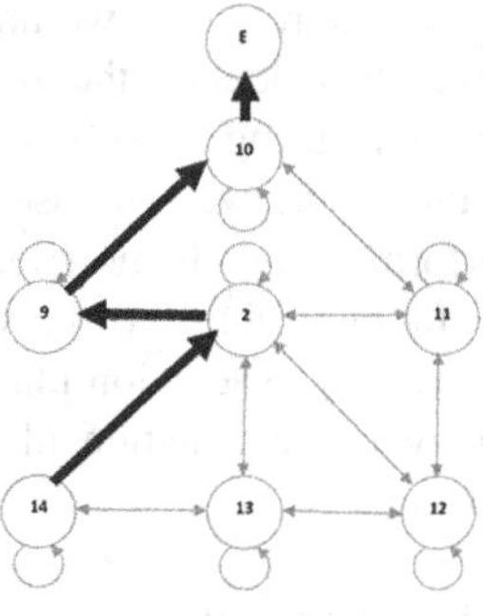

T60:
14(0.83) → 2 (0.13) → 9 (0.17) → 10 (0.12) → E

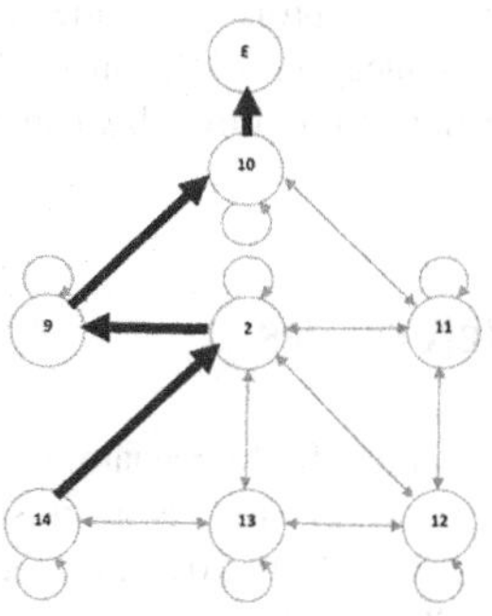

T80:
14(0.75) → 2 (0.2) → 11(0.5) → 10 (0.75) → E

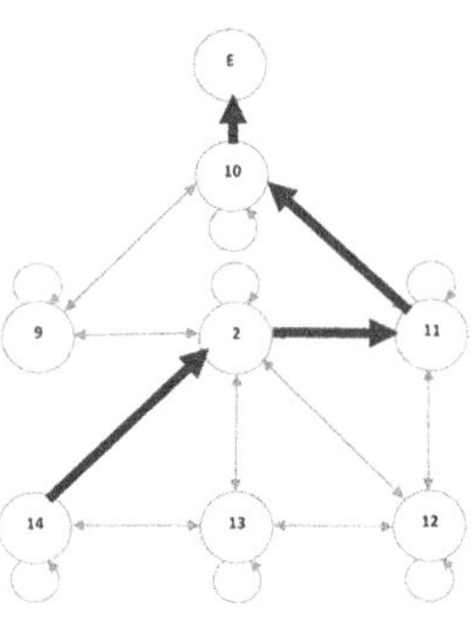

7 Conclusions and Future Work

This paper tries to take in input some Cyber-Physical Space models under SiA monitoring, to define an architectural-map-based Dynamic Bayesian Network (DBN) and predict crowd and hazard behavior. Quickest flow model for consecutive time intervals to minimize the total evacuation time. As a conclusion, the importance of hazard quiddity, and crowd behavior on the evacuation efficiency in emergency situations realized to be strongly important.

As future work, we are developing a model for SiA-based outdoor crowd monitoring to calculate the waiting time for ticketing, security check and entering the museum, using Two-Stage Stochastic Integer Programming Approach. As a similar future work, we will use dynamic mathematical model on our case to have some performance evaluation on, for instance, the shortest and quickest path calculation time.

In our future work, we will have a deep comparison between the traditional emergency evacuation plans with our model, taking into account the traditional safety emergency evacuation plan provided for the researcher's night of the university of L'Aquila.

Acknowledgment. We acknowledge that the work is a part of cyber-physical Situational Awareness project with the UFFIZI galleries, Florence, Italy. In addition, we would like to thank our colleagues Mohammad Sharaf and Fabrizio Rossi for their valuable comments and suggestions to improve this paper

References

Chiappino, S., Marcenaro, L., Morerio, P., Regazzoni, C.: Run length encoded dynamic bayesian networks for probabilistic interaction modeling. In: Signal Processing Conference (EUSIPCO), 2013 Proceedings of the 21st European, pp. 1–5. IEEE (2013)

Ensdley, M.R.: Toward a theory of situation awareness in dynamic systems. J. Hum. Factors Ergon. Soc. **37**(1), 32–64 (1995)

Endsely, M.R.: Theoretical underpinnings of situation awareness: a critical review. In: Endsley, M.R., Garland, D.J. (eds.) Situation Awareness Analysis and Measurement, pp. 3–32. Lawrence Erlbaum Associates, Mahwah (2000)

Feng, T., Yu, L.-F., Yeung, S.-K., Yin, K., Zhou, K.: Crowd-driven mid-scale layout design. ACM Trans. Graph. **35**(4), 132:1–132:14 (2016)

Franke, U., Brynielsson, J.: Cyber situational awareness–a systematic review of the literature. Comput. Secur. **46**, 18–31 (2014)

Gendreau, A.A.: Situation awareness measurement enhanced for efficient monitoring in the internet of things. IEEE (2015). doi:10.1109/TENSYMP

He, Y., Zhong, L., Jianmai, S., Yishan, W., Jiaming, Z., Jinyuan, L.: K-shortest-path-based evacuation routing with police resource allocation in city transportation networks (2015)

http://www.sweethome3d.com/it/ H. SWEETHOME-SWEET, Sweet Home 3D. "3d (2015)"

Muccini, H., Sharaf, M.: CAPS: architecture description of situational aware cyber physical systems. In: 2017 IEEE International Conference on Software Architecture (ICSA). IEEE (2017)

Naderpour, M., Lu, J., Zhang, G.: A fuzzy dynamic bayesian network-based situation assessment approach. In: 2013 IEEE International Conference on Fuzzy Systems (FUZZ), pp. 1–8. IEEE (2013)

Pretz, K.: Smarter sensors. IEEE Inst. **38**(2), 6–7 (2014)

Radianti, J., Granmo, O.-C., Sarshar, P., Goodwin, M., Dugdale, J., Gonzalez, J.J.: A spatio-temporal probabilistic model of hazard-and crowd dynamics for evacuation planning in disasters. Appl. Intell. **42**(1), 3–23 (2015)

Tadda, G.P., Salerno, J.S.: Overview of Cyber Situation Awareness. Springer Science+Business Media, pp. 15–35 (2010)

Tashakkori, H., Rajabifard, A., Kalantari, M.: A new 3D indoor/outdoor spatial model for indoor emergency response facilitation. Build. Environ. **89**, 170–182 (2015)

TranSafety, Inc.: Study compares older and younger pedestrian walking speeds. Road Engineering Journal (1997)

Tolstikov, A., Xiao, W., Biswas, J., Zhang, S., Tham, C.-K.: Information quality management in sensor networks based on the dynamic bayesian network model. In: 3rd International Conference on Intelligent Sensors, Sensor Networks and Information, ISSNIP 2007, pp. 751–756. IEEE (2007)

Co-engineering Safety and Security in Industrial Control Systems: A Formal Outlook

Inna Vistbakka[1(✉)], Elena Troubitsyna[1], Tuomas Kuismin[2], and Timo Latvala[2]

[1] Åbo Akademi University, Turku, Finland
{inna.vistbakka,elena.troubitsyna}@abo.fi
[2] Space Systems Finland, Espoo, Finland
{tuomas.kuismin,timo.latvala}@ssf.fi

Abstract. An increasing openness and interconnectedness of safety-critical industrial control systems makes them vulnerable to security attacks. Hence, we should establish the integrated approaches enabling safety-security co-engineering. Such approaches should support an analysis of interdependencies between the mechanisms required for safety and security assurance. In this paper, we demonstrate how formal modelling can facilitate reasoning about the impact of certain security solutions on safety and vise versa. We rely on modelling and refinement in Event-B to systematically uncover mutual interdependencies and the constraints that should be imposed on the system to guarantee its safety even in the presence of security attacks. The approach is illustrated by a case study – a battery charging system of an electric car.

Keywords: Formal modelling · Event-B · Refinement · Safety-critical systems · Security

1 Introduction

Modern industrial systems integrate novel information and communication technologies in controlling a wide range of systems. Increasing reliance on networking not only offers a variety of benefits but also introduces security threats. Exploiting security vulnerabilities might result in loss of control and situation awareness directly threatening safety of human lives. Therefore, we need to create the techniques that facilitate a systematic analysis of safety and security interdependencies from the early development stages.

In this paper, we propose a formal approach to integrating security consideration into a formal development of safety-critical systems in Event-B [1]. Event-B is a rigorous approach to correct-by-construction system development by refinement. Development typically starts from an abstract specification that models the most essential system functionality. In the refinement process, the abstract model is transformed into a detailed specification. While refining the system model, we can explicitly represent both nominal and failure behaviour of

A. Romanovsky and E.A. Troubitsyna (Eds.): SERENE 2017, LNCS 10479, pp. 96–114, 2017.
DOI: 10.1007/978-3-319-65948-0_7

the system components as well as define the mechanisms for error detection and recovery. Moreover, we can also explicitly represent the effect of security vulnerabilities such as tampering, spoofing and denial-of-service attacks and analyse their impact on system safety.

The stepwise refinement process allows us to systematically derive the constraints and explicitly define the assumptions that should be fulfilled to guarantee system safety even in presence of security attacks. In our formal development, we adopt systems approach, i.e., specify controlling software together with the relevant behaviour of its environment – sensors, actuators and controlled process. The security failures are modelled by their effect on the system – altering or blocking messages sent over the communication channels. The proposed approach is illustrated by a case study – a battery charging system.

We believe that the proposed approach facilitates an integration of the security consideration into the safety-driven design of control systems. It allows us to capture the dynamic nature of safety and security interplay, i.e., analyse the impact of deploying the security mechanisms on safety assurance and vice versa.

2 Systems View on Safety and Security Interdependencies

Nowadays safety-critical systems – the systems whose failures might cause loss of human lives or environmental damage [16] – are increasingly rely on networked technologies in their functioning. In this section, we analyse a generic architecture of a networked control system and discuss the constraints and properties that should be imposed on its design to guarantee safety.

The generic architecture of a control system is shown in Fig. 1. The goal of the system is to control a certain physical process. The state of the process is defined by some physical value *p_real*. The value of *p_real* is measured by the sensor. The sensor can be a physical device, i.e., a hardware component that converts the physical value *p_real* into its digital representation *p_sen*. However, it can be also a logical sensor – a module of a controlling program that computes an estimate of *p_real* based on some other measurements of the controlled process.

In a general case, sensing is remote, i.e., the measured value *p_sen* is transmitted over the network to the input of the controller. Since the transmission

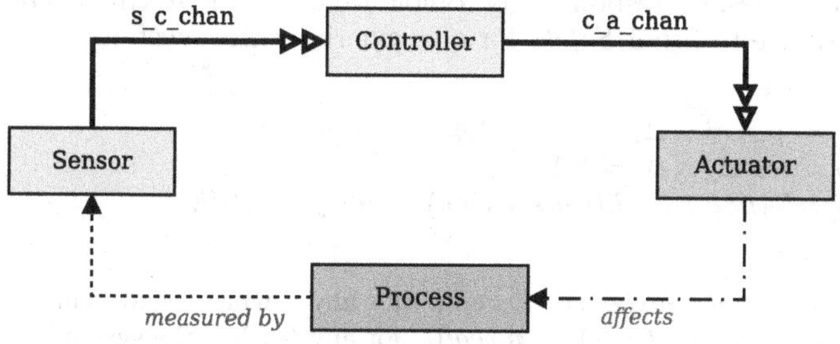

Fig. 1. Generic architecture of a control system

channel between the sensor and the controller *s-c-chan* might be untrusted, i.e., it might be a subject of security attack, the value that is received by the controller – *p_est* might be different from *p_sen*. The controlling software should check the reasonabless of the received *p_est* and decide to use it as the current estimate of *p_real*, i.e., *p:=p_est* or ignore it. The value p that the controller adopts as its current estimate of the process state should pass the feasibility check, i.e., should coincide with the predicted value and the freshness check, i.e., should be ignored if the transmission channel is blocked due to a DOS attack. If the controller ignores the received value *p_est*, it uses the last good value of *p_est* and the maximal variation of the process dynamics to compute p.

The value of p is then used to calculate the next state of the actuator – the physical device that affects the controlled process, i.e., causes the changes in the value of *p_real*. The command from the controller to the actuator is transmitted over a network. In the similar way, the transmission channel from the controller to the actuator $c-a-chan$ might be attacked. Hence, in general, the command *cmd_trans* received by the actuator might be different from the command *cmd* computed by the controller.

In this paper, we focus on the failsafe systems, i.e., consider the control systems that can be put into a safe non-operational state to preclude an occurrence of a safety failure [16]. Often system safety is defined over the parameters of the controlled physical process. For example, in our generic control system, we can define safety as the following predicate

$$Safety = p\_real \leq safe\_threshold \ \vee \ failsafe{=}TRUE$$

Essentially, it means that the controlled process should be kept within the safety boundaries while the system is operational. Otherwise, a safe shutdown should be executed.

Design of any system relies on certain assumptions and properties of the domain. In case of a safety-critical software-intensive control system, the aim of the design is to construct controlling software, which under the given assumptions and properties guarantees safety, i.e., allows us to proof the following

$$(\boldsymbol{ASM},\ \boldsymbol{DOM},\ \boldsymbol{SW}\ ) \vdash Safety,$$

where ***ASM, DOM*** and ***SW*** stand for assumptions, domain and controlling software properties, correspondingly. Below we define these three types of properties that suffice to proof *Safety* for our generic control system:

ASM

A1. $p\_sen \ = p\_real \pm \Delta_1$

A2. $p \ = \ p\_sen \pm \Delta_2 \wedge \Delta_2 = k\Delta_3$

A3. $(failsafe{=}FALSE \wedge cmd\_trans = cmd) \vee failsafe{=}TRUE$

DOM

D1. $cmd = incr \Rightarrow p\_real(t+1) > p\_real(t)$ for any t, while the system is operational

D2. $cmd = decr \Rightarrow p\_real(t+1) \leq p\_real(t)$ for any t, while the system is operational

D3. $max|(p\_real\ (t+1) - p\_real(t)\ )| = \Delta_3$

D4. *failsafe=TRUE* $\Rightarrow$ *p_real*$(t+1) \leq$ *p_real*(t) for any t, while the system is shut down

SW

S1. *p_est* $+ \Sigma_{i=1}^{3} \Delta_i \geq$ *safe_threshold* $\wedge$ *failsafe=FALSE* $\Rightarrow$ *cmd* $=$ *decr*

Straightforward logical calculations allow us to prove

$$(A1, \ldots, A3, D1, \ldots, D4, S1) \vdash Safety.$$

Let us now discuss the introduced assumptions and properties and link them with safety and security requirements. The assumption ***A1*** means that the sensor measurement are sufficiently precise and unprecision is bounded. It implies a safety requirement: sensor should have high reliability.

The assumption ***A2*** states that the controller adopts a measurement of the value of the process parameter that either coincides with *p_sen*, i.e., $k = 0$, or is calculated on the basis of the last good value and the maximal possible increase of the value *p_real* per cycle, where k is the number of cycles. This assumption implies both safety and security requirements. Firstly, we should guarantee that the channel $s - c - chan$ is tamper resistant and the sensor is spoofing resistant. Secondly, we should ensure that the controlling software checks the validity of the input parameter and ignores it, if the check fails. The assumption ***A2*** also implies that, in case of DOS attack on the channel $s - c - chan$, the system continues to function for some time by relying of the last good value.

The assumption ***A3*** implies that if a failure or an attack on the channel $c - a - chan$ is detected then the system is shut down. It means that the system should have some (possibly non-programmable) way to execute a shutdown in case the channel $c - a - chan$ becomes unreliable.

The domain properties explicitly define certain axioms about the physical environment of the system and their interdependencies. The property ***D1*** states that an execution of the command *incr* results in the increase of the value *p_real*. The property ***D2*** is similar to ***D1***. The domain property ***D3*** states that the maximal possible increase of *p_real* per cycle is known and bounded. ***D4*** stipulates that when the system is put in the failsafe state, the value of the physical parameter does not increase.

Finally, the software property ***S1*** corresponds to the safety invariant that controller should maintain: the controller issues the command *decr* to the actuator if at the next cycle the safe threshold can be exceeded.

Our system level analysis has demonstrated that both safety and security aspects are critical for fulfilling the system-level goal of ensuring safety. Hence, both these aspects should be explicitly addressed during the system development.

It is easy to observe, that we had to define a large number of requirements even for a generic high-level system architecture. To facilitate a systematic requirements derivation, we propose to employ formal development framework Event-B, which we overview next.

3 Modelling and Refinement in Event-B

Event-B [1] is a state-based framework that promotes the correct-by-construction approach to system development and formal verification by theorem proving. In Event-B, a system model is specified using the notion of an *abstract state machine* [1]. An abstract state machine encapsulates the model state, represented as a collection of variables, and defines operations on the state, i.e., it describes the dynamic behaviour of a modelled system. A machine also has an accompanying component, called *context*, which includes user-defined sets, constants and their properties given as model axioms.

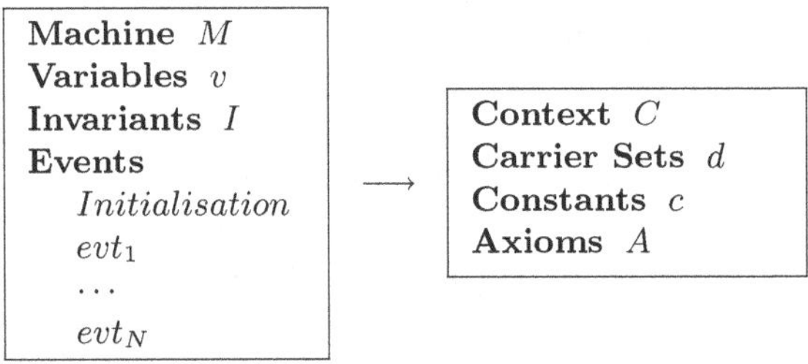

Fig. 2. Event-B machine and context

A general form for Event-B models is given in Fig. 2. The machine is uniquely identified by its name M. The state variables, v, are declared in the **Variables** clause and initialised in the *Initialisation* event. The variables are strongly typed by the constraining predicates I given in the **Invariants** clause. The invariant clause might also contain other predicates defining essential properties (e.g., safety invariants) that should be preserved during system execution.

The dynamic behaviour of the system is defined by a set of atomic *events*. Generally, an event has the following form:

$$e \mathrel{\widehat{=}} \textbf{any } a \textbf{ where } G_e \textbf{ then } R_e \textbf{ end},$$

where e is the event's name, a is the list of local variables, the *guard* G_e is a predicate over the local variables of the event and the state variables of the system. The body of an event is defined by a *multiple* (possibly nondeterministic) assignment over the system variables. In Event-B, an assignment represents a corresponding next-state relation R_e. Later on, using the concrete syntax in our Event-B models, we will rely on two kinds of assignment statements: deterministic ones, expressed in the standard form $x := E(x, y)$, and non-deterministic ones, represented as $x :| \ some\_condition(x, y, x')$. In the latter case, the state variable x gets non-deterministically updated by the value x' which may depend on the initial values of the variables x and y.

The guard defines the conditions under which the event is *enabled*, i.e., its body can be executed. If several events are enabled at the same time, any of them can be chosen for execution nondeterministically.

Event-B employs a top-down refinement-based approach to system development. Development typically starts from an abstract specification that nondeterministically models the most essential functional requirements. In a sequence of refinement steps, we gradually reduce nondeterminism and introduce detailed design decisions. We can add new events, split events as well as replace abstract variables by their concrete counterparts, i.e., perform *data refinement*.

The consistency of Event-B models, i.e., verification of well-formedness and invariant preservation as well as correctness of refinement steps, is demonstrated by discharging a number of verification conditions – proof obligations. For instance, to verify *invariant preservation*, we should prove the following logical formula:

$$A(d,c),\ I(d,c,v),\ G_e(d,c,x,v),\ R_e(d,c,x,v,v') \vdash I(d,c,v'), \qquad \text{(INV)}$$

where A are the model axioms, I are the model invariants, d and c are the model constants and sets respectively, x are the event's local variables and v, v' are the variable values before and after event execution. The full definitions of all the proof obligations are given in [1].

The Rodin platform [23] provides an automated support for formal modelling and verification in Event-B. In particular, it automatically generates the required proof obligations and attempts to discharge them. The remaining unproven conditions can be dealt with by using the provided interactive provers.

In the next section, we illustrate how to use Event-B framework to formally develop a safety-critical control system and derive safety and security constraints in a systematic manner.

4 Case Study: The Battery Charging System

We start by briefly describing our case study – a battery charging system. Then we demonstrate how to develop a detailed specification of the system by refinement and uncover the mutual interdependencies between safety and security requirements through the process of formal development.

Case Study Description. Our case study is a battery charging system of an electric car. Charging of the car battery is initiated when the vehicle gets connected to an external charging unit [24]. Figure 3 shows the main components of the system: the battery module, the battery management system, the CAN bus, the charging station (with the associated charging interface and the external charging unit). When the charging station detects that an electrical vehicle got connected to its external charging unit, it starts the charging procedure. While charging, the battery management system (BMS) – the controlling software of the system, monitors the measurements received from the battery element and issues the signal to the charging station to continue or stop charging. The communication between the BMS and the charging station goes through the CAN bus. The system behaviour is cyclic: at each cycle the charging station receives

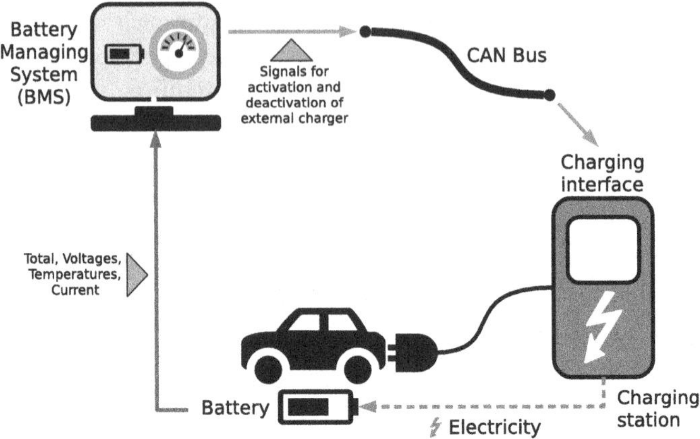

Fig. 3. Architecture of battery charging system

the command from BMS to continue or stop charging. Correspondingly, it either continues or stops to supply the energy to the battery of the car.

The main hazard associated with the system is overcharging of the car's battery, which might result in an explosion. Therefore, the safety goal of the system is to avoid overcharging. In case the system cannot reliably assess the current battery charge or stop charging using the programmable means, a safe shutdown should be executed. Hence, the system architecture should have a reliable mechanism for controlling the charging procedure and, in case of hazardous deviations, be able to abort charging, i.e., make a transition to failsafe state.

The top-level safety goal of the battery charging system is to keep a battery level parameter within the predefined boundaries. Let bl_real correspond to the real physical value of such a parameter. Then the system safety property can be formulated as follows: $0 \leq bl\_real \leq bl\_max\_crit$, where 0 and bl_max_crit denote the lowest and highest boundaries. The safety goal is achieved by changing the state of the charging unit that supplies an electricity to the battery.

The battery charging system is a typical example of a *control system* discussed in Sect. 2. Indeed, the BMS acts as a *controller*, the charging station (with its associated charger unit) – as an *actuator* and the battery unit as the *process* that the system controls. The battery level parameter can be directly measured by the *sensor* of BMS or computed on the basis of the alternative measurements obtained from the battery. At each cycle, BMS assesses the value of the battery level and sends the corresponding control command.

The charging station and in-car CAN bus are linked by the corresponding communication channel that could be possibly vulnerable to the security attacks. In particular, the attacker can use the in-car charging interface as an entry point by compromising the external charger interface or tampering with the communication between the interfaces to inject a malicious content into the CAN bus. Therefore, while reasoning about the behaviour of such a system, we should also reason about the impact of security threats on its safety. The analysis presented in Sect. 2 shows that safety cannot be guaranteed when the controller-actuator channel is attacked. Therefore, the battery charging system should include an additional hardware component that should be installed in the car to break the charging circuit if the battery charge level becomes dangerously high. Such a non-programmable switch can override the commands from the controller and put the system in the failsafe state to guarantee safety.

Next we present an abstract Event-B specification of our case study.

Abstract specification. In the initial Event-B specification, we introduce the abstract representation of the system architecture according to Fig. 3. The abstract model BatteryCharging_Abs represents the overall behaviour of the system as an interleaving between the events modelling the phases of the control cycle defined in Sect. 2.

First we introduce the variable *phase*, where $phase \in PHASES$. The enumerated set *PHASES={BAT, EST, BMS, TRANSM, CHARGST}* is defined in the model context BatteryCharging_c0. The variable *phase* is used to enforce the pre-defined cyclic execution order of events:

Battery → BMS_estimation → BMS_act → CAN_bus → ChargingStation → Battery → ...

Here the event Battery models the changes of the battery parameter *bl_real* while charging and the event BMS_estimation models the BMS estimation of this parameter (that is defined by *bl* variable). The event BMS_act specifies the BMS actions (i.e., sending the signal to continue or stop charging) and the event CAN_bus models transmission of the corresponding signal to the charging station. Finally, the event ChargingStation models the required actions from the charging station upon receiving the signal from the BMS. The some events of the abstract model – the machine BatteryCharging_Abs – is given in Fig. 4. In addition to modelling the control cycle, we define the event Connect that represent the beginning of the charging procedure (i.e., when a vehicle connects to the charging station) and the event ChargingComplete representing its completion.

Let *signal* be a variable modelling the control commands issued by the BMS to continue or abort the charging. The abstract constants *CONT* and *STOP* correspond to the external charger being switched on and off correspondingly. The initial value of the signal is designated by the constant *S0*. We also define a variable *status* to denote the status of charging. It can obtain any of three possible values from the set *STATUSES={IDLE, CHARGING, CHARGED}*. When the external charger unit is not connected to the vehicle, *status* has the value *IDLE*. The variable *status* obtains the value *CHARGING* if charging is in progress and the value *CHARGED* when charging has been recently stopped.

Let us note that the BMS estimate of the battery level value *bl* is not necessarily equal to the measurements produced by the battery sensor that monitors *bl_real*. In our model, *bl* is an abstraction representing the BMS's "perception" of the battery capacity. This perception is accumulative in a sense that it accounts for any possible deviations (e.g., due to the sensor imprecision) from *bl_real*, as

```
Machine BatteryCharging_Abs
Sees BatteryCharging_c0
Variables phase, signal, bl, bl_real, status, failsafe
Invariants phase ∈ PHASES ∧ signal ∈ SIGNALS ∧ status ∈ STATUSES ∧ bl ∈ ℕ ∧
           bl_real ∈ ℕ ∧ failsafe ∈ BOOL ∧ failsafe=TRUE ⇒ status=IDLE ∧ ...
Events
...
Battery ≙
  where phase=BAT ∧ status=CHARGING ∧ failsafe=FALSE
  then  bl_real :∈ ℕ || phase:=EST
  end
BMS_estimation ≙
  where phase=EST ∧ failsafe=FALSE
  then  bl :∈ ℕ || phase:=BMS
  end
BMS_act ≙
  where phase=BMS ∧ failsafe=FALSE
  then  signal :∈ {CONT, STOP} || phase:=TRANSM
  end
ChargingComplete ≙
  where status = CHARGED ∧ failsafe=FALSE
  then  bl := 0 || status:=IDLE || signal:=S0 || phase=BAT
  end
...
```

Fig. 4. The machine BatteryCharging_Abs

we explained in Sect. 2. The value *bl_real* is updated in the event Battery, while *bl* is estimated in the event BMS_estimation.

Finally, the transition into a safe but non-operational state is modelled by the event FailSafe. An execution of this event results in an immediate aborting of charging, which is modelled by assigning the variable *status* the value *IDLE*.

Let us note that at this modelling step we have not formulated the safety system property as a model invariant yet. Since the initial model defines only the control flow at the component level, we do not have sufficiently detailed "knowledge" to prove the desired safety property. In the next section, we demonstrate how to refine the abstract model to achieve this goal.

5 Event-B Development of the Battery Charging System

The refinement process facilitates requirements structuring and allows us to introduce their detailed representation in a systematic disciplined manner. In the following sequence of model refinements, we will consider different cases of the component behaviour and model the impact of the security attacks on system behaviour. In the refinement process, more detailed assumptions and constraints are defined in the form of abstract data structures and their properties. Once the sufficient level of details is reached, we formulate and prove the desired system safety invariant.

The First Refinement. Our first refinement step aims at introducing a detailed specification of the BMS logic. We define the control algorithm, i.e., model the behavior of the controller. The controller calculates the control commands to be send to the charging station using the current estimate of the battery level. Moreover, at this refinement step, we also elaborate on the dynamics of the controlled process, i.e., define the changes in the real battery level *bl_real* and model different cases of the behaviour of the charging station.

At each control cycle, the controller receives the current estimate of the battery level from the sensor. The controller checks whether the battery is still not fully charged and it is safe to continue to charge it or charging should be stopped. The decision to continue to charge can be made only if the controller verifies that the battery level at the end of the next cycle will still be in the safe range $[0 \dots bl\_max\_crit]$. The event BMS_estimation modelling estimation the current value of battery parameter made by the BMS is refined. Consequently, the variable *bl* gets any value from the range $(bl\_real - bl\_delta .. bl\_real + bl\_delta)$, where *bl_delta* is the maximal imprecision value for the battery sensor introduced as a constant in the model context.

We also specify our knowledge about the process of battery charging by introducing the following abstract function into the model context: $bl\_fnc \in \mathbb{N} \rightarrow \mathbb{N}$. The function models the next predicted value for the battery level parameter *bl_real*. It takes the previous value of *bl_real* and returns its predicted value in the next cycle. Obviously, while the battery is charging, its battery level is increasing. Hence we impose this restriction on *bl_fnc* function and formulate it as the following model axiom defined in the context BatteryCharging_c1:

$$\forall n \cdot n \in \mathbb{N} \Rightarrow n < bl\_fnc(n).$$

Moreover, the following constraint in the context component

$$\forall n \cdot n \in 0 .. bl\_max + bl\_delta \Rightarrow bl\_fnc(n) \leq bl\_max\_crit$$

requires that, if the battery level is currently in the safe range, it cannot exceed the critical range within the next cycle, i.e., the safety gap between *bl_max* and *bl_max_crit* is sufficiently large. The refined event Battery modelling the changes of the battery level parameter is presented in Fig. 5.

We also refine the abstract event BMS_act to represent different alternatives. The first alternative defines a reaction to the monitored parameter exceeding *bl_max*. The second alternative models continuing the charge when the monitored parameter is in the completely safe range $[0..bl\_max)$. Note that the monitored value *bl* that BMS relies on here is different from the actual value of the physical process (*bl_real*) updated by the event Battery.

We can formulate correctness of the BMS logic by the following invariants:

$$phase = TRANSM \wedge bl \geq bl\_max \Rightarrow signal{=}STOP$$
$$phase = TRANSM \wedge bl < bl\_max \Rightarrow signal{=}CONT.$$

The invariants postulate that the BMS issues the signal to stop when the parameter *bl* is approaching the critically high value (*bl_max_crit*), and vice

```
Machine BatteryCharging_M1 refines BatteryCharging_Abs
Sees BatteryCharging_c1
Variables phase, signal, bl, bl_real, status, failsafe
Invariants  phase = TRANSM ∧ bl ≥ bl_max ⇒ signal=STOP ∧
            phase = TRANSM ∧ bl < bl_max ⇒ signal=CONT ∧ ...
Events...
Battery refines Battery
  where phase=BAT ∧ status = CHARGING ∧ failsafe = FALSE
  then bl_real := bl_fnc(bl_real) || phase := EST
  end
BMS_estimation ≙ refines BMS_estimation
  where phase=EST ∧ failsafe = FALSE
  then bl :∈ bl_real − bl_delta..bl_real + bl_delta || phase := BMS
  end
BMS_cont ≙ refines BMS_act
  where phase=BMS ∧ failsafe = FALSE ∧ bl < bl_max
  then signal:=CONT || phase := TRANSM
  end
ChargingStation ≙ refines ChargingStation
  any sg
  where phase=CHARGST ∧ sg ∈ {CONT, STOP} ∧ failsafe = FALSE
  then status :| (sg = CONT ⇒ status′ = CHARGING)∨
                 (sg = STOP ⇒ status′ = CHARGED)
       phase := BAT
  end
...
```

Fig. 5. The machine BatteryCharging_M1

versa. To give the system a time to react, BMS sends the stopping command to the station whenever the value bl breaches the predefined value bl_max.

Moreover, in this refinement step, we elaborate on the behaviour of the charging station. Upon receiving the command from BMS, the charging station either deactivates the charging unit or continues to supply an energy to the battery. Such a behaviour is defined by the refined event ChargingStation (see Fig. 5).

In this refinement step, we have elaborated on the control algorithm and the model of the controlled physical process. However, we have abstracted away from modelling the fact that the charging station reads the signal from the CAN bus. Such an abstraction allows us to further refine the communication model and explicitly define the impact of the security attacks on the system behaviour, as we demonstrate in the next refinement step.

The Second Refinement. In the architecture of battery charging system the CAN bus represents the communication channel in the in-car system. This component is used to transmit the signal issued by BMS to the charging station (specifically, to the charging interface). However, such a channel could be possibly vulnerable to security attacks. Specifically, the attacker can use the in-car charging interface as an entry point by compromising the external charger interface or tampering with the communications between the interfaces to inject malicious content into the CAN bus. Therefore, the goal of our second refinement step is to incorporate into the model architecture a certain mechanism that would allow the system to transmit the signal in a secure way. The possible solution here is to add a new component – security gateway – between the CAN bus and the external charging unit. In general, such a security gateway could control the network access according to predefined security policies and can also inspect the packet content to detect the intruder attacks and anomalies. However, while adding security protection to the system architecture, a security gateway might introduce latency into communication between the CAN bus and the charging station, and, in its turn, increase the reaction time of charging unit.

To address this new functionality, we add several new events and new variables into the refined system specification (see Fig. 6). Firstly, we introduce a new event Attack to model a possible attack on the system. The attack can happen anytime while transmitting the signal to the charging interface. The variable $attack \in BOOL$ indicates whether the system is under attack. If the event Attack is triggered, the value of *attack* becomes *TRUE*, otherwise it equals to *FALSE*.

Secondly, we introduce a new event SecurityGateway and a new variable *charg_in* that specifies the input buffer of the charging interface. It might obtain values from the set of possible signals, i.e., $charg\_in \in SIGNALS$. If no attack happens, then signal transmission results in copying the signal from one-place output buffer of the CAN bus (represented by *bus_out* variable) to the input buffer *charg_in* of the charging interface. If a security failure occurred (e.g., the system has been under attack) then the output signal would differ from the sent signal. The DOS attack (or in general channel unavailability) results in no values being transmitted over the channel. For the sake of simplicity, we model it by introducing the *DOS* constant that the input buffer of the charging interface will get in this case. However, we also could have modelled it by defining a behaviour of a watchdog process triggering the timeout signal. This behaviour is modelled by the event SecurityGateway presented in Fig. 6.

The event ChargingStation is now refined by two events ChargingStation_cont and ChargingStation_stop modelling the continuation of the charging procedure or stopping it. In case of the DOS attack, the system will make a transition to failsafe mode and the charging will be aborted (that modelled by the event FailSafe_DOS). We can formulate correctness of the charging station logic by the following invariants:

$$phase = BAT \wedge charg\_in{=}STOP \Rightarrow status{=}CHARGED,$$
$$phase = BAT \wedge charg\_in{=}CONT \Rightarrow status{=}CHARGING.$$

The model.invariants postulate that the charging station deactivates the charging unit when it receives the signal to stop the charging, and vice versa.

Let us note that adding a security gateway can introduce latency into communication between the CAN bus and the charging station that might increase the reaction time of charging unit. It can be crucial for ensuring that the signal to abort charging *STOP* is issued in time. Thus, a careful analysis should be performed while choosing a suitable value *bl_max* to ensure:

$$bl\_max + bl\_delta + max\_increase \leq bl\_max\_crit,$$

```
Machine BatteryCharging_M2 refines BatteryCharging_M1
Sees BatteryCharging_c2
Variables phase, signal, bl, bl_real, status, failsafe, attack, bus_out, charg_in
Invariants charg_in ∈ SIGNALS ∧ attack ∈ BOOL ∧
           phase = CHARG ∧ bl ≥ bl_max ⇒ bus_out=STOP ∧
           phase = CHARG ∧ bl < bl_max ⇒ bus_out=CONT ∧
           attack = FALSE ∧ phase = CHARG ∧ bus_out=STOP ⇒ signal=STOP ∧
           attack = FALSE ∧ phase = CHARG ∧ bus_out=CONT ⇒ signal=CONT ∧
           phase=BAT ∧ status=CHARGING ⇒ bl_real ≤ bl_max + bl_delta ∧
           bl_real ∈ 0 .. bl_max_crit ∧ ...
Events
...
SecurityGateway ≙
  where phase=CHARG ∧ failsafe=FALSE ∧ charg_in=S0
  then charg_in : |(attack = FALSE ⇒ charg_in' = bus_out)∨
                   (attack = TRUE ⇒ charg_in' = DOS)
  end
ChargingStation_stop ≙ refines ChargingStation
  where phase=CHARG ∧ charg_in = STOP ∧ failsafe = FALSE
  with sg=STOP
  then status := CHARGED || phase := BAT || charg_in := S0
  end
...
end
```

Fig. 6. The machine BatteryCharging_M2

where *max_increase* is the maximal increase of the batter level value peer cycle that can be introduced as a constant in the model context.

As a result of this refinement step, we arrive at a sufficiently detailed specification to define and prove the following safety invariant:

$$bl\_real \in 0 \,..\, bl\_max\_crit.$$

Discussion. In our modelling, we adopt an implicit discrete model of time. We define the abstract function representing the change in the dynamics of the controlled process as well as the constraints relating the components behavior in the successive iterations. Such an approach significantly improves the scalability of formal modelling because it enables modular layered reasoning [13,14] which is not well supported by the frameworks with the explicit representation of time. To enable verification of real-time properties, we can rely on the approach proposed by Iliasov et al. [6] allowing to map Event-B specification into UPPAAL.

To support reasoning about safety-security interplay, we have to explicitly model the impact of accidental and malicious faults on the system behaviour, i.e., introduce in our specification an explicit representation of failure modes of system components and communication links. As a result, the complexity of the specification is significantly increased. To addressed this issue, we can rely on the modularisation approach [5], which supports compositional reasoning and specification patterns [7]. FMEA into the formal models [17].

To cope with the complexity of a formal specification, which explicitly integrates the failure behaviour, we can employ such an architectural mechanism as the mode-based reasoning, as proposed in [8,9]. We can distinguish between the normal operational mode, the degraded mode caused by the accidental component failures as well as the attacked and failsafe modes. By defining and verifying such a high-level mode logic, we can facilitate a structured analysis of the complex failure behaviour.

Construction of Evidence for a System Safety Case. To ensure safety, we have to demonstrate satisfaction of the safety requirements imposed on the system. Traditionally, to assure safety of critical systems in a structured way, safety cases have been proposed. A safety case justifies why a system is safe and whether the design adequately implements the imposed safety requirements. To represent the safety case, a graphical notation called Goal Structured Notation can be used [11]. It explicitly represents how goals are decomposed into subgoals until claims can be supported by the direct evidences. Next we demonstrate how formal modelling and refinement-based development can allow us to systematically construct the evidence justifying safety goals (and subgoals, consequently). The results of formal modelling can be used to provide the required evidence for a system safety. The guidelines for constructing the safety cases from the formal specification in Event-B are described in [22].

The fragment of resulting safety case for our system is presented in Fig. 7. Rectangles contain definitions of goals (if the rhombus is attached then the goal needs to be further developed), parallelograms show the definitions of the strategies, while circles represent solutions (will be presented on a figure later).

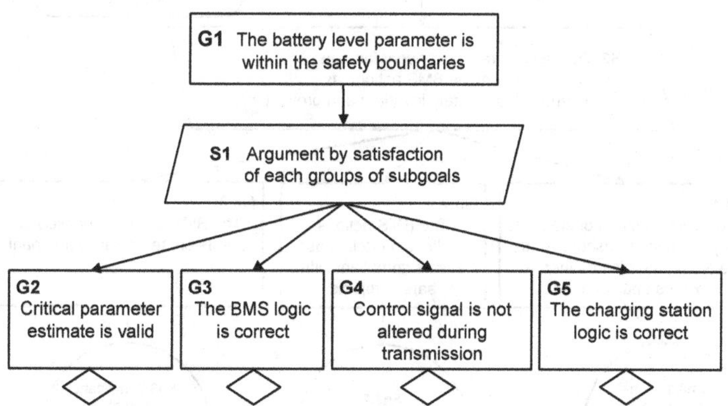

Fig. 7. Decomposition of top-level safety goal

We introduce the main goal ***G1***: *The battery level parameter is within the safety boundaries.* To provide evidence that this goal holds, strategy ***S1*** is applied. It leads to obtaining a number of sub-goals, i.e., ***G2***, ***G3***, ***G4***, ***G5***. The decomposition of subgoals into even more detailed subgoals can be continued until we reach a statement that can be directly supported by some evidence, e.g., formal verification results. On the Fig. 7 ***G2–G5*** goals are left undeveloped meaning that we further elaborate on it in order to support by direct evidence. The Event-B system specification and the associated proofs allow us to justify achieving the ***G2, G3, G4, G5***.

Lets consider the goal ***G3***: *"The BMS logic is correct"*. It is considered in the **Context** of *formal modelling in Event-B with Rodin platform tool* (***C1***). To support that claim ***G3*** holds, we state a strategy ***S2*** to be used in solution of a goal. Namely, we need to define constrains over constants as axioms. Moreover, we have to model the BMS actions as well as define the safety invariant and prove it preservation during system execution. Consequently, we further decompose the goal ***G3*** into three subgoals and define the solutions that support the claims.

Indeed, in our Event-B specification, presented in the Sect. 5.1-3, we introduce constraints over the system constants as axioms in the model context (e.g., $bl\_max \in \mathbb{N}$, $bl\_max\_crit < bl\_max\_crit$, etc.) and additionally prove noncontradictiveness of axioms. We model the BMS actions as the corresponding events (e.g., BMS_cont and BMS_stop.) and prove the preservation of the invariants that described the correctness of the BMS actions. We also formulate the main safety invariant and prove it preservation during system execution. Thereby, the derived Event-B specification and the associated proofs allows us to justify achieving the goal ***G3*** (see Fig. 8).

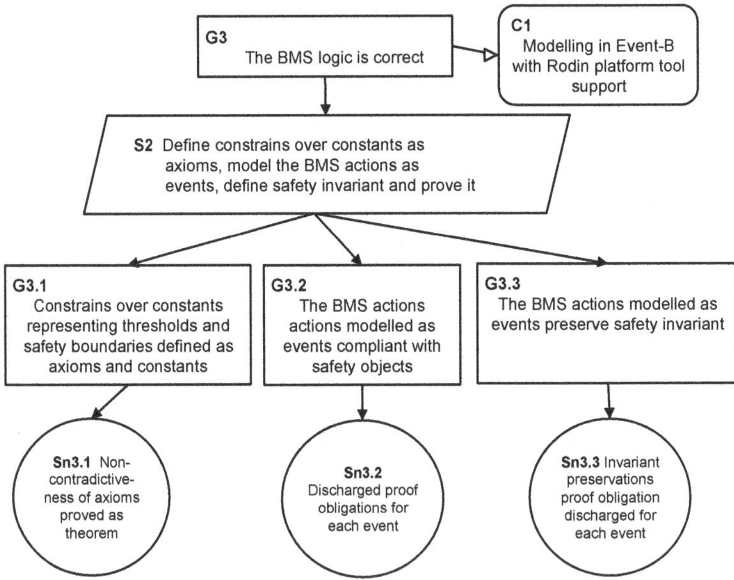

Fig. 8. Decomposition of top-level safety goal

6 Related Work and Conclusions

Related Work. Research investigating safety and security interaction has recently received a significant attention. It has been recognised that there is a clear need for the approaches facilitating an integrated analysis of safety and security [19,33,34].

This problem has been addressed by several techniques demonstrating how to adapt conventional techniques for analysing safety risks (e.g., FMECA, fault trees, etc.) to perform a security-informed safety analysis [4,25]. The techniques aim at providing the engineers with a structured way to discover and analyse security vulnerabilities that have safety implications. Since the use of such techniques facilitates a systematic analysis of failure modes and results in discovering safety and security requirements, the proposed approaches can provide a valuable input for our modelling. A large set of formal modelling approaches to reasoning about the impact of failures on system dependability is presented in [2].

There are several works that address formal analysis of safety and security requirements interactions [12,21]. Majority of these works demonstrate also how to find conflicts between them. A typical scenario used to demonstrate this is a contradiction between the access control rules and safety measure. In our approach, we treat the problem of safety-security interplay at a more detailed level, i.e., we analyse the system architecture, investigate the impact of security failures on safe implementation of system functions. Such an approach allows us to analyse the dynamic nature of safety-security interactions.

The MILS approach [3] employs a number of advanced modelling techniques to create a platform for a formal architectural analysis of safety and security. The approach supports an analysis of the properties of the data flow using model checking and facilitates derivation of security contracts. Since our approach enables incremental construction of complex distributed architectures, it would be interesting to combine these techniques to support an integrated safety-security analysis throughout the entire formal model-based system development.

An important aspect of demonstrating system safety is its quantitative evaluation. The foundations of the quantitative probabilistic reasoning about safety using formal specifications was established in [10,18,30,31]. This work has been further extended to enable probabilistic assessment of safety and reliability using Event-B specifications [28,29]. It would be interesting to quantitatively assess the impact of accidental and malicious faults on safety.

In this paper, we have assumed that the hazards associated with the system has been already identified and correspondingly, focused on modelling system behaviour guaranteeing hazard avoidance. Our work can be complemented with the approaches proposed in [15,26,32], which address hazard identification and elicitation of safety requirements.

Conclusions. In this paper, we have proposed a formal approach enabling safety-security co-engineering. Our approach supports an analysis of interdependencies between the architectural patterns and mechanisms required for safety and security assurance. We have demonstrated how the formal construction of evidences required to substantiate system safety case results in derivation of both safety and security requirements. Instead of contraposing safety and security, we consider them as the interdependent constraints required for building robust system. Relying on modelling and refinement in Event-B we systematically uncover mutual interdependencies and the constraints that should be imposed on the system to guarantee its safety even in the presence of security attacks.

The approach presented in this paper generalises the results of our experiment with formal refinement-based development in the Event-B conducted in the context of verification of safety-critical control system. The results have demonstrated that the formal development significantly facilitates derivation of safety and security requirements.

We have also observed that the integrated safety-security modelling in Event-B could be facilitated by the use of external tools supporting constraint solving and continuous behaviour simulation. Such an integration would be interesting to investigate in our future work. Moreover, we are also planning to investigate the problem of enhancing safety via the advanced reconfiguration mechanisms similar to the once proposed in [20,27].

References

1. Abrial, J.R.: Modeling in Event-B. Cambridge University Press, New York (2010)
2. Butler, M., Jones, C.B., Romanovsky, A., Troubitsyna, E. (eds.): Rigorous Development of Complex Fault-Tolerant Systems. LNCS, vol. 4157. Springer, Heidelberg (2006)
3. Cimatti, A., DeLong, R., Marcantonio, D., Tonetta, S.: Combining MILS with contract-based design for safety and security requirements. In: Koornneef, F., Gulijk, C. (eds.) SAFECOMP 2015. LNCS, vol. 9338, pp. 264–276. Springer, Cham (2015). doi:10.1007/978-3-319-24249-1_23
4. Fovino, I.N., Masera, M., Cian, A.D.: Integrating cyber attacks within fault trees. Rel. Eng. Sys. Safety **94**(9), 1394–1402 (2009)
5. Iliasov, A., Troubitsyna, E., Laibinis, L., Romanovsky, A., Varpaaniemi, K., Ilic, D., Latvala, T.: Supporting reuse in Event-B development: modularisation approach. In: Frappier, M., Glässer, U., Khurshid, S., Laleau, R., Reeves, S. (eds.) ABZ 2010. LNCS, vol. 5977, pp. 174–188. Springer, Heidelberg (2010). doi:10.1007/978-3-642-11811-1_14
6. Iliasov, A., Romanovsky, A., Laibinis, L., Troubitsyna, E., Latvala, T.: Augmenting Event-B modelling with real-time verification. In: Proceedings of the FormSERA 2012, pp. 51–57. IEEE (2012)
7. Iliasov, A., Troubitsyna, E., Laibinis, L., Romanovsky, A.: Patterns for refinement automation. In: Boer, F.S., Bonsangue, M.M., Hallerstede, S., Leuschel, M. (eds.) FMCO 2009. LNCS, vol. 6286, pp. 70–88. Springer, Heidelberg (2010). doi:10.1007/978-3-642-17071-3_4
8. Iliasov, A., Troubitsyna, E., Laibinis, L., Romanovsky, A., Varpaaniemi, K., Ilic, D., Latvala, T.: Developing mode-rich satellite software by refinement in event-B. Sci. Comput. Program. **78**(7), 884–905 (2013)
9. Iliasov, A., Troubitsyna, E., Laibinis, L., Romanovsky, A., Varpaaniemi, K., Väisänen, P., Ilic, D., Latvala, T.: Verifying mode consistency for on-board satellite software. In: Schoitsch, E. (ed.) SAFECOMP 2010. LNCS, vol. 6351, pp. 126–141. Springer, Heidelberg (2010). doi:10.1007/978-3-642-15651-9_10

10. Sere, K., Troubitsyna, E.A.: Probabilities in action systems. In: Proceedings of the 8th Nordic Workshop on Programming Theory, pp. 373–387 (1996)
11. Kelly, T.P., Weaver, R.A.: The goal structuring notation - a safety argument notation. In: DSN 2004, Workshop on Assurance Cases (2004)
12. Kriaa, S., Bouissou, M., Colin, F., Halgand, Y., Pietre-Cambacedes, L.: Safety and security interactions modeling using the BDMP formalism: case study of a pipeline. In: Bondavalli, A., Di Giandomenico, F. (eds.) SAFECOMP 2014. LNCS, vol. 8666, pp. 326–341. Springer, Cham (2014). doi:10.1007/978-3-319-10506-2_22
13. Laibinis, L., Troubitsyna, E.: Fault tolerance in a layered architecture: a general specification pattern in B. In: SEFM 2004, Beijing, China, pp. 346–355. IEEE Computer Society (2004)
14. Laibinis, L., Troubitsyna, E.: Refinement of fault tolerant control systems in B. In: Heisel, M., Liggesmeyer, P., Wittmann, S. (eds.) SAFECOMP 2004. LNCS, vol. 3219, pp. 254–268. Springer, Heidelberg (2004). doi:10.1007/978-3-540-30138-7_22
15. Laibinis, L., Troubitsyna, E.: Fault tolerance in use-case modeling. In: Proceedings of RHAS 2005 (2005)
16. Leveson, N.G.: Safeware: System Safety and Computers. Addison-Wesley, Boston (1995)
17. Lopatkin, I., Iliasov, A., Romanovsky, A., Prokhorova, Y., Troubitsyna, E.: Patterns for representing FMEA in formal specification of control systems. In: HASE 2011, Boca Raton, FL, USA, pp. 146–151. IEEE Computer Society (2011)
18. McIver, A., Morgan, C., Troubitsyna, E.: The probabilistic steam boiler: a case study in probabilistic data refinement. In: Proceedings of the International Refinement Workshop, Canberra, Australia, pp. 250–265. Springer (1998)
19. Paul, S., Rioux, L.: Over 20 years of research into cybersecurity and safety engineering: a short bibliography. Saf. Secur. Eng. VI **151**, 335 (2015)
20. Pereverzeva, I., Troubitsyna, E., Laibinis, L.: Formal development of critical multi-agent systems: a refinement approach. In: EDCC 2012, pp. 156–161 (2012)
21. Ponsard, C., Dallons, G., Massonet, P.: Goal-oriented co-engineering of security and safety requirements in cyber-physical systems. In: Skavhaug, A., Guiochet, J., Schoitsch, E., Bitsch, F. (eds.) SAFECOMP 2016. LNCS, vol. 9923, pp. 334–345. Springer, Cham (2016). doi:10.1007/978-3-319-45480-1_27
22. Prokhorova, Y., Laibinis, L., Troubitsyna, E.: Facilitating construction of safety cases from formal models in Event-B. Inform. Softw. Technol. **60**, 51–76 (2015)
23. Rodin: Event-B platform. http://www.event-b.org/
24. Schmittner, C., Ma, Z., Puschner, P.: Limitation and improvement of STPA-Sec for safety and security co-analysis. In: Skavhaug, A., Guiochet, J., Schoitsch, E., Bitsch, F. (eds.) SAFECOMP 2016. LNCS, vol. 9923, pp. 195–209. Springer, Cham (2016). doi:10.1007/978-3-319-45480-1_16
25. Schmittner, C., Ma, Z., Smith, P.: FMVEA for safety and security analysis of intelligent and cooperative vehicles. In: Bondavalli, A., Ceccarelli, A., Ortmeier, F. (eds.) SAFECOMP 2014. LNCS, vol. 8696, pp. 282–288. Springer, Cham (2014). doi:10.1007/978-3-319-10557-4_31
26. Sere, K., Troubitsyna, E.: Hazard analysis in formal specification. In: Proceedings of the 18th International Conference, SAFECOMP 1999, pp. 350–360 (1999)
27. Tarasyuk, A., Pereverzeva, I., Troubitsyna, E., Latvala, T., Nummila, L.: Formal development and assessment of a reconfigurable on-board satellite system. In: Ortmeier, F., Daniel, P. (eds.) SAFECOMP 2012. LNCS, vol. 7612, pp. 210–222. Springer, Heidelberg (2012). doi:10.1007/978-3-642-33678-2_18

28. Tarasyuk, A., Troubitsyna, E., Laibinis, L.: Quantitative verification of system safety in Event-B. In: Troubitsyna, E.A. (ed.) SERENE 2011. LNCS, vol. 6968, pp. 24–39. Springer, Heidelberg (2011). doi:10.1007/978-3-642-24124-6_3
29. Tarasyuk, A., Troubitsyna, E., Laibinis, L.: Integrating stochastic reasoning into Event-B development. Formal Asp. Comput. **27**(1), 53–77 (2015)
30. Troubitsyna, E.: Enhancing dependability via parameterized refinement. In: PRDC 1999, Hong Kong, p. 120. IEEE Computer Society (1999)
31. Troubitsyna, E.: Stepwise Development of Dependable Systems. Technical report (2000)
32. Troubitsyna, E.: Elicitation and specification of safety requirements. In: ICONS 2008, Cancun, Mexico, pp. 202–207. IEEE Computer Society (2008)
33. Troubitsyna, E., Laibinis, L., Pereverzeva, I., Kuismin, T., Ilic, D., Latvala, T.: Towards security-explicit formal modelling of safety-critical systems. In: Skavhaug, A., Guiochet, J., Bitsch, F. (eds.) SAFECOMP 2016. LNCS, vol. 9922, pp. 213–225. Springer, Cham (2016). doi:10.1007/978-3-319-45477-1_17
34. Young, W., Leveson, N.G.: An integrated approach to safety and security based on systems theory. Commun. ACM **57**(2), 31–35 (2014)

Software

Evaluation of Open Source Operating Systems for Safety-Critical Applications

Petter Sainio Berntsson[1], Lars Strandén[2], and Fredrik Warg[2(✉)]

[1] Chalmers University of Technology, Göteborg, Sweden
petter.berntsson@gmail.com
[2] RISE Research Institutes of Sweden, Borås, Sweden
{lars.stranden, fredrik.warg}@ri.se

Abstract. There are many different open source real-time operating systems (RTOS) available, and the use of open source software (OSS) for safety-critical applications is considered highly interesting by industrial domains such as medical, aerospace and automotive, as it potentially enables lower costs and more flexibility. In order to use OSS in a safety-critical context, however, evidence that the software fulfills the requirements put forth in a functional safety standard for the relevant domain is necessary. However, the standards for functional safety typically do not provide a clear method for how one would go about certifying systems containing OSS. Therefore, in this paper we identify some important RTOS characteristics and outline a methodology which can be used to assess the suitability of an open source RTOS for use in a safety-critical application. A case study is also carried out, comparing two open source operating systems using the identified characteristics. The most suitable candidate is then assessed in order to see to what degree it can adhere with the requirements put forth in the widely used functional safety standard IEC 61508.

Keywords: Functional safety · IEC 61508 · Open source software · Real-time operating systems · Software quality

1 Introduction

The last few years have seen a remarkable rise in the use of embedded systems, for instance in the automotive industry where modern cars are typically equipped with dozens of embedded electronic systems. A real-time system is defined as a system in which the correctness of the system does not only depend on the result of a computation but whether or not the correct result is produced within the set time constraint [1]. The use of a Real-Time Operating System (RTOS) is common in embedded systems due to the multitasking requirement in many applications [2]. During the last two decades RTOSs have undergone continuous evolution and there are many commercially available RTOSs.

For various reasons, including cost of commercial alternatives or lack of desired features in existing products, people have developed their own versions of such software and made it publicly available as Open Source Software (OSS). A common use of OSS is in operating systems since they are normally application independent and can

A. Romanovsky and E.A. Troubitsyna (Eds.): SERENE 2017, LNCS 10479, pp. 117–132, 2017.
DOI: 10.1007/978-3-319-65948-0_8

therefore attract a large user base and be ported to different hardware platforms. The use of OSS for safety-critical applications is considered highly interesting by industrial domains such as medical, aerospace and automotive, as it potentially enables lower costs and more flexibility. Open source projects that have well-established communities (e.g. Linux and Apache) usually employ stringent development processes [3, 4] and deliver high quality software. However, they do not fulfill the requirements of current safety standards such as IEC 61508 [5] and ISO 26262 [6]. These standards impose strict demands on e.g. project management, developer qualification, risk management, requirements management, quality assurance and documentation. This becomes a problem since many OSS projects do not follow a strict development process [7], which makes the requirements impossible to achieve after the software has already been developed. However, software that has been developed with a non-compliant process can in some cases still be qualified if the software fulfills the requirements for reuse. This can be done by providing enough evidence to support its suitability for safety-critical applications.

In this paper we investigate criteria such as software metrics, support and maintainability issues, real-time and dependability properties that can be used to evaluate, mainly from a software perspective, an open source RTOS with regards to its use in safety-critical applications. We then propose a methodology for such evaluation; the methodology is based on using the Capgemini Open Source Maturity Model [14] together with a set of characteristics influence by earlier work in [12], but adapted to better suit an RTOS. The aim of our proposed methodology is to collect information to help determine if an RTOS is a potential candidate for use in a safety-critical application, and also to be able to choose which candidate is the most promising when several candidates exist. For use in an application that is to be certified against a functional safety standard, however, an assessment of the RTOS against the relevant requirements in the standard must also be conducted. We show a case study where the two OSS RTOSs ChibiOS [16] and ContikiOS [17] are compared using the methodology, and where ChibiOS is subsequently evaluated against the requirements for use of pre-existing software elements using non-compliant development according to the functional safety standard IEC 61508.

2 Related Work

There are multiple different open source quality and maturity models available and a comparative study [8] has been done. It showed two models that satisfied all eight factors under product quality in the ISO/IEC 25010 standard [9]. However, most of the models compared in the study seem to be abandoned, and the tools used for retrieval and analysis of metrics are no longer available. One of these is the QualOSS [10] model, which was one of the two models satisfying all eight factors under product quality in ISO/IEC 25010. High test coverage is one of the most impacting activities in order to qualify software for safety certification. The study in [11] investigates the relationship between software complexity and the effort to achieve high test coverage with the objective of figuring out to what extent it is possible to predict the effort needed for certification. By looking at software complexity metrics this would enable a preliminary screening and benchmarking of OSS. A previous study [12] has been made regarding the use of Linux in safety-related systems and it has been helpful for identifying important characteristics for comparing the suitability of open source RTOS for safety-critical applications.

3 Evaluation of OSS RTOS

In this chapter, we discuss how existing software quality models can be leveraged to evaluate the maturity and quality of OSS. The rationale behind using such models is that they take into account organizational aspects that will give an indication of whether the maturity of the project is acceptable, that the software it suitable for the intended application, and that there is potential for fulfilling the process requirements of safety standards. We also look at previous work for identifying characteristics and metrics of the software which will give an indication of how well the product requirements of the standards can be fulfilled.

3.1 Software Quality and ISO/IEC 25010

Quality is the level of which a product meets the mentioned requirements or fulfils customer needs and expectations. OSS developers and organizations are facing many challenges and questions regarding the quality when compared to proprietary software, as there are worries about the level of satisfaction that can be achieved with respect to robustness, support, maintenance and other quality attributes when the software is written by volunteer developers. Software quality is an external software measurement attribute. Therefore, it can be measured only indirectly with respect to how the software, software development processes and resources involved in software development, relate to software quality.

The ISO/IEC 25010 [9] standard defines a product quality model composed of eight characteristics (which are further subdivided into sub-characteristics) that relate to static properties of software and dynamic properties of the computer system:

1. Functional suitability: How well the product meets stated and implied needs.
2. Performance efficiency: The performance relative to the amount of resources used.
3. Compatibility: How well the product can exchange information with other products, and if it can share hardware or software environment with other products.
4. Usability: If the product is useful in a specified context.
5. Reliability: How reliably the product performs its specified functions.
6. Security: The degree to which a product protects information and data.
7. Maintainability: Effectiveness and efficiency of product modifications.
8. Portability: Effectiveness and efficiency with which a product can be transferred from one usage environment to another.

The product can either be a complete system or a component. The characteristics are described in more detail in the standard. In addition to the product quality model there is a quality in use model which we do not further discuss or make use of.

The quality model proposed in ISO/IEC 25010 is well established. However, it does not provide sufficient support for assessing the quality of OSS. This is due to the particularities present in OSS development, specifically how to judge the impact of community, collaboration, licensing, and support aspects. Several quality models have been designed specifically for assessing the quality of OSS, but most of them predate ISO/IEC 25010, and are therefore based on its now obsolete precursor ISO/IEC 9126 [13]. A comparative study [8] has been made between different OSS quality models and the newer ISO/IEC 25010 model. The study showed that the Capgemini Open Source Maturity Model (OSMM) [14] was the most comprehensive model satisfying all eight factors under Product Quality. Therefore, we use the Capgemini OSMM in our proposed evaluation methodology.

3.2 Capgemini Open Source Maturity Model

Capgemini OSMM is a model where software is graded against a set of product indicators and application indicators. The product indicators are described as objective and measurable facts that focus on the product and the model includes scoring criteria for each indicator. The application indicators are used to assess how well the product fits a specific context. That is, they take into account environmental aspects and the present and (expected) future demands of the users. Therefore these indicators cannot be assessed without an intended context, and they are evaluated in two dimensions: the score (S) – how well the characteristic is fulfilled, and the priority (P) – how important the indicator is relative to other indicators. The final weight is the product of these (P*S). Both indicator scores and priority are judged on a scale 1–5 where 5 are the highest.

The model points out the significance of information, both of the product itself and the community that surrounds it, and thus it incorporates various criteria such as product development, developer and user community, product stability, maintenance and training. It was designed as a tool that can be used to compare and decide on the most suitable open source product option for an organization based on the product's maturity.

The product indicators are categorized into four categories, namely:

1. Product: Focuses on the product's inherent characteristics, age, selling points, developer community, human hierarchies and licensing.
2. Integration: Measures the product's modularity, adherence to standards as well as options to link the product to other products or infrastructure.
3. Use: Informs on the ease of which the product can be deployed and the way in which the user is supported in the everyday use of the product.
4. Acceptance: Tells about the market penetration of the product and the user base formed around the product.

A brief overview of the defined application indicators:

- Usability: Taking into account the intended users.
- Interfacing: Required connectivity, applicable standards.

- Performance: The performance demands that must be met.
- Reliability: Required level of service.
- Security: Required security measures.
- Proven technology: Is the technology proven in daily production?
- Vendor independence: Level of commitment between supplier and user.
- Platform independence: Is the product available for a wide range of platforms?
- Support: What level of support is required?
- Reporting: What kind of reporting is required?
- Administration: Use of existing maintenance tools, demands for management?
- Advice: Is validation by independent parties required?
- Training: Required training.
- Staffing: How is product expertise acquired?
- Implementation: Preferred implementation scenario.

For a more described description of the indicators see [14].

3.3 Dependability-Critical Aspects of an RTOS

Relevant parts of the international standards for functional safety IEC 61508 and ISO 26262 have been analyzed, and a literature survey made (see [18] for more details), in order to find characteristics that can be used to assess and compare the suitability of an open source RTOS for use in safety-critical applications. In particular, a study [12] has been made regarding the use of Linux in safety-critical applications and three basic criteria were set out in order to assess the suitability of an operating system and a simplified version of these three criteria are the following:

1. The behavior of the operating system shall be sufficiently well defined.
2. The operating system shall be suitable for the characteristics of the application.
3. The operating system shall be of sufficient integrity to allow the system safety integrity requirements to be met.

Considering the first criterion, it is important that the software developer of the safety-critical application has full knowledge of the intended behavior of the operating system. This is necessary so that hazards don't arise due to misconceptions that the application developer might have about the intended functionality of the operating system. It shall also be clear that the second criterion is necessary, since no matter how well specified an operating system might be, if it does not provide the desired functionality to support the software design chosen for the safety-critical application, it won't be suitable for use. This can be most clearly seen in the timing domain: if the application has hard real-time requirements and the operating system cannot support deadlines then the operating system cannot be used with confidence. The third and final criterion is fairly self-evident. However, it shall be noted that what is sufficient will depend on the complete system design, including any system level measures that can mitigate operating system failures and thus allow the operating system to have a lower safety requirement than would be the case without system mitigation measures.

An RTOS differs from a regular non-real-time operating system which is optimized to reduce response time while an RTOS is optimized to complete tasks within the set time constraint [1] often referred to as a deadline. However, in most RTOSs (soft real-time) one is not guaranteed that the system will always meet its deadlines, just generally. Only hard real-time systems can deterministically meet its deadlines.

An RTOS needs to satisfy a number of requirements. These are usually similar to high-reliability systems requirements. The operating system features listed below were identified in [12] as necessary to evaluate if the system is to be used in safety-critical applications:

1. Executive and scheduling: The process switching time and the employed scheduling algorithm of the operating system must meet all time-related application requirements.
2 Resource management: The internal use of resources must be predictable and bounded.
3 Internal communication: The task synchronization mechanisms must be robust and the risk of a corrupt message affecting safety shall be adequately low.
4. External communication: The mechanisms used for communication with external devices must be robust and the risk of a corrupt message shall be adequately low.
5. Internal liveness failure: The operating system shall allow the application to meet its availability requirements.
6. Domain separation: If an operating system is used, functions shall be provided that allow safety functions of lower integrity levels to not interfere with the correct operation of higher integrity safety functions.
7. Real-Time: Timing facilities and interrupt handling features must be sufficiently accurate to meet all application response time requirements.
8 Security: Risk of safety implications of security issues in connected systems.
9. User interface: When the operating system is used to provide a user interface, the risk of interface corrupting the user input to the application or the output data of the application must be sufficiently low.
10. Robustness: The operating system shall be able to detect and respond appropriately to the failure of the application process and external interfaces.
11. Installation: Installation procedures must include measures to protect against a faulty installation due to user error.

These features have been helpful for identifying the characteristics that are used for comparison in this paper and these are described in Sect. 4.1, but we have modified some characteristics and omitted some in order to better suit an embedded RTOS.

We will also look at the implementation and test coverage of the OSS. Embedded software systems are often implemented in the C programming language and in order to increase the quality of the implementation it is common to define a set of coding rules that must be followed. The coding rules can include for example the conventions used to format the source code, complexity limits for modules, hierarchical organization of the modules and language subsets. For safe and reliable software written in C, a commonly used subset is the MISRA C [15] which effectively defines a subset of the C programming language, removing features which are usually responsible for implementation errors or compiler dependencies. The MISRA C 2012 subset is sometimes considered a strongly typed subset of C.

As mentioned we will also take test coverage into account since high test coverage is one of the most impacting activities in order to qualify software for safety certification [11]. Test-driven development has become widespread both in proprietary software and OSS projects, in particular, the possibility to perform automated tests. The purpose of testing is to detect faults in the software component under test in order to find discrepancies between the specification and the actual behavior of the software. For example, running the automated test after every single commit to the code base may facilitate the detection of bugs ensuring the intended functionality of the software. Test coverage is one of the measures often required by standards to help make sure the test suite is adequate, and it is commonly defined as a percentage of the software that is covered by the tests. There are different ways in which this percentage can be defined; some common metrics are the percentage of code lines or statements executed, or the percentage of branch paths (edges) tested. These are often referred to as code (or line) coverage, statement coverage, and branch coverage respectively. For complex software components such as an RTOS the state space is potentially huge and it may be difficult to achieve 100% coverage in a practical amount of time (depending on which metric is used or prescribed in the standards). When this is the case, the test cases shall be chosen in a manner such that they test the different aspects of the RTOS, and an argument made for justifying why certain input combinations don't require testing (based on e.g. equivalence classes or other forms of analysis).

4 Selecting and Qualifying an OSS RTOS for Use in Safety-Critical Applications

In this chapter we present an approach on how to select and qualify an OSS RTOS for use in safety-critical applications.

4.1 Characteristics for Comparison

Based on the discussion in previous sections and common requirements in functional safety standards we have put together a list of characteristics that are relevant for an open source RTOS used in a safety-critical context. Although some characteristics in the list partly overlap with Capgemini OSMM indicators, this list is more focused on characteristics that will be relevant when trying to assess the RTOS suitability in safety-critical applications and map it to the requirements in functional safety standards, whereas the main purpose of OSMM is to determine whether the software is mature enough to consider in a wider perspective. It should be noted that this is a first attempt at identifying such criteria, and thus the list of characteristics should not be seen as exhaustive. In addition, we currently rate the characteristics only as 'available' or 'not available', while in reality some of them might be somewhere in between non-existent and sufficient for the intended purpose (for instance 'documentation' and 'test suite'). This may be refined in an improved version of these characteristics, e.g. using a scoring range with specified criteria for each level, or possibly more detailed sub-characteristics. The current characteristics we use are:

- Coding rules: Is the RTOS implemented using coding conventions throughout the entire code base?
- Language subset: Is the RTOS implemented using any defined language subset to reduce the likelihood of faults?
- Version-control: Is version control being used to track changes in the code base?
- Documentation: Is documentation available?
  - What functionality does it cover?
- Static resource allocation: Does the RTOS use static memory allocation? Dynamic memory allocation is not recommended in the standards since it can give rise to hazards.
- Priority-based preemptive scheduling: The scheduling policy needs to be priority-based preemptive in order to be used with confidence.
- Real-time support: Does the RTOS support deadlines?
- Domain separation: Is there support for domain separation?
- Synchronization primitives: Are there synchronization primitives available (e.g. semaphores, mutexes etc.) to allow safe inter-task communication.
- Verification: Are there any verification procedures to verify the functionality of the RTOS?
  - Test suite: Is there a test suite available?
- Does the test suite provide test coverage metrics? (e.g. code/branch coverage)
- Configuration options: Is there an option to turn off undesired functionality in the RTOS so that the unused functionality won't be compiled at all?
- Active community: Is the community behind the open source RTOS active?
  - Quality assurance: Are measures made in order to keep out "bad" code from the projects code base?
  - Bug tracking: Is there a list of known bugs?
  - Bug fixing: Are bugs being fixed at regular intervals?

If the open source RTOS fulfills all of the above characteristics it is a good candidate since it holds some of the functionality that is desirable for a safety-critical RTOS and some attributes that are preferred from an open source perspective. If it does not fulfill all of the above characteristics it could still be possible to adapt it, but the effort to achieve compliance with a functional safety standard is likely considerably higher.

4.2 Workflow

Based on the material from the previous sections, the process for choosing and assessing a suitable open source RTOS candidate against a functional safety standard is described below and a workflow can be seen in Fig. 1. The first step is identifying promising open source RTOS candidates. When enough candidates have been identified the quality and maturity of the OSS project is evaluated. As mentioned, we are using the Capgemini OSMM in order to see what support options there are for the project. If there are different licensing options available, does it have a stable and active community with regular updates, bug tracking and bug fixing etc. These and other criteria are then graded with a certain number of points based on the guidelines given in [14]. When the quality and maturity assessment has been made, a comparison of the characteristics presented in Sect. 4.1 is made. The best candidate is chosen based on the results of these two assessments. In the end, determining if there is a suitable candidate and which one to choose is not a mathematical exercise, the results must be judged within the context of what one is trying to achieve and the main point of the exercise is to gather the relevant information to make such a judgment.

When a candidate has been identified, one has to study the documentation and other information available for the open source RTOS and compare it with the applicable requirements in a functional safety standard. In our case study we have looked at the requirements for reuse of software components with non-compliant development (i.e. development has not been performed according to the standard) that are given in sub-clause 7.4.2.13 of IEC 61508-3. If the documentation or other material is insufficient or unavailable, the missing pieces may be supplemented by the developer of the safety-critical application, but in the case study we have only evaluated the RTOSs based on existing artefacts. The methodology is not only applicable for IEC 61508 however; other functional safety standards could also be used.

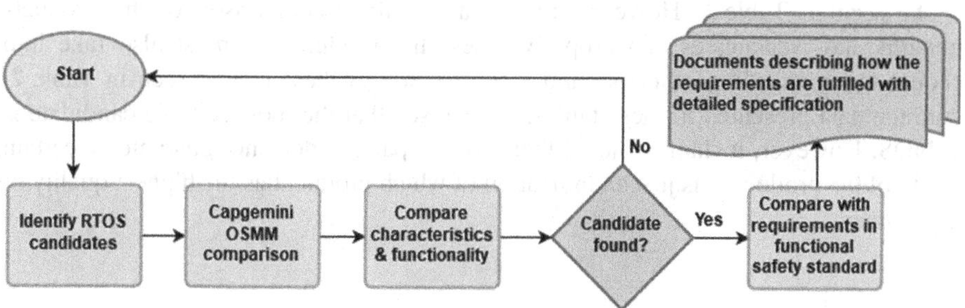

Fig. 1. Proposed workflow for assessing an RTOS for safety-critical applications.

5 Case Study: Comparing ChibiOS and ContikiOS

In this chapter, the two open source operating system ChibiOS [16] and ContikiOS [17] are compared. ChibiOS is an OSS RTOS implemented compliant with MISRA C and ContikiOS is a lightweight OSS operating system that is designed to run on Internet of Things (IoT) devices with limited resources. These operating systems are compared in order to find the most suitable candidate for use in a supposed safety-critical function. The most suitable candidate is then assessed to see to what degree it can adhere to the requirements of non-compliant development put forth in Part 3: Software Requirements of the functional safety standard IEC 61508. In the case study we assume the function shall be certified according to IEC 61508 with safety integrity level (SIL) 2. In a real case, the required SIL is determined using a hazard analysis and risk assessment for the function being implemented. SIL is a measure of the level of risk reduction provided by a safety function, and IEC 61508 specifies four levels 1–4, where higher levels require more risk reduction and hence imply more stringent demands on the electrical/electronic system (including the software). In the case study we have chosen to evaluate against SIL 2 as the higher levels have requirements that will be much more difficult to achieve for a component developed with a non-compliant development process.

Note that the evaluation has been made by one person for demonstration purposes, and not by a team of experts as recommended in Capgemini OSSM, nor by a qualified assessor as required for an actual assessment against IEC 61508. Therefore, the case study should be seen as a working example of evaluating an OSS RTOS, and not as reliable results for the two RTOSs used in the study.

5.1 Project Maturity

The quality and maturity of the two open source operating systems are evaluated with the Capgemini OSMM described in Sect. 3.2 and with the help of the guidelines given in [14]. First the product indicators form the basis of the model. Using these indicators, the quality of the open source products can be determined. Product indicators receive a score valued between one and five. One is poor, five is excellent and 3 is average. All the scores are summed to produce a product score. A comparison of the two products can be seen in Table 1. However, this data is only a comparison of the products strengths and weaknesses. To properly assess the product, we must also take into account the application indicators and a comparison of these can be seen in Table 2. From the data presented in these tables, we can see that the most suitable candidate is ChibiOS. However, it shall be noted that this comparison does not guarantee a certain quality of the product, it is just an indication of which product has the highest quality of development.

5.2 RTOS Characteristics

In this section, we will give a brief description of the two operating systems in this study and compare them based on the characteristics that are described in Sect. 3.3 and the result of this comparison can be seen in Table 3. The results have been obtained by going through the documentation and test suites, running PC-Lint, and researching how community activities are performed.

ChibiOS. This is an open source RTOS implemented in MISRA C. A code analysis has been performed using the PC-Lint static analyzer, on the ChibiOS 16.1.7 release and it reported no violations of the checked MISRA rules using the configuration provided with the source code. Additionally, the coding standard in terms of naming conventions and design patterns are explicit and consistently used on all the software.

The scheduler of ChibiOS is implemented as a priority-based preemptive scheduler with round-robin scheduling for tasks at the same priority level and it is suited for real time systems since it supports deadlines. A test suite is also used to verify the functional correctness of the core mechanisms in the operating system like priority

Table 1. Comparison of product indicators according to Capgemini OSMM.

Indicator	ChibiOS	ContikiOS
Product		
Age	5	3
Licensing	5	3
Human hierarchies	5	5
Selling points	3	3
Developer community	3	3
Integration		
Modularity	5	5
Collaboration with other products	3	3
Standards	5	3
Use		
Support	3	3
Ease of deployment	3	3
Acceptance		
User community	3	1
Market penetration	3	1
Total	46	38

Table 2. Comparison of application indicators according to Capgemini OSMM.

Indicator	Priority (P)	ChibiOS		ContikiOS	
		Score (S)	P*S	Score (S)	P*S
Usability	5	5	25	5	25
Interfacing	3	3	9	3	9
Performance	5	4	20	3	15
Reliability	5	5	25	4	20
Security	3	3	9	3	9
Proven technology	3	3	9	3	9
Vendor independence	4	4	16	4	16
Platform independence	2	4	8	4	8
Support	4	3	12	2	8
Reporting	2	4	8	2	4
Administration	2	3	6	3	6
Advice	1	1	1	1	1
Training	3	3	9	3	9
Staffing	3	2	6	2	6
Implementation	3	4	12	2	6
Total			175		151

Table 3. Comparison of characteristics. An "X" indicates availability and "–" non-availability.

Characteristic	ChibiOS	ContikiOS
Coding rules	X	X
Language subset	X	–
Version control	X	X
Documentation	X	X
Static resource allocation	X	X
Priority-based preemptive scheduling	X	–
Real-time support	X	–
Domain separation support	X	–
Synchronization primitives	X	–
Verification	X	X
Test suite	X	X
Configuration	X	X
Active community	X	X
Quality assurance	X	X
Bug tracking	X	X
Bug fixing	X	X

inversion, priority-based scheduling, timers and all the synchronization primitives that are offered by the RTOS. The test suite can be executed both on a simulator and on real hardware. By running the test suite on hardware, one can benchmark the given hardware platform where the time overhead of operations like context-switch, interrupts and synchronization primitives can be obtained.

Separation of different tasks can be done in the time domain by utilizing the implemented scheduling policy. However, care must be taken while using critical regions, since they can introduce unexpected latency. To avoid this, the tasks must be developed coherently to avoid timing interference between the different tasks. The only execution model available for ChibiOS is single process-multi thread. Some of the supported architectures can provide memory separation by using a Memory Protection Unit (MPU) or Memory Management Unit (MMU), while memory separation is not available in other architectures. For the case study we have rated domain separation as available, but keep in mind that this depends on the hardware to be used.

ContikiOS. This is a lightweight open source operating system that is designed to run on IoT devices with limited resources. It provides three network mechanisms: the uIP TCP/IP stack which provides IPv4 networking, the uIPv6 stack which provides IPv6 networking, and the Rime stack [19] which is a set of custom lightweight networking protocols designed for low-power wireless sensor networks.

ContikiOS is mainly developed in standard C (ISO C) and is portable to various platforms. The coding rules only cover the formatting style. A MISRA C compliance check has been performed using PC-Lint static analyzer with the default configuration for MISRA C checking. All the files under dev/, cpu/, platform/ and core/directories of the ContikiOS 3.0 code base have been checked. In total over 70 000 messages were generated, most of them relating to either styling issues or errors that are easily correctable. However, there were also reports of more severe errors such as recursive functions, discarding of volatile or constant qualifiers, variable shadowing, uninitialized variables, buffer overrun, and unused return codes.

The scheduler in ContikiOS does not support priorities for tasks. However, they can be either cooperative or preemptive and a number of timer modules exist and these can be used to schedule preemptive tasks. There are also no well-defined mechanisms for inter-task communication and concurrency issues must be handled manually. On every new version of ContikiOS regression tests are performed. However, they seem to mostly cover the communication protocols and not the functionality of the operating system like scheduling, inter-task communication and synchronization primitives. Also, memory separation is not used due to lack of support in most of the supported architectures.

5.3 Compliance with IEC 61508

As we can see by the data presented in Sect. 5.2, the most suitable option for assessment is ChibiOS. Therefore, we have assessed ChibiOS according to the requirements for reuse of software components with non-compliant development in IEC 61508. The RTOS is in this case regarded as a context free software component and in order to assess ChibiOS we have gone through the available documentation and compared it with the requirements given under sub-clause 7.4.2.13 in IEC 61508-3. However, a detailed description of the requirements is not given here. For a detailed description of the requirements, see [5]. Due to space restrictions, this is an abbreviated version of our assessment; more details can be found in [18]. Note that we make no claim that this assessment is exhaustive.

Under sub-clause 7.4.2.13 in IEC 61508-3 there is a requirement that a software safety requirements specification shall exist for the software element. This specification shall contain all system safety requirements, in terms of system safety function requirements and the system safety integrity requirements, in order to achieve the required functional safety. This specification must be valid in the specific system context and it shall also cover the functional and safety behavior of the software element in its new application. However, a pre-existing RTOS is unlikely to have any specific safety requirements defined since it is not bound to a specific context, therefore, in this study we assume that the requirement of this specification can be fulfilled if the behavior of the RTOS is precisely defined supplemented with its use in the target application. This requirement can then be fulfilled by ChibiOS since there is a detailed reference manual covering all the functionality of the kernel together with a supporting book that describes the architecture of the RTOS and how all the submodules work.

According to IEC 61508, the use of semi-formal methods (e.g. finite state machines) to express parts of a specification so that some types of mistakes such as wrong behavior can be detected is recommended for safety functions considered to be of SIL 1 or SIL 2 and highly recommended for SIL 3. These methods are used to model, verify, specify or implement the control structure of a system, and the IEC 61508 standards states that state transition diagrams can apply to the whole system or to some objects within it. The documentation available for ChibiOS shows that the behavior of the kernel and other submodules are specified in detail with the help of UML and finite state machines.

The IEC 61508 standard provides recommended practices for verification and how the architectural design of the software shall be structured. Some of these techniques are not applicable to an operating system such as graceful degradation which is something that needs to be implemented on the application level. However, high integrity software shall be designed with a modular approach that is verifiable and testable with measurements indicating the test coverage. It is also recommended to use static resource allocation, time-triggered architecture with cyclic behavior etc. These requirements can be fulfilled by ChibiOS since it has a modular design; it is internally divided in several major independent components. It uses static resource allocation and it has a time-triggered architecture with cyclic behavior. The test suite provided is used in order to verify the proper working of the kernel and it can be used to test if a ported version of the RTOS is working and all the test results are included as reports in the RTOS distribution.

Another requirement is that when software elements are present which are not required for achieving the functional safety, evidence shall be provided that this functionality will not prevent the system from meeting its safety requirements. In ChibiOS unwanted functions can be removed from the build by disabling them in the ChibiOS configuration file so that they won't be compiled at all. Functionality that can be disabled/enabled or modified can vary from hardware peripheral drivers, software subsystems, debugging options, speed optimization and system tick frequency. This will make it easier to prove that unwanted functionality will not interfere.

There shall also be evidence that all credible failure mechanisms of the software element have been identified and that mitigation measures exist. ChibiOS provides support for domain separation of different tasks in the time domain, which is done by using priority-based preemptive scheduling, but care must be taken while using critical regions, since they can introduce unexpected latency. The only execution model available for ChibiOS is the single process-multi thread execution model, which means that all the tasks share the same addressing space unless an MMU is used. But memory separation is not implemented on all architectures. Mitigation measures shall also be used at the application level, if considered necessary in the context of use. This requirement may therefore require significant work to fulfill.

There are requirements that coding rules are followed and each module is reviewed. Also, a suitable strongly typed language and language subset is required. In the core ChibiOS codebase, the code is thoroughly tested and maintained, bugs are tracked and fixed, and the code is released in stable packages regularly. In order for code to be added to the core codebase, the code has to follow strict coding guidelines and go through extensive reviews and testing. ChibiOS also implements the C subset MISRA C 2012 which is sometimes considered a strongly typed subset of C. Although C was not specifically designed for this type of application, it is widely used for embedded and safety-critical software for several reasons. Some advantages are control over memory management are simple and well debugged core runtime libraries and mature tool support. While manual memory management code must be carefully checked to avoid errors, it allows a degree of control over application response times that is not available with languages that depend on e.g. garbage collection. The core runtime libraries of the C language are relatively simple, mature and well understood, so they are amongst the most suitable platforms available.

6 Conclusions and Future Work

ChibiOS holds many of the desirable characteristics that are required by an RTOS in safety-critical applications and for the IEC 61508 standard. On the basis of the limited evidence and analysis presented in this study, we have concluded that ChibiOS may be acceptable for use in safety-critical application of SIL 1 and SIL 2. Of course, this statement must be qualified by stating that the hardware must be of suitable SIL and the fact that we may have stretched the definitions of the standard somewhat since sub-clause 7.4.2.13 of IEC 61508-3, reuse of software components with non-compliant development, is not really intended for assessing an operating system.

The assessment done in this thesis project is by no means complete and a real assessment would require trained professionals from an accredited certification body to perform the analysis of the available code and documentation. A follow up project could therefore be to perform a real assessment of ChibiOS with regards to IEC 61508 to determine whether the requirements for SIL 1 or SIL 2 can be fulfilled. Other relevant standards such as ISO 26262 could also be considered.

It should also be noted that the list of characteristics and evaluation methodology is our first attempt for evaluating the use of an RTOS in safety-critical applications. Future work is needed to refine the characteristics and methodology to match the requirements in functional safety standards even better.

Acknowledgements. This work is from of a Master's thesis project at RISE Electronics; and is partly funded by the Swedish government agency for innovation systems (VINNOVA) in the NGEA step 2 project (ref 2015-04881).

References

1. Hambarde, P., Varma, R., Jha, S.: The survey of real time operating system: RTOS. In: IEEE International Conference on Computer and Communication Technologies (ICCCT), pp. 34–39 (2014)
2. Tan, S., Nguyen Bao Anh, T.: Real-time operating system (RTOS) for small (16-bit) microcontrollers. In: IEEE 13th International Symposium on Consumer Electronics (ISCE), pp. 1007–1011 (2009)
3. Corber, J.: How the Development Process Works (The Linux Foundation) (2011)
4. Mockus, A., Fielding, R.T., Herbsleb, J.D.: Two case studies of open source software development: apache and Mozilla. ACM Trans. Softw. Eng. Methodol. (TOSEM) **11**, 309–346 (2002)
5. IEC 61508, International standard. Functional Safety of Electrical/Electronic/Programmable Electronic Safety-Related System (2010)
6. ISO 26262, International Standard. Road vehicles – Functional Safety (2011)
7. Zhao, L., Elbaum, S.: Quality assurance under the open source development model. J. Syst. Softw. **66**, 65–75 (2003)

8. Adewumi, A., Misra, S., Omoregbe, N.: Evaluating open source software quality models against ISO 25010. In: IEEE International Conference on Computer and Information Technology; Ubiquitous Computing and Communications; Dependable, Automatic and Secure Computing, Pervasive Intelligence and Computing, pp. 872–877 (2015)
9. ISO/IEC 25010, International Standard. Systems and Software Engineering – Systems and Software Quality Requirements and Evaluation (2011)
10. Soto, M., Ciolkowski, M.: The QualOSS open source assessment model measuring the performance of open source communities. In: Proceedings of the 3rd International Symposium on Empirical Software Engineering and Measurement (ESEM), pp. 498–501 (2009)
11. Cotroneo, D., Di Leo, D., Natella, R.: Prediction of the testing effort for the safety certification of open-source software: a case study on a real-time operating system. In: IEEE 12th European Dependable Computing Conference (EDCC), pp. 141–152 (2016)
12. Pierce, R.H.: Preliminary Assessment of Linux for Safety Related Systems. In: HSE Contract research report RR011/2002 (2002)
13. ISO/IEC 9126, International Standard. Information Technology – Software Engineering – Product Quality (2001)
14. Dujinhouwer, F.W., Widdows, C.: Capgemini Expert Letter Open Source Maturity Model, Capgemini, pp. 1–18 (2003)
15. Motor Industry Software Reliability Association, MISRA-C Guidelines for the Use of the C Language in Critical Systems, UK (2004)
16. ChibiOS. https://www.chibios.org. Accessed 29 May 2017
17. ContikiOS. https://www.contiki-os.org. Accessed 29 May 2017
18. Berntsson, P.S.: Evaluation of open source operating systems for safety-critical applications. Master's thesis, Chalmers University of Technology (2017)
19. Dunkels, A., Österlind, F., He, Z.: An adaptive communication architecture for wireless sensor networks. In: Proceedings of the Fifth ACM Conference on Networked Embedded Sensor Systems (SenSys 2007), Sydney, Australia, November 2007

100 Years of Software - Adapting Cyber-Physical Systems to the Changing World

Hayley Borck[1(✉)], Paul Kline[2], Hazel Shackleton[1], John Gohde[1], Steven Johnston[1], Perry Alexander[2], and Todd Carpenter[1]

[1] Adventium Labs, 111 3rd Ave S, Minneapolis, MN 55401, USA
{hayley.borck,hazel.shackleton,john.gohde, steven.johnston,todd.carpenter}@adventiumlabs.com

[2] Information and Telecommunication Technology Center, The University of Kansas, 2335 Irving Hill Road, Lawrence, KS 66045, USA
{paulkline,palexand}@ittc.ku.edu

Abstract. Cyber-Physical Systems (CPS) are software and hardware systems that interact with the physical environment. Many CPSs have useful lifetimes measured in decades. This leads to unique concerns regarding security and longevity of software designed for CPSs which are exacerbated by the need for CPSs to adapt to ecosystem changes if they are to remain functional over extended periods. In particular, the software in long-lifetime CPSs must adapt to unanticipated trends in environmental conditions, aging effects on mechanical systems, and component upgrades and modifications. This paper presents the Toolkit for Evolving Ecosystem Envelopes (TEEE) system created to help address these challenges in CPSs. TEEE is able to detect environmental changes which have caused errors within the CPS without directly sensing the environmental change. TEEE uses dynamic profiling to detect the errors within the CPS, determine the root cause of the error, alert the user, and suggest a possible adaption.

Keywords: Cyber-Physical systems · Resilient systems · Requirements-based testing

1 Introduction

Cyber-Physical Systems can interact with the physical environment by sensing external state, transferring kinetic and potential energy, computing solutions to affect desired outcomes, and driving electrical, optical, and mechanical actuators to achieve those outcomes. Unlike software applications, CPSs sense, depend upon, and actuate physical phenomena. The software in long-lifetime CPS must adapt to unanticipated changes in environments, mechanical, or use. The CPS, however, might not directly sense all aspects of its environment, especially those aspects of the environment which were not considered significant during original development. For example our System Under Test (SUT) is a specific patient controlled analgesia (PCA) pump which requires medical tubing with an inner

A. Romanovsky and E.A. Troubitsyna (Eds.): SERENE 2017, LNCS 10479, pp. 133–148, 2017.
DOI: 10.1007/978-3-319-65948-0_9

diameter of 0.054″. However, residents of less developed countries are often forced to use whatever equipment is available to them, often without standard safety procedures or support resources. These users may have access to tubing with a smaller 0.0033″ inner diameter which will affect the rate of flow of medication.

This paper presents the Toolkit for Evolving Ecosystem Envelops (TEEE) system to detect changes in the environment that are not directly sensible and semiautomatically adapt to them. Neches et al. [18] described resilient systems as: "trusted and effective out of the box in a wide range of contexts, easily adapted to many others through reconfiguration or replacement, with graceful and detectable degradation of function." TEEE aims to add this sort of resiliency to CPSs. Further, TEEE adds root cause analysis and adaption to errors, whether they are expected (i.e., degradation due to longevity in the field) or unexpected. TEEE uses dynamic profiling tools and techniques to explore CPS performance envelopes, subject to its evolving environment, that will ultimately allow software to adapt as internal and external conditions change. TEEE leverages model-based development techniques for requirements, design, architecture, configuration, and automated measurement and stimulus to identify root causes of anomalies. In contrast, the state of the practice development processes still largely use trial-and-error test-based software coding.

The remainder of this paper is structured as follows. Section 2 presents the TEEE system design and architecture. Section 3 describes the background and related research. Section 4 describes how TEEE models the CPS system. Sections 5 and 6 go into detail on the Synthesis of Stimulus and Measurements algorithms respectively. Section 7 presents a real world use case and the results of running it through TEEE. Finally, Sect. 8 concludes the paper.

2 TEEE Overview

When an error in the system is detected, currently by the user, the TEEE system uses CPS models and design to create and inject profiling code to identify the root cause of the error. The aim of the Synthesize Stimulus Algorithm (SSA) and Dynamic Measurements component is to infer the root cause of the error, especially in cases which the error is not directly sensible by the CPS. When a root cause is determined alternative system hardware or software components (i.e., motor or motor controller software) are suggested to the user.

The primary components of the TEEE architecture are AADL models of the SUT and dynamic profiling components to synthesize measurements and stimulus of the SUT. The current prototype, developed in JAVA and Coq [4], has all of the components built with manual data transfers. TEEE interfaces with the developer (or trained user) before the SUT is deployed. During this step (shown by the circled 1, in Fig. 1) the developer indicates which AADL model will be deployed as the SUT. For example the user would indicate the specific implementation of the system motor controller. The SUT is constantly monitored by the user for errors, a process we intend to automate in the future. If a variable in the system has different values than the requirements specify (for example flow

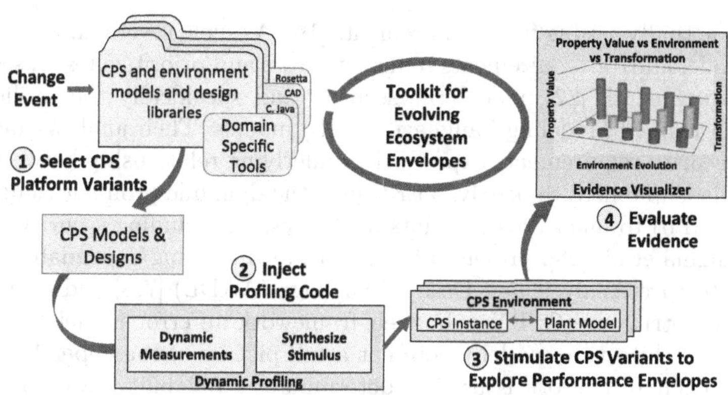

Fig. 1. The TEEE system architecture.

rate on the medical tubing does not fall within a specified range in the requirement) the user indicates to TEEE that an error occurred. Dynamic profiling code is injected into the system using the TEEE CPS Synthesized Stimulus and Dynamic Measurement synthesis tools (circled 2). TEEE generates synthesized stimuli, driven by requirements in the model of the SUT, using the Synthesize Stimulus component. The stimuli drives exploration of the overall operational envelopes of the SUT. Operational envelopes are regions in which the CPS is intended to correctly operate as per its requirements. For the PCA pump SUT, an example envelope might include a space defined by flow rate, environmental temperature, and fluid viscosity. The stimuli can also be used to focus on specific cyberphysical characteristics to evaluate, with input from the user. For example, the user may specify prioritization of stimuli on a certain component (i.e., tubing, motor, sensors etc.). The Synthesize Stimulus component explores operational envelopes by creating a test case suite from requirements. A potential drawback of the current TEEE implementation is the manual process of creating requirements for the SUT; If a requirement is missing in the model there will be no test case created. The user of the SUT is tasked to test the SUT according to the test cases within the suite. Information on the operational envelopes is sent to the Dynamic Measurement component. The Dynamic Measurement component synthesizes measurements, consists of properties about the SUT, and reasons with the architecture models to infer system behaviors. The results of the Dynamic Measurement system is a set of components from which the error may have originated. In Sect. 7 we will dive into an example of TEEE doing exactly this in a real world scenario.

3 Related Work

Typical design-for-test and unit-test approaches evaluate the SUT against requirements, but these methods only address a small fraction of issues, with the majority of defects actually arising from requirements [16]. As such, several approaches use a SUT model and/or requirements to detect errors and prioritize test cases.

Rodriguez et al. [22], model the security and specifically the resilience of systems in Unified Modeling Language (UML) models. Their analysis and modeling of security requirements exposes the underlying relationship between security and dependability. Similarly, TEEE uses the dynamic profiling components (Sects. 5 and 6) to uncover constraints in the system including security requirements. Rugina et al. [23], present a framework for modeling dependability using the Architecture Analysis and Design Language (AADL) [7,8] and Generalized Stochastic Petri Nets (GSPNs). In their framework an error model is added to the AADL architecture model to present a full picture of the dependability for the user. Their framework is used to determine the reliability, availability, and safety prior to system deployment. TEEE focuses on determining if the requirements, including these dependability properties, are satisfied in the event of an environment change or off-specification use when the system has been deployed.

Arafeen and Do [2] use requirements to prioritize test cases and more quickly determine faults. Their prioritization scheme clusters the requirements and prioritizes the cluster based on the priority of the requirements within. TEEE's test case prioritization scheme (Sect. 5) also takes uses system requirements to create and prioritize test cases. However, TEEE also takes into account whether the test case (and subsequently requirement) has previously exposed an error. The merging of these prioritization techniques may prove interesting and will be explored in further work. Dreossi et al. [6] detect errors in machine learning components of CPS systems, such as in Lane Keeping Assist Systems in cars, by formulating it as a falsification problem for the model. TEEE similarly uses the model requirements to create test cases and determine errors within the CPS.

Adaption in systems (CPS or software) research is focused primarily on automatically creating patches for software. The GenProg system, Le Goues et al. [14], uses genetic programming to automatically repair software defects given a set of test cases. The ClearView system [19] automatically patches errors in deployed software without access to source code or debugging info. ClearView learns normal execution, detects failures while monitoring execution, and generates a patch. While ClearView works on deployed systems, as TEEE does, it discovers errors by learning 'normal' execution and would be unable to discover error if the 'normal' execution changes (such as a system use case change). Converse to these software only approaches TEEE is able to find and repair issues stemming from the underlying architecture (with a human in the loop) as well as software errors. TEEE models alternate components in the CPS architecture and, when an issue arises, is able to suggest possible alternate architecture configurations.

The TEEE project is a seedling effort to augment the DARPA Building Resource Adaptive Software Systems (BRASS) program [10], which is tasked with creating resilient systems that have robust and functional 100+ year software. This program has roots in autonomic computing [12] in which systems manage themselves given high-level objectives. TEEE only tries to monitor the system for errors in order to determine error causes and possible adaptations however, rather than the larger task of managing goals and objectives of the system administrator. Part of ensuring resilient long lifetime software includes accounting for unanticipated uses of systems as well as unintended environmental changes. The TEEE approach uses dynamic profiling components to determine whether environmental changes and/or changes to the SUT use cases are the cause of current errors. Stoicescu et al. [24] expanded upon Neches description of resilient systems to be "expected to continuously provide trustworthy services despite changes in the environment or in the requirements they must comply with." The authors outlined an overall approach to defining fault tolerant applications that automatically adapt during the systems lifetime. Their approach monitors the system and analyzes the observations to determine if adaptation is necessary. Stoicescu et al. and TEEE share the goal of adapting to changes in requirements and/or the environment. Adjepon-Yamoah [1] modeled fault tolerant methods via petri nets in systems interfacing with unpredictable environments (i.e., the cloud). Similarly, TEEE interfaces with the highly unpredictable physical world to evaluate the cause of errors in the SUT.

4 Modeling Cyber-Physical Systems

The SUT used with the TEEE prototype is a PCA pump. The PCA pump's components and requirements are modeled in AADL. While our current SUT is a PCA pump there is no reason TEEE cannot be generalized to other CPSs, as long as the models are given to the system.AADL was chosen due to it's focus on *architecture* rather than the functional/behavior emphasis that underlies other modeling languages. In particular, it better enables modeling and trading-off *what* components comprise a system and the relationships between the components, rather than *how* the system works. AADL has been shown beneficial to risk management activities using medical devices [13]. One of the salient features of AADL is the ability to model design alternatives coherently within a single AADL model. AADL defines component types that include all externally visible features, separately from implementations, which model component internals. Component `implementations`, an instantiation of a component, may have subcomponents which themselves may be component types or implementations. A component type may have any number of implementations, all of which look identical from outside. By having multiple implementations for a component, different design alternatives can be modeled. This allows many alternatives for fault management to be captured in a single model so they may be evaluated and compared. We anticipate over the lifetime of the CPS additional alternative implementations and components will be added to the model as technology advances. Lastly AADL is a rich enough language and does not require extensions to model CPSs. Requirements are scraped from the AADL model of the CPS system by a custom OSATE [11] plugin. The requirements are consumed (via XML) by the Stimulus Synthesis Algorithm (SSA) (Sect. 5) and Dynamic Measurement algorithm (Sect. 6). Listing 1.1 shows a snippet of one implementation of the motor component in the PCA pump. In this snippet the specific motor modeled is called ‘motor’, its parents are defined under the <Parents> tag. The criticality of the component is defined by the user and annotated with the <Criticality> tag. Lastly the requirements of the component are defined using the <Variable> tag. Each variable may define an allowable and test range as well as the actual value. Often the actual functioning range of a variable will be larger than the allowed range indicates, which is why we include the option of a test range. The requirement on the motor component in Listing 1.1 defines the variable *Operating Temperature* as having an allowed range of −10 to 40 °C.

Listing 1.1. A XML requirement on the motor component of the PCA pump that has been extracted from the AADL model.

```
<Component type="device" implementation="motor">
  <Parents>
    <SystemRef type="system" implementation="motorSystem"/>
    <SystemRef type="system" implementation="pump"/>
    <SystemRef type="system" implementation="Full_sys_inst"/>
  </Parents>
  <Criticality>0</Criticality>
  <Variable name="OperatingTemperature" units="c">
    <allowed>
        <real min="-10.0" max="40.0"/>
    </allowed>
  </Variable>
</Component>
```

5 Stimulus Synthesis Algorithm

The Stimulus Synthesis Algorithm (SSA) probes the SUT operating envelope by creating a set of test cases from the model requirements. The SSA is a combination of state of the art approaches which are described further in this section. The SSA consists of two sub-algorithms (1) Create all test cases from the system specifications and requirements, (2) Reduce test cases to N-wise subsets where possible, and prioritize the test cases. The results are sent to the Dynamic Measurements component.

5.1 Create Test Cases from Requirements

For each component in the model, the SSA creates a test case that corresponds to each variable’s allowable range and test range. Our algorithm to create test cases from requirements is derived from Ranganathan’s [21] work using the Rosetta modeling language. A *test case* is defined in our work as a *test scenario*, a boolean condition to be applied to a variable; and a *test vector*, a set of inputs to be substituted for the variable in the boolean condition. The system requirements for the motor component (Listing 1.1) only define one variable with an allowable range, therefore, one test case will be created. The test scenario is the boolean condition: $-10 \leq temp \ \wedge \ temp \leq 40$. This example test case will test if a particular component in the CPSs, the motor, is operating under the temperature range it for which it was designed. The test vector for each test case is created using the step value in the requirement. If there is no step value present in the model, a step value of the nearest 1 at the lowest non-zero decimal place is used (i.e., 200 has a step = 100, 0.34 has a step = 0.01). We expect the AADL model to be hand created by system designers and therefore, have all of the necessary information such as step value. However, in the case of a legacy model or if a designer does not know the step value we have implemented a rest step creation algorithm. A test vector is created by the SSA for the operating temperature variable by enumerating each value between -10 and 40 with a step of 10 $(-10, 0...30, 40)$. Boundary values have been implicated in faults within the SUT [17], therefore an additional n, where $n = 2$ in the current prototype, vector values are added on each boundary. The SSA also adds test vector values for the actual variable value, if available. The resulting test case suite has sufficient coverage over the specified requirements.

5.2 Combine and Prioritize

To reduce the number of test cases and subsequently the time it takes to test the SUT, the SSA combines test cases using the method by Lott et al. [15]. As previously mentioned a test case is created for each variables allowable range and test range. The large number of test cases is not scalable to large CPSs which is why we combine the test cases. The combination algorithm is a simple greedy algorithm described by Cohen et al. [5], which combines test cases into pairwise randomly until there are none (or only one) left to combine. The SSA does not pair test cases which test the same variable (i.e., temperature) in the test scenario. We found, as Lott et al. did, that a higher order combination yields greater test pattern savings. Though currently the SSA algorithm uses pairwise combination to reduce the risk of combining differently named variables which are actually the same (i.e., operating temperature vs temperature). With pairwise combination, assuming independence, growth of the test space increases $log_2(x)$ where x is the number of independent requirements. Increasing the order of combination of test cases, changes it to $log_n(x)$.

The test suite is prioritized to find failure quickly using a the fault-recorded test prioritization (FRTP) technique [20]. At this stage the user may request prioritization on a specific component. Each time a test case is marked as failed, its Failure Detection Number (FDN) is incremented. This indicates a fault has been found at the component(s) being tested within the test case. The FRTP method iteratively extracts information from the testing process and does not need to be bootstrapped with information from prior test executions. The FRTP method prioritizes test cases based on previously found faults (FDN). Some components are necessarily 'more important' than others. For example, if the motor in the PCA pump fails then the PCA pump will not work. If instead a sensor on the motor fails then the PCA pump will error but may continue to work. To encode this we added the criticality of the component to the prioritization algorithm by using an equation derived from the *Risk Exposure* metric [3] to prioritize the test suite.

$$RiskExposure(TS) = \frac{\sum_{tc \in TC} P(f) * C(f)}{|f|} \tag{1}$$

Chen et al., defines the risk exposure metric (Eq. 1) as the probability of failure ($P(f)$) of a component in the current test case tc multiplied by the cost of failure of the components in the current test case ($C(f)$) and then divided by the total number of components in the current test case. In place of determining the probability of failure for each component in the test case we redefined $P(f)$ in TEEE to represent the number of times the components in the current test case previously failed any test case. Equation 2 shows the TEEE definition of $P(f)$ which is a novel extension of the Chen Risk Exposure metric. In TEEE the $P(f)$ is defined by the sum of the FDN for each component in the current test case over the entire test suite (denoted by TS). The cost of failure ($C(f)$), or criticality of a component, is annotated by the user in the AADL model (`<Criticality>` tag). The default criticality is to zero, which means not critical. In future iterations we plan to explore ways of automatically inferring criticality to give the SSA more meaningful and complete information to reason on.

$$P(f) = \sum_{tc \in TS} \left(\sum_{c \in tc} FDN(c) \right) \tag{2}$$

Finally Grindal et al. [9] looked at the effectiveness of test case combination and found better results when pair-wise test cases are combined with a single variable test strategy. The SSA's final step is to randomly add k one-wise test cases to the test suite from the pre-combined list of one-wise test cases for the SUT. We choose a random k between 25% and 75% of the test suite size to test the prototype.

Figure 2 shows the prototype GUI for the SSA algorithm. The requirements file for the PCA pump has been loaded and the SSA algorithm has been run in the figure. The left side of the GUI shows statistics on the number of test cases created and the number of *test patterns* (the test scenarios from the test case and one test vector value from each test case) before and after combination. It is worth noting that combining the test cases into pair-wise test cases creates a test pattern savings of 24% for the PCA pump. The right side of the GUI shows a pairwise test case. The test scenarios test the tube component (top) and power system component (bottom). The user is requested to test the test vector values highlighted in red by substituting the vector values for their respective variable. In this example the variables are length for the tube component and power for the power system. The user is expected to record the results using the 'passed' or 'did not pass' buttons.

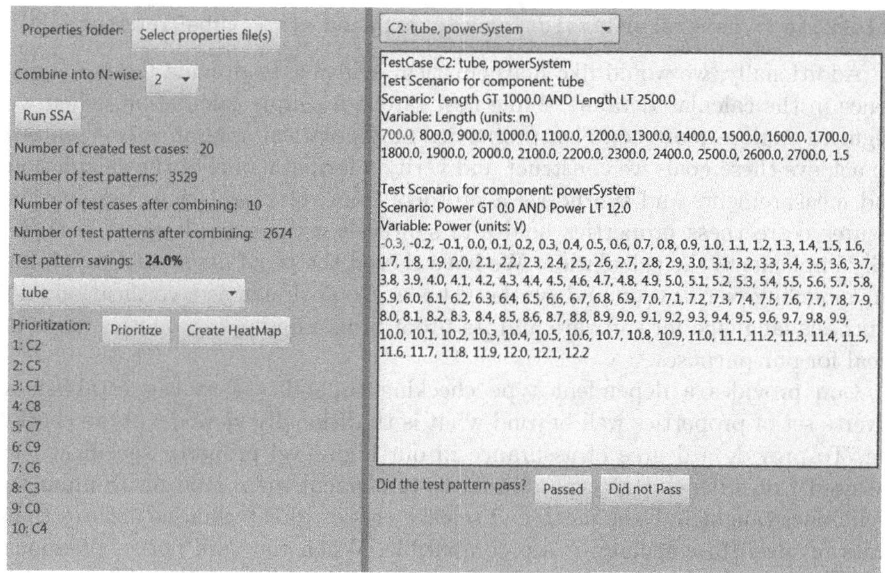

Fig. 2. A GUI of the SSA algorithm showing a combined test case testing a tube and motor sensor

6 Dynamic Measurements

Some of the properties in CPSs necessary for engineering design decisions or operational decisions are not directly sensed by the SUT. To calculate the measurements of these properties TEEE uses dynamic measurements of properties which can be sensed. By synthesizing these measurements TEEE alleviates the need to measure properties directly in the environment (i.e., the user may not need to buy new sensors for the SUT in order to determine newly encountered errors). For example, flow rate is a critical property both the user and designer need for their respective tasks. The most obvious way to determine flow rate is to sense it. However, in our working example (PCA pump) flow rate sensors are not usually built into the system. This forces us to calculate flow rate from other known quantities. Currently the PCA pump calculates flow rate from system parameters input by the user. While this has some utility, it is an indication of what the flow rate *should* be and not what it actually is. For both engineering and use case scenarios determining the actual delivered flow rate is critical.

TEEE constructs measurements which are not directly sensible by the SUT using dynamic, physical measurements from other properties. The measurement calculation is performed much as it currently is, but using physical measurements rather than exclusively user input. For example, flow rate can be calculated by taking the following measurements: motor speed, distance (meters) plunger traveled per motor rotation, and vial diameter and then calculating a flow rate value:

$$\texttt{flowRate} := \texttt{metersPerRevolution} * \texttt{motorSpeed} * (\pi * (\texttt{tubeDiameter}/2)^2)$$

Additionally, we would like mathematical evidence to provide further confidence in the calculated value. While flow rate is a simple calculation, when we begin to explore more complex properties mathematical assurance is essential. To achieve these goals we construct and verify a formal model of the calculation and measurements and synthesize a protocol from the calculation. Verification assures correctness properties hold and synthesis assures resulting code faithfully implements the calculation. We have chosen the proof assistant Coq [4] for our modeling, verification and synthesis tasks. Coq's design as a verification and synthesis language for software and its proof programming capabilities make it ideal for our purposes.

Coq provides a dependent type checking capability that can establish a diverse set of properties well beyond what is traditionally viewed as type checking. To provide a degree of assurance in our high-level property specifications we used Coq's dependent type system to implement units analysis. Similar to techniques taught in basic math and science classes, this technique ensures that units involved in calculations are compatible. When they are not, expressions will not type check and thus cannot be used in any computation. Thus, units analysis provides a simple static analysis that predicts errors prior to processing.

Every measurable quantity in our engineering domain is expressible by some combination of the seven base units (Ampere, Candela, Kelvin, Kilogram, Meter, Mole, and Second). For example, a Newton is $\frac{Kgm}{s^2}$, and a Volt is $\frac{Kgm^2}{s^3A}$. To our surprise, we could find no existing Coq library for keeping track of units. Therefore, we created a Units library and a dependently typed expression language implementing Units. With these libraries, we can create a *typed expression* where the simplification of the subterms are guaranteed to evaluate to the stated units of the expression itself. If the units do not match, the statement cannot be constructed.

We know that the end result of our flow rate calculation has units or type $\frac{m^3}{s}$. Thus, any calculation of flow rate must result in that type. The following Coq pseudo-code calculates flow rate using the previous equation with units:

```
var flowrate :: m^3/s := (metersPerRevolution :: m/Void)
                         * (motorSpeed :: Void/s)
                         * (3.14 * (tubeDiameter :: m / 2)^2)
```

During type checking Coq examines the types of various quantities with associated units and determines compatibility. The type of the tube cross section area is m^2 and is calculated by squaring the `tubeDiameter` variable of type m. The Meters Per Revolution (MPR) type is $\frac{m}{Void}$, meters divided by a unit-less number. When multiplying the MPR by motor speed of type $\frac{Void}{s}$ the $Void$ values cancel giving $\frac{m}{s}$. Finally when multiplying the result by tube cross section results in $\frac{m^3}{s}$, the unit associated with flow rate. One cannot make a correctness assertion of the tube diameter based on this result, but it is evidence that the formula is correct.

In addition to properties which are not directly sensible, but may be calculated using other properties measurements, some properties may not be calculated using properties, or may not be directly measurable from the operational environment. For example, the distance traveled by the plunger per motor revolution is not easily measurable in our SUT because the gear train is sealed preventing counting teeth or relying on them all being the same. The value is also not likely to change without severe modification and abnormal use of the system. However, the value may be derivable if we are able to determine flow rate from more than one method. The differing values are detected, and we can deduce what environmental factors may have changed to explain the discrepancy. Therefore it may be possible to adjust predefined assumption values as needed. The assumed or given value for distance traveled is identified in the SUT AADL model.

To reason about the measurement process we must have a model of the pump's operational `Environment`. To model this environment in Coq we create a class containing measurable quantities. The instance of this class must have every possible measurement enumerated and defined as either an assumption or a measurable value. Assumptions and their assumed values are provided in the AADL model. Measurable values must define how the value is measured. Additionally, a proof must be provided to confirm every measurement is present in exactly one of these two categories. When the measurement code is synthesized from the Coq model, the environment model falls away and is replaced by the actual environment.

7 Scenario Walkthrough

CPSs developed for first world countries are retired to developing countries after their service life expires in the first world countries. In these situations resources are not always available to run these systems in the environment they are designed for. We will validate two scenarios which came from real world observations of PCA pumps being used in developing countries. Then we will walk through one of the scenarios, showing the output of each of the TEEE components, and demonstrate TEEE is able to determine possible root causes and suggestion an adaption. As this is a unique system a full system evaluation was not able to be run, however, we show through the scenario walkthrough the validity of the system. First we will look at the viscosity of the material being pumped. Untrained or overworked users may put the wrong medication into the pump. While there is a bar code reader on the PCA pump, it is easily bypassed. Additionally, temperature has an affect on the viscosity of liquids. Egg whites are similar in viscosity to blood plasma, which is commonly used to treat patients with shock. If, for example, the PCA pump is used in an area which is very hot and without air conditioning the medication could be more viscous. In the walk through we will show that TEEE is able to determine the root cause of this error is the viscosity of the medication in the pump. A second common issue found is how a brown out may affect the SUT. Brown outs can cause the motor to run slower and subsequently the amount of medication expelled is less. To continue regular functionality, many medical devices contain a battery. However, very few working batteries last or even arrive in the developing world, and black/brown outs can have a significant effect on the device that the programmers thought would never occur[1]. The motor, in this particular PCA pump, does not have a sensor to determine the motor rate nor does it have a sensor to determine the flow of the material being pumped. If a brown out occurs there could be no way for the CPS software to determine the cause of the problem.

We ran experiments to confirm the validity of these scenarios. Water and egg whites were run through the PCA pump for 5 min and varied the speed of the motor (100 Hz, 50 Hz, and 25 Hz). We ran 5 experiments for each variant. The experiments showed a significant difference, using a paired t Test with $p < .005$, between uL expelled per tick of the motor between 100 Hz and 25 Hz as well as 50 Hz and 25 Hz when using egg whites. Water showed a significant difference between 100 Hz and 50 Hz as well as 100 Hz and 25 Hz. The t Test resulted in a value of $p = 0.007$ when comparing 50 Hz and 25 Hz using water. The results of this experiment can be seen in Fig. 3. The test results also indicated a significant difference in uL expelled per tick of water versus egg whites at 100 Hz and 25 Hz ($p < .005$). These experiments confirm the validity of the brownout scenario by showing the rate of the motor affects the amount of material dispensed. They also confirm the validity of the viscosity scenario showing materials at different viscosities affect the amount of material dispensed.

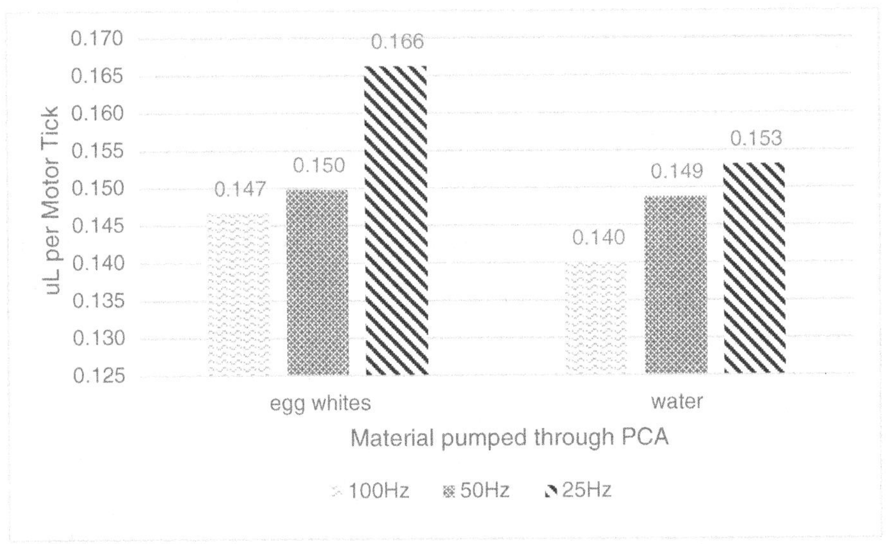

Fig. 3. Comparison of the uL of material (egg whites or water) expelled from the PCA pump when the motor was running at 100 Hz, 50 Hz, and 25 Hz.

[1] In one of the authors person experience, we once came across some donated defibrillators none of which had batteries. While the defibrillators are designed to still function without a battery (slightly slower charge build up), they were clearly never intended to be used this way as one of steps in the daily self test *required* the presence of a battery despite the battery itself not being present in the test. Luckily, we were able to find an alternate method of ensuring proper functionality.

Confirmation of Adaptation Within TEEE. The data from the PCA pump experiments shows that there is a difference in amount of material expelled when using materials of difference viscosities. Viscosity of the medication in the PCA pump, however, is a change within the environment that cannot be known via it's sensors. To confirm that TEEE is able to determine the root cause of this scenario (material is of a different viscosity than is expected) and adapt to such changes we will dive into the output of each component. The first step is to model the PCA pump in AADL.

Listing 1.2. A snippet showing requirements in the viscosity scenario.

```
<Component type="device" implementation="tube">
 <Variable name="FlowRate" units="ulps" varType="real">
    <allowed> <real min="0.141" max="0.147"/> </allowed>
 </Variable>
<\Component>

<Component type="device" implementation="medication">
 <Variable name="DynamicViscosity" units="cP" varType="real">
   <allowed> <real min="1" max="1.5"/> </allowed>
 </Variable>
<\Component>
```

A requirement is put on the tube component of the model that the flow rate of the medication must be between 0.141 and 0.147 and viscosity of the medication must be between 1 and 1.5. (Listing 1.2). The SSA algorithm created 20 test cases from the requirements within the model which enumerated 3529 test patterns (the test scenarios of the test case and one value from each of the test vectors). After the SSA pair-wise combination step is run the test case suite size is reduced to 10 cases and 2674 test patterns, yielding a test pattern savings of 24% (results shown in the SSA GUI in Fig. 2. The test cases in Table 1 corresponds to the requirements.

Table 1. Test cases created for requirements on tube flow rate and medication viscosity

Component	Test scenario	Test vector	Actual value
Tube	$0.141 < FlowRate < 0.147$	0.139, 0.140, 0.141, 0.142, 0.143, 0.144, 0.145, 0.146, 0.147, 0.148, 0.149, 0.166	0.166
Medication	$1.0 < Viscosity < 1.5$	0.8, 0.9, 0.94, 1.0, 1.1, 1.2, 1.3, 1.4, 1.5, 1.6, 1.7	0.94

A randomized user was simulated testing the PCA pump, i.e., running through the test cases and marking them passed or failed. Each test pattern had a 50% chance to mark its parent test case as failed, except the test case for the Tube component, shown in Table 1, which was marked failed each time. The test case suite was then prioritized on the tube component. The resulting prioritization along with failure detection number and risk exposure score is found in Table 2.

Table 2. The prioritization of test cases for the tube component based on randomized user data.

Case Id	Component A	Component B	FDN	Risk exposure
C5	Tube	Medication	2070	.60
C2	Tube	Power system	144	.35
C8	Interface logic system	Tube	44	.17
C1	Motor	Power system	114	.09
C7	Pump	Power system	120	.08
C9	Environment	Power system	110	.06
C4	Pump	Pump	12	.04
C0	Pump	Interface logic system	46	.02
C3	Motor sensor	Motor controller	18	.01
C6	Motor controller	Motor sensor	30	.01

The information on the test case failures was sent to the Dynamic Measurement component to provide more information concerning the cause of the error. The Dynamic Measurement component models the calculation of mass flow rate as described previously. Working from measured values back to flow rate provides an alternative perspective on the failure. The mass flow rate equation is defined using Coq and verified using units analysis and using an execution semantics for the protocol description. Using information from testing and measurement, the user is able to determine the failure is likely that the medication is the incorrect viscosity rather than the alternative of improper tube diameter. With the root cause of the failure found a recommendation is presented to the user to change the viscosity of the medication based on evidence from the SSA and Dynamic Measurement system. A new test suite is set up and tested to confirm the issue was solved.

8 Conclusion

In this paper we presented the Toolkit for Evolving Ecosystem (TEEE) system, to address challenges in CPSs due to changing environment or use over time. We presented a real world example of environmental changes affecting the use of a PCA pump. The scenario was verified valid by a series of experiments using a Hospira PCA pump. We showed the TEEE prototype is able to determine the root cause of the issue in the scenario using the Stimulus Synthesis and

Dynamic Measurements algorithms. Further work will focus on automating the components of TEEE. The SSA creates a bottleneck by requiring a human in the loop to manually mark test cases as passed/failed. In the future we plan to create tools using OSATE-based analysis to determine if a test case will pass/fail. Future work on the Dynamic Measurement algorithm will focus on deducing more complex or obscured environmental changes, such as vial diameter or faulty sensors. To do this we will create a number of verified measuring programs for each property within the AADL model. This will allow the algorithm to dynamically answer requests like "measure flow rate every possible way and compare the results". We are also aiming to create a Dynamic Measurement algorithm which is able to determine the property measurement without using assumptions in the current environment.

Acknowledgments. This material is based upon work supported by the United States Air Force and DARPA under Contract No. FA8750-16-C-0273. Any opinions, findings and conclusions or recommendations expressed in this material are those of the author(s) and do not necessarily reflect the views of the United States Air Force or DARPA.

References

1. Adjepon-Yamoah, D.E.: *cloud-ATAM*: method for analysing resilient attributes of cloud-based architectures. In: Crnkovic, I., Troubitsyna, E. (eds.) SERENE 2016. LNCS, vol. 9823, pp. 105–114. Springer, Cham (2016). doi:10.1007/978-3-319-45892-2_8
2. Arafeen, M.J., Do, H.: Test case prioritization using requirements-based clustering. In: 2013 IEEE Sixth International Conference on Software Testing, Verification and Validation (ICST), pp. 312–321. IEEE (2013)
3. Chen, Y., Probert, R.L., Sims, D.P.: Specification-based regression test selection with risk analysis. In: Proceedings of the 2002 Conference of the Centre for Advanced Studies on Collaborative Research, p. 1. IBM Press (2002)
4. Chlipala, A.: Certified Programming with Dependent Types: A Pragmatic Introduction to the Coq Proof Assistant. MIT Press, Cambridge (2013)
5. Cohen, D.M., Dalal, S.R., Fredman, M.L., Patton, G.C.: The AETG system: an approach to testing based on combinatorial design. IEEE Trans. Softw. Eng. **23**(7), 437–444 (1997)
6. Dreossi, T., Donzé, A., Seshia, S.A.: Compositional falsification of cyber-physical systems with machine learning components. In: Barrett, C., Davies, M., Kahsai, T. (eds.) NFM 2017. LNCS, vol. 10227, pp. 357–372. Springer, Cham (2017). doi:10.1007/978-3-319-57288-8_26
7. Feiler, P., Lewis, B., Vestal, S.: The SAE avionics architecture description language (AADL) standard: a basis for model-based architecture-driven embedded systems. In: Real-Time Applications Symposium Workshop on Model-Driven Embedded Systems (2003)
8. Feiler, P.H., Gluch, D.P., Hudak, J.J.: The architecture analysis & design language (AADL): an introduction. Technical report, DTIC Document (2006)
9. Grindal, M., Lindström, B., Offutt, J., Andler, S.F.: An evaluation of combination strategies for test case selection. Empir. Softw. Eng. **11**(4), 583–611 (2006)

10. Hughes, J., Sparks, C., Stoughton, A., Parikh, R., Reuther, A., Jagannathan, S.: Building resource adaptive software systems (brass): objectives and system evaluation. ACM SIGSOFT Softw. Eng. Notes **41**(1), 1–2 (2016)
11. Software Engineering Institute. Open source AADL tool environment (osate). http://la.sei.cmu.edu/aadlinfosite/OpenSourceAADLToolEnvironment.html
12. Kephart, J.O., Chess, D.M.: The vision of autonomic computing. Computer **36**(1), 41–50 (2003)
13. Larson, B., Hatcliff, J., Fowler, K., Delange, J.: Illustrating the AADL error modeling annex (v. 2) using a simple safety-critical medical device. ACM SIGAda Ada Lett. **33**(3), 65–84 (2013)
14. Le Goues, C., Nguyen, T., Forrest, S., Weimer, W.: Genprog: a generic method for automatic software repair. IEEE Trans. Softw. Eng. **38**(1), 54–72 (2012)
15. Lott, C., Jain, A., Dalal, S.: Modeling requirements for combinatorial software testing. ACM SIGSOFT Softw. Eng. Notes **30**, 1–7 (2005). ACM
16. Mogyorodi, G.: What is requirements-based testing? Technical report, Crosstalk (2003)
17. Myers, G.J., Sandler, C., Badgett, T.: The Art of Software Testing. Wiley, New York (2011)
18. Neches, R.: Engineered resilient systems (ers) s&t priority description and roadmap (2011)
19. Perkins, J.H., Kim, S., Larsen, S., Amarasinghe, S., Bachrach, J., Carbin, M., Pacheco, C., Sherwood, F., Sidiroglou, S., Sullivan, G., et al.: Automatically patching errors in deployed software. In: Proceedings of the ACM SIGOPS 22nd Symposium on Operating Systems Principles, pp. 87–102. ACM (2009)
20. Qi, Y., Mao, X., Lei, Y.: Efficient automated program repair through fault-recorded testing prioritization. In: 2013 29th IEEE International Conference on Software Maintenance (ICSM), pp. 180–189. IEEE (2013)
21. Ranganathan, K., Rangarajan, M., Alexander, P., Regan, T.: Automated test vector generation from rosetta requirements. In: VHDL International Users Forum Fall Workshop, Proceedings, pp. 51–58. IEEE (2000)
22. Rodríguez, R.J., Merseguer, J., Bernardi, S.: Modelling and analysing resilience as a security issue within UML. In: Proceedings of the 2nd International Workshop on Software Engineering for Resilient Systems, pp. 42–51. ACM (2010)
23. Rugina, A.-E., Kanoun, K., Kaâniche, M.: A system dependability modeling framework using AADL and GSPNs. In: Lemos, R., Gacek, C., Romanovsky, A. (eds.) WADS 2006. LNCS, vol. 4615, pp. 14–38. Springer, Heidelberg (2007). doi:10.1007/978-3-540-74035-3_2
24. Stoicescu, M., Fabre, J.-C., Roy, M.: Architecting resilient computing systems: overall approach and open issues. In: Troubitsyna, E.A. (ed.) SERENE 2011. LNCS, vol. 6968, pp. 48–62. Springer, Heidelberg (2011). doi:10.1007/978-3-642-24124-6_5

Fault Tolerance, Resilience and Robustness

Improving Robustness of AUTOSAR Software Components with Design by Contract: A Study Within Volvo AB

Yulai Zhou[1], Patrizio Pelliccione[1(✉)], Johan Haraldsson[2], and Mafjiul Islam[2]

[1] Chalmers University of Technology, University of Gothenburg, Gothenburg, Sweden
patrizio.pelliccione@gu.se
[2] Volvo AB, Gothenburg, Sweden
{johan.haraldsson,mafijul.islam}@volvo.com

Abstract. The increasing volume of software in vehicles makes robustness a significant quality attribute. In this paper, we investigate the use of Design by Contract to improve the robustness of existing AUTOSAR software components. The main idea of DbC is to view the relationship between two components as a formal contract that expresses component's rights and obligations.

The proposed solution is validated by testing both the original and modified components and by comparing the results. The results prove that Design by Contract greatly increases the robustness of AUTOSAR software components: none of the tests for the modified software components failed. We also identified some weaknesses of the proposed approach, such as (i) potential additional errors brought by the newly-built components, and (ii) difficulty in modifying components that are automatically generated through some model-to-code generation tools.

1 Introduction

Software volume in vehicles has been keeping increasing for years; it is expected to increase by 50% by 2020 [1]. 80% to 90% of the innovation within the automotive industry is based on electronics, and a big part of electronics is software [2,3]. The increasing complexity of software causes an increasing request for robustness. According to some reports, software errors led to almost 60–70% of all the recalls of vehicles in Europe and North America [1]. These errors might endanger people's life, affect manufacturers' reputation and lead to economic losses.

To increase the quality and the efficiency of the embedded system of the vehicle, many large manufacturers and suppliers in the automotive industry in Europe have been joined up to establish a shared standard for vehicle system architecture since 2003. The output for this effort is AUTOSAR (Automotive Open System Architecture - https://www.autosar.org/). Its goal is to get a defacto open industry standard for automotive E/E architectures [4], by which automotive systems can get better modularity, scalability, transferability and re-usability. Since then, AUTOSAR has been a popular open standard in the

A. Romanovsky and E.A. Troubitsyna (Eds.): SERENE 2017, LNCS 10479, pp. 151–168, 2017.
DOI: 10.1007/978-3-319-65948-0_10

automotive industry. However, AUTOSAR just defines the architecture of the vehicle software system, while the implementation of the functionality is done by the manufacturers and suppliers themselves. Moreover, it is in general quite difficult to ensure that the quality expectations are met. This includes the robustness of the developed AUTOSAR software components.

In this paper we describe an industrial investigation made within Volvo AB in Gothenburg about using Design by Contract (DbC) as a means for improving the robustness of AUTOSAR software components. In DbC, the relationship between a class and its clients is viewed as a formal agreement in which each party's right and obligations are described [5]. In practice, it sets precise conditions to both the input and output of the components. Since the output of one component is often the input of another component, this enables to check that the communication among components is correct. DbC helps both checking the correctness of input and output of one software component, and the preservation of invariants inside the software component.

The proposed approach is implemented and applied to the components of two AUTOSAR applications. The output of our approach is a set of components enhanced with contracts. These components are then tested by black-box testing with ARUnit testing tool. By comparing the test results of the original and modified components, we can conclude saying that DbC greatly increases the robustness of AUTOSAR software components. In the paper we also identify and discuss limitations and weaknesses of the proposed approach.

The paper is structured as follows: Sect. 2 provides background information. Related works are discussed in Sect. 3. Section 4 presents the approach and Sect. 5 describes its implementation. The validation of the approach is discussed in Sect. 6. The paper concludes with final remarks and future research directions in Sect. 7.

2 AUTOSAR and ARUnit

AUTOSAR (AUTomotive Open System ARchitecture) [4] is a collaborative project initiated by several large manufactures and suppliers in automotive industry to establish a shared standard for automotive E/E architectures. It is driven by the intention of getting better flexibility, scalability, reliability, and quality when the complexity of E/E system is greatly increasing. This kind of increased complexity is mainly concerned with the growth of the functional scope. Besides the goal of making the developers concentrate on the realization of the functionality rather than the design of the architectures, the standard of AUTOSAR also makes components developed by different manufacturers or software companies be able to be integrated with well-defined interfaces.

AUTOSAR is a standard architecture to make vehicle software applications independent of the hardware. AUTOSAR also makes components developed by different manufacturers or software companies able to be integrated through well-defined interfaces. Every AUTOSAR application is distributed to one or more Electronic Control Units (ECUs). An AUTOSAR software component is defined as the encapsulation of part of the functionality of the AUTOSAR application [4]. An AUTOSAR application is composed of one or several software components (SW-Cs). How to describe the interfaces of these AUTOSAR SW-Cs is defined and standardized within AUTOSAR. Each component can only be distributed to one AUTOSAR ECU. This is the reason why a AUTOSAR SW-C is called as "Atomic Software Component" [4]. In order to be able to integrate several AUTOSAR SW-Cs correctly, one formal and complete description for one SW-C is needed when it is implemented.

Communication between AUTOSAR software components are conducted by well-defined ports. A port is defined by an AUTOSAR interface. It can either be a *Provided Port*, which provides data, or a *Required Port*, which receives data. There are two main types of communication patterns supported by AUTOSAR. One is *Client-Server* and another one is *Sender-Receiver*. An AUTOSAR software component (SW-C) can be both a client and a server. The *Sender-Receiver* pattern realizes asynchronous communication. A sender sends information to one or several receivers without receiving back an answer. The time and way to send back information are decided by the receivers.

Communication between different ECUs is performed via a shared virtual bus, which consists of hardware interfaces provided by the basic software in AUTOSAR infrastructure. The Runtime Environment (RTE) is an implementation of the Virtual Functional Bus (VFB). It provides a uniform environment for communication between components [4]; when moving a component to another ECU, developers do not need to change any code of the component. This work focuses on the application layer.

Robustness of software refers to the capability of the system or component to (i) handle data correctly even when the input volume is very large, and (ii) handle invalid inputs to ensure the successful running of the system or component. In the vehicle embedded system most applications run repeatedly over a time period, i.e., 5 ms, 10 ms or 20 ms according to the requirements of the application.

In order to test AUTOSAR software components we make use of ARUnit[1], which is a lightweight unit testing environment based on Eclipse. After importing the components that need to be tested, it can compile the components and generate the run-time environment for each single AUTOSAR software component. Test cases can be defined directly within the tool and moreover it provides an API to stimulate and query the state of the RTE from the outside. It is a quite convenient tool for operating unit testing effectively and efficiently.

3 Related Works

Design by Contract, also known as programming by contract, is an approach for designing software, by which software can get better robustness. The key concept is "viewing the relationship between a class and its clients as a formal agreement, expressing each party's right and obligations" [5]. The agreements are

[1] https://www.artop.org/arunit.

similar to the contracts in business. These contracts set conditions for input and output of software components. The conditions have three types: pre-condition, post-condition and invariant. When a client component calls an operation on a server component, the client component needs to meet the pre-condition which is specific for that operation. For the return of that operation, the requirements of the post-condition need to be meet, which are an obligation for the server component. Invariant is a certain property that holds for both client and server components. In this way, different components of a software system can collaborate with each other with high robustness.

Design by Contract was popularized by Bertrand Meyer [6] and included in his Eiffel programming language [7]. The work in [7] shows that building software components on the basis of carefully designed contracts might reduce bugs and then improve software reliability. In the last two decades DbC started to be popular in several programming languages, either through native support or with third-party solutions. The work in [8] exploits DbC to concurrent programs. Java Modeling Language (JML) is extended with constructs to specify contracts and to verify assertions of concurrent Java programs. The same authors apply then the approach to a case study in the telecommunications domain to assess the effectiveness of contracts as test oracles in detecting and diagnosing functional faults in concurrent software [9]. The work shows that DbC can be a valuable tool to improve the economics of software engineering.

The work in [10] shows how to specify the functionality of software components with the theory and methods of the DbC approach. The conclusion of the author is that the reliability and reusability of components can be enhanced by encapsulating operations within the components and by managing communications through the interfaces. The work in [11] introduces an approach to check DbC assertions without referring to the program states; this makes the assertions more readable and maintainable.

The work in [12] introduced an approach for integrating DbC with feature-oriented programming. In the C programming language, the application of DbC is not obvious. The subjects of the conditions are the functions: the caller function must meet all the preconditions of the callee function, and the callee function must meet its own post-conditions. The failure of either parts of the contract is a bug in the software [5]. Invariants in C are the conditions that must be hold for a structure or type[2].

The work in [13] presents a methodology for contract-based system design. The authors identify also AUTOSAR software components as an interesting direction to be investigated. However, to the best of our knowledge, the use of DbC for AUTOSAR software components still need to be investigated and experimented deeply. Our paper contributes exactly in this direction.

As Design by Contract is used for objected-oriented languages in most situations and AUTOSAR SW-Cs are developed by C without any existing third-party tools that support Design by Contract, we need to explore a new way for

[2] www.onlamp.com/pub/a/onlamp/2004/10/28/design_by_contract_in_c.html.

applying Design by Contract in AUTOSAR SW-Cs and evaluate the effect of improvement of robustness.

4 DbC for AUTOSAR SW-Cs

This work has been organized in three iterations, each of them including the following phases: (i) problem identification, (ii) discussion and suggestion, (iii) design and development, (iv) evaluation, and (v) conclusion and report. The first two attempts were abandoned for their weaknesses as it is described in the following. Finally, in the third iteration we identified the method that we implemented and used.

4.1 First Iteration and Attempt

This first attempt focuses on the direct use of `assert()` to add input and output checks into the code. For example, there are two types of input and one type of output for one component. And the requirements for them are `input_1 > 0`, `input_2 < 0 and output > 0`. Then we need to add `assert(input_1 > 0 & input_2 <0)` at the beginning of the code and `assert(output > 0)` at the end of the code. And also, if there are C-style structures or types in any places of the code, assertions are needed at these places as well. These assertions are used as the pre-conditions, post-conditions, and invariants for this component.
Problems and Limitations: A C-style assertion is not suitable for error handling especially in embedded software. In most situations, there are no screens available to show the information of the errors. What such software needs is an approach to detect and handle the errors. Moreover, there are many weaknesses of using assertions:

- Assertions lack robustness, there is a high intermix between application code and contracts, and there is a high code redundancy;
- The use of `assert()` requires to add extra code into the original component and this may also bring errors that might show up when running the preconditions, post-conditions and invariants checks;
- Assert statements tend to intermix with application code and this is not good for readability, understandability, and reusability of the code;
- Duplicate code is needed when invariants for a common structure or type exist in many different places in the code.

Summarizing, `assert()` in C programming language does not make DbC reach desired effects to improve software components' robustness in AUTOSAR.

4.2 Second Iteration and Attempt

As second attempt, we tried to set independent components for every type of input, output and structures in the original AUTOSAR software components. More precisely, there should be 3 components around the original component for

every type of input, output and structures in the original component. In each of these components, there is a function which is used to check the value. These functions are invoked when needed by the original component.
Problems and Limitations: This solution suffers of some limitations:

- Typically, there is a huge number of types of input, output, and structures for one AUTOSAR software component. This will cause the creation of a large number of components and it will be hard to manage so many components;
- In most conditions the requirements for one type of input, output or structure are not complex. It is not worth the effort of building so many new components just for one original component;
- Other problems, such as redundancy of invoking these functions in the code of the original component and bad readability of the code, also exist.

Summarizing, this second solution is not exactly the best solution to improve software components' robustness in AUTOSAR.

4.3 Third Iteration and Successful Attempt

In this final attempt, we tried to build a pre-condition component, a post-condition component and an invariant component for one original component. The pre-condition component contains a function to check all types of input. The post-condition component contains a function to check all the types of output. Also, the invariant component has functions to check all the structures or types in the original AUTOSAR software components. This method effectively limits the number of newly-built components and functions. It is also the method that we finally implemented and experimented.

As mentioned in Sect. 2, the DbC approach considers the two sides of the contract as the caller and the callee (or the client and the server). For this reason, the traditional client-server pattern in the software architecture design is a very good reference pattern.

We got inspiration also from the Proxy pattern for what concerns the handling of the invoked service. When a client component invokes a service from a server component, the proxy component will make pre-processing for the input and post-processing for the output. The idea is to exploit the pattern for input and output checking and to combine it with the widely approach.

When combining the DbC approach with the two reference patterns, the most significant point is where to define the pre-conditions, post-conditions, and invariants. Figure 1 shows the design for the new components enhanced with DbC and how the components work together. The main processing component is almost unchanged. It is responsible for calculating or handling the input data and generating the output data. The newly-built pre-condition, post-condition and invariant components around it are responsible for data check.

In the *Pre-condition component*, there is a function that works for checking all the input data. If the input is invalid or erroneous, it can be throw away or, if possible, it can be changed in a default and valid value. How to deal

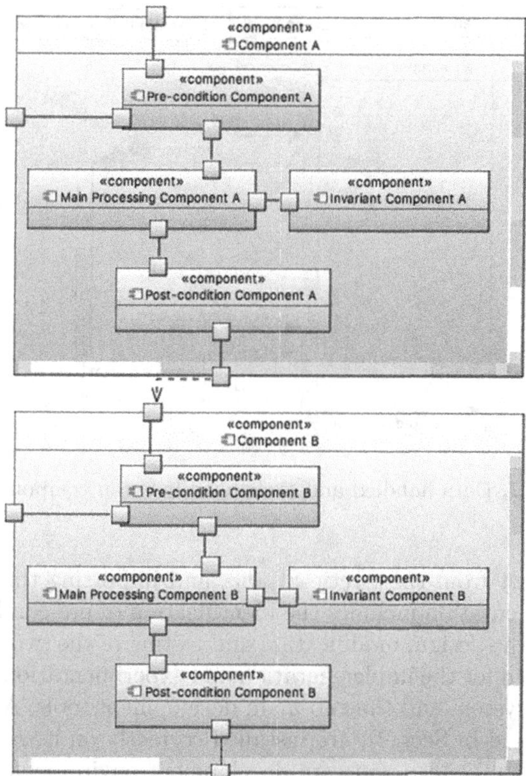

Fig. 1. Design for AUTOSAR SW-Cs with DoC

with it depends on the specific requirements. The *Pre-condition component* will then give the checked input data to the main processing component for further calculation. In the *Invariant component* one or more functions are defined. Each function is used for checking one structure or type in the code of the main processing component. When there is a structure or type in the code, it will invoke the corresponding function to check this structure before using it. In the *Post-condition component* there is a function that works for checking all the output data. It will make sure that the output is in the reasonable range.

Considering how Proxy pattern handles input and output data, the newly-built pre-condition, post-condition and invariant components can be viewed as proxy components. Figure 2 shows how the input data are handled and exchanged between the components.

5 Implementation

This section introduces the process of setting up the development environment including exporting the Brake-Pedal-Input-Handler component and Brake-Light-

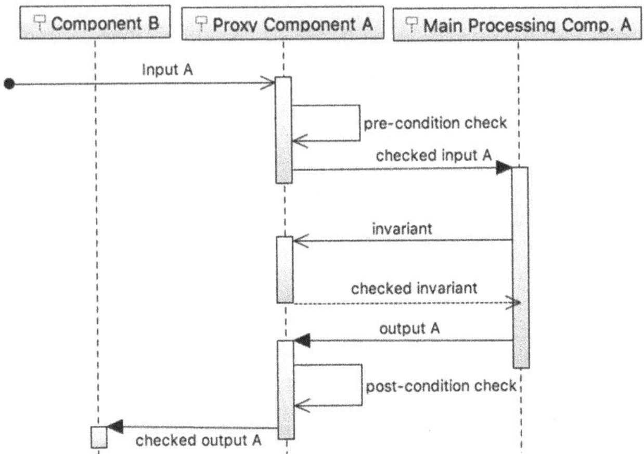

Fig. 2. Data handled and exchanged between components

Control component from the Arctic Studio, and importing them into ARUnit. Then, the implementation includes the identification of pre-conditions and post-conditions[3], and the design, modification and testing of the two software components. The PC used for the implementation and experimentation uses Windows 7 as the operating system and the two main development tools, Arctic Studio and ARUnit (introduced in Sect. 2), are installed correctly on it. Arctic Studio provides a complete embedded software development environment for automotive embedded software based on AUTOSAR[4].

Arctic Studio is the original development tool for the existing AUTOSAR SW-Cs. It makes the architecture easy to understand and the components easy to recognize and read. Driven by the industrial co-authors, and by reading through the code of the components and the available documentation, we selected the Brake-Pedal-Input-Handler Component and the Brake-Light-Control Component from the applications in this package as the components to be considered for the experiment. These two components are described in Sect. 5.1.

Arctic Studio and ARUnit are built for different purposes. ARUnit is more efficient for running and testing one single component or certain components. In order to modify and test the two selected components independently from the relevant components in the applications, the ECU, and the real running environment, we exported them from the whole package in Arctic Studio and imported them into ARUnit. The files that we imported into ARUint are the

[3] In the considered components there was no need for invariant checks. As the functioning of the invariant component is similar to the functioning of the functions in the pre-condition and post-condition components, this will not affect the evaluation of our solution. In the AUTOSAR software components of other projects or applications, there are structures or types. Therefore, invariant component can be used in those software components though it is not used here.

[4] http://www.arccore.com/products/arctic-studio.

source files of the components and the software component description files of them. ARUnit is then used to generate the run-time environment for them. Finally, code files used for testing are built in ARUnit as well.

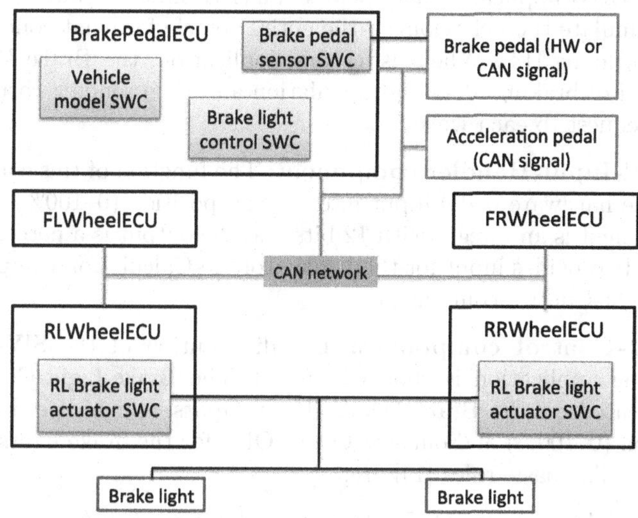

Fig. 3. Brake lighting SW-Cs distribution on ECUs [14]

5.1 Selected AUTOSAR Software Components

An AUTOSAR software component is defined as the encapsulation of part of the functionality of the AUTOSAR application [4]. An AUTOSAR application is composed of one or several SW-Cs. How to describe the interfaces of these AUTOSAR SW-Cs is defined and standardized within AUTOSAR. Each component can only be distributed to one AUTOSAR ECU. This is the reason why the AUTOSAR SW-C is called as "Atomic Software Component" [4]. AUTOSAR does not prescribe the size of the SW-Cs and how the SW-Cs are implemented. But in order to be able to integrate several AUTOSAR SW-Cs correctly, one formal and complete description for one SW-C is needed when it is implemented. The description introduces how to configure the infrastructure for the component when building the system. In this section we describe the AUTOSAR software components we selected for the evaluation. These two components have been selected with the support of experts within Volvo AB and they are representative of the set of the existing AUTOSAR software components for the purpose of studying robustness. These components are used in many research projects within Volvo AB. To better understand the functionality of these components we first introduce the software application that includes them, i.e. the Brake-By-Wire application (BWB).

The Brake-By-Wire is an application that is used in several research projects within Volvo AB. It implements a brake-by-wire function distributed over five ECUs. It is not the real system that is used in the real trucks. It is proposed to give an example of distributed safety-critical system for validating research projects. The BBW application also includes an environment model of the vehicle in order to simulate the behaviour of the entire vehicle for what concerns acceleration and braking [14]. When using this application, the Brake Pedal ECU gets the signal of braking, does the calculation and then sends a corresponding brake force request to each wheel.

Brake-Pedal-Input-Handler component: The function of this component is to convert the hardware pedal input into a pedal position (0–100%). The input of this component is an integer with 12 bits and the output is a percentage from 0% to 100%. It provides input for the Brake-Torque-Calculation component and the Brake-Light-Control component.

Brake-Light-Control component: The distribution of the SW-Cs in the Brake-Lighting application is shown in Fig. 3. The Brake-Light-Control component is located on the BrakePedalECU. It inputs vehicle speed and brake pedal position (0–100%) and outputs ON or OFF for the brake lights according to some rules. The basic rules [14] are:

1. The brake light is always OFF when the pedal input is 0%;
2. The brake light is always fixed ON whenever the pedal input >0% and the vehicle speed is <10 km/h;
3. From 10 km/h and above the brake light will blink ON/OFF if emergency braking is active otherwise it is fixed ON.

5.2 Process of Modifying the Brake-Pedal-Input-Handler Component

In this section, we describe the analysis of the original component, the process of design, the modification and testing of the Brake-Pedal-Input-Handler component according to the Design by Contract approach.

Issues of the Current Component: Several issues were raised when reviewing the original component that may threaten the realization of the expected functionality and the robustness of the whole component. One issue is that there are no complete input checks for the component. The component does not handle the input in all the possible ranges of values that are mentioned in the documentation. In other words, the input check is too simple to deal with all the possible conditions.

Another issue is that there is no output check to ensure that the data gotten from the component is completely correct for the next component that uses the data. Although the calculation in this component is not complex, the errors cannot be completely avoided at runtime. That is why output check is necessary.

Finally, other issues concern the internal logic and the readability of the component code. In the original component, the simple and incomplete input checks are mixed with the code that is responsible for the calculation. This makes the code hard to read and understand for developers. This may also threaten the robustness when modifying the code.

Identification of Pre-conditions and Post-conditions: According to the documentation and the package of all the program code, the Brake-Pedal-Input-Handler component is used to convert the analogue input from the pedal into a pedal position which is from 0% to 100%. The pedal provides an analogue input with the range from 10% to 90% of supply voltage (5 V direct current), which means the voltage is about from 0.5 V to 4.5 V. If the analogue input is 0–0.5 V, it means that it is an open circuit or short to ground. If the analogue input is 4.5–5 V, it means that the battery level is too low. Both of them are errors. For the reason that the AD (Analog-to-Digital) converter of the micro-controller has not been calibrated, this inaccuracy has to be considered when building the software. The output from the AD converter is the input for the software component we considered. The input is a 12 bit value, which uses 0 to represent 0 V and uses 4095 to represent 5 V. Of course, if considering that the input values of the test cases for this component can come also from the ARUnit, the input can possibly be less than 0 or greater than 4095. Thus, input values in these ranges are seen as invalid.

All the possible inputs of the Brake-Pedal-Input-Handler component are:

- value < 0;
- 500 <= value <= 3500;
- 0 <= value <= 400;
- 3501 <= value <= 3700;
- 401 <= value <= 499;
- 3701 <= value <= 4095;
- value > 4095.

What we need to do next is to set contracts for the component. In the considered components there was no need for invariant checks. As the functioning of the invariant component is similar to the functioning of the functions in the pre-condition and post-condition components, this will not affect the evaluation of our solution. In the AUTOSAR software components of other projects or applications, there are structures or types. Therefore invariant component can be used in those software components though it is not used here.

When setting pre-condition part of the contracts, the information from requirements specification should be carefully considered to cover all the possible inputs. In this specific example the precondition considers as a valid input only an input value in the range 401–3700. When the input value is less than 0 or greater than 4095, it is an invalid input. Input value in this range just appears in the testing environment in ARUnit[5]. When the input value is in the range of 0–400 and 3701–4095, it is erroneous. Input values in this range represents 0–0.5 V or 4.5–5 V. They can be generated by the errors of hardware in the vehicles.

[5] These values should not really come in real environments.

For the post-condition, it should meet two requirements. Firstly, the output of the software component should be an integer from 0 to 100 to represent values from 0% to 100%. Then, the correctness check for the calculation within the component is needed. There are not structures or types used in this component. Hence, we do not need to set invariant checks for them.

Design and Modification: In the pre-condition component, there is a function that gets the pedal signal as input and verifies it for the main processing component. Only the valid and faultless data, which are greater than 401 and less than 3700, can enter into the main processing component. The invalid and erroneous data are detected and handled. In order to see the testing results intuitively, in our design it directly shows in the console of ARUnit that it is invalid or erroneous. For example, if the input is −100, the console shows it is an invalid input. But when running in the real ECU, other approaches should be used to handle an invalid or erroneous input because of lack of a screen. The possible approaches may be the correction of the data or getting the next input data after some time. The main processing component works for calculation of the data and giving the results to the post-condition component for checks. The code for data processing in the main processing component is the same of the original component. In the post-condition component, a function used for checking the calculation results of the main processing component is defined. It checks if the calculation is correct and the output is in the range of 0%–100%.

Test: In order to check whether the modified component improves the robustness of the component, we test both the original and the modified components in ARUnit. When running the testing program, the input data are sent into the component and the output data are shown on the console in ARUnit through the testing program. Table 1 shows some examples of input data in all possible ranges of the Brake-Pedal-Input-Handler Component. According to the documentation, the expected outputs of the software component are also included to help readers better understanding the testing.

Table 1. Examples of input and the expected output.

Range of input value	Input example	Expected output
Value < 0	−100	Invalid input
0 <= value <= 400	200	Erroneous input
401 <= value <= 499	450	0, Successful
500 <= value <= 3500	2100	53, Successful
3501 <= value <= 3700	3600	100, Successful
3701 <= value <= 4095	3900	Erroneous input
Value > 4095	6000	Invalid input

In the testing period, 70 different input data are tested for both the original component and the modified component. If the output received from the component matches the expected output, we are in the case of a successful running. Referring to the Table 1, the tests that get valid output data such as 0, 53 and 100 are considered as successful tests that can be used by other components. Moreover, also the tests that successfully detect invalid or erroneous inputs are seen as successful tests. The results of the testing are described in Sect. 6. The robustness of the tested software component can be measured in terms of number or percentage of test cases that are successful.

5.3 Process of Modifying the Brake-Light-Control Component

In this section, we describe the process of modifying the Brake-Light-Control component with the Design by Contract approach. This section emphasizes on the collaboration between the Brake-Light-Control component and the Brake-Pedal-Input-Handler component.

Analysis and Identification of Pre-conditions and Post-conditions: The existing issues for the Brake-Light-Control component are similar to the Brake-Pedal-Input-Handler component. It does not have complete input checks for the input data to cover all the possible input data. Some simple input data checks are mixed with the program code. Also, it lacks output checks. The modification for the original component is expected to solve these issues. The Brake-Pedal-Input-Handler component is used to control the brake lights by the rules described in Sect. 5.1. Its input should be the pedal position and the vehicle speed. The pedal position is an output of the Brake-Pedal-Input-Handler component. The pedal position should be in the range 0%–100%. The range of the vehicle speed depends on different situations. Here, we set the highest vehicle speed as 300 km/h, which is obviously out of the range. Another factor that affects the output of the component is the status of emergency braking. The status of emergency braking can be active or inactive. In order to concentrate on the collaboration of the two modified components, the status of emergency braking is directly sent into the Brake-Light-Control component as another input without being included in the pre-condition. Thus, the pre-condition for this component is that the pedal position should be in the range 0%–100% and the vehicle speed should be in the range 0 km/h–300 km/h. For the post-condition, it should check if the calculation in the component is correct.

Design and Modification: The design of the new Brake-Light-Control component is similar to the new Brake-Pedal-Input-Handler component. The pre-condition and post-condition are separated from the main processing component as the pre-condition component and the post-condition component.

A function in the pre-condition component of the Brake-Light-Control component gets as input data from the Brake-Pedal-Input-Handler component and other sources, and then verifies the data for the main processing component. Only the input data with pedal position from 0% to 100% and vehicle speed from

0 km/h to 300 km/h are valid. The code for data processing in the main processing component is the same of the original component. In the post-condition component, a function used for checking the calculation results of the main processing component is defined. It checks if the status of braking light is correct.

Test: In order to know if the two modified components can collaborate with each other and improve the robustness, a testing program is created for the original components and for the modified components in ARUnit. When running the testing program, the input data are sent into both the two components. Data similar to those in Table 1 are passed to the Brake-Pedal-Input-Handler component. Its output data are used as the input data for the Brake-Light-Control component with the vehicle speed and the emergency braking status. The output is the status of the brake lights. It can be ON/OFF/BLINK. Some comments are attached to the output to know which input is detected as invalid or erroneous.

Table 2 shows some examples of input data. According to the documentation, the expected outputs of the software component are also included to help readers better understanding the testing.

Table 2. Examples of input for the two selected components and the expected output

Brake Pedal Input	Vehicle speed	Emergency braking status	Expected output
2000	5	Active	ON
450	35	Inactive	OFF
3000	35	Active	BLINK
200	35	Inactive	Erroneous brake pedal input
500	400	Inactive	Erroneous vehicle speed

In the testing period, 30 different sets of input data are tested for both the original components and the modified components. If the output received from the components matches the expected output, it means that it is a successful testing. If it successfully detects the invalid or erroneous input, it is still seen as a successful testing. The results of the performed tests are described in the next section. The robustness of the tested software component can be measured in terms of number and percentage of successful test cases.

6 Evaluation

In the evaluation stage, black-box testing is performed with the ARUnit test tool. The code of the software components is also in ARUnit. The steps of robustness evaluation are: (i) Perform robustness testing in ARUnit of the original version of the software component; (ii) Input a list of valid and invalid data, and calculate the percentage of test cases that are successful - this percentage is stored in the D1 variable; (iii) In Eclipse, replace the original version of the software component with the software component which has been enhanced with Design by Contract; (iv) Input the same list of valid and invalid data of step 2, and calculate the percentage of test cases that are successful - this percentage is stored in the D2 variable; (v) Compare D1 and D2 - if D2 is greater than D1, it means that the software component that is enhanced with Design by Contract has better robustness.

The testing results for the Brake-Pedal-Input-Handler component are shown in Table 3. For the original component, it failed 15 times in the 70 test cases. The modified component failed 0 time in the 70 test cases. The success rates of them are 78.6% and 100.0% respectively. Obviously, the modified component has better robustness and can handle more input data successfully.

Table 3. Results of tests for Brake-Pedal-Input-Handler

	Successful tests	Total tests	Success rates
Original component	55	70	78.6%
Modified component	70	70	100.0%

The testing results for the Brake-Pedal-Input-Handler component are shown in Table 4. The original components failed 9 times in the 30 test cases. The modified component failed 0 time in the 30 test cases. The success rates of them are 70% and 100%, respectively. Obviously, the modified component has better robustness and can handle more input data successfully.

Table 4. Results of tests for the two modified components

	Successful tests	Total tests	Success rates
Original component	21	30	70%
Modified component	30	30	100%

Analysis of results: There are two main reasons that make the modified components get better results. The first one is that all possible input data have been considered by carefully analysing the documented specification. The invalid input data and erroneous input data have been handled in the pre-condition component and do not have the chance to get into the main processing component. The second reason is that the data from the main processing component are checked again in the post-condition component to ensure its correctness. The pre-condition and post-condition components are like two guards that check all the input and output data of the main processing component.

Table 5. Strengths and weaknesses of the Design by Contract approach in AUTOSAR

Strengths
• Better robustness of the components and applications • Increase readability and understandability of the code • Convenient to refactor manually coded software components • Low redundancy
Weaknesses
• Add more components which may also bring errors to the components • Strict data checks may slow the components and applications down • Hard to modify the components of which the code is automatically generated from some models

The prerequisite of setting such pre-condition and post-condition components that can accurately cover all the possible input and output data, is that we need to have complete requirements for the components. According to experts within the company, the two software components used in this work are representative for the entire set of the existing components for the purpose of studying robustness. It is important to highlight that, when developing AUTOSAR software components in the company, the bottom line for the requirements of the components is that the whole range of every input and output must be specified. And if they are not, someone will revise or update the requirements. It means that almost for every component the requirements specify the ranges of the input and output; this information can be used to set accurate pre-conditions and post-conditions for the components.

Components' code produced via code generators: The code of some components is generated from TargetLink, which is a modeling and development tool. Generated code is hard to read, import into ARUnit, and modify manually. Components with automatically generated code should follow a different approach. Contracts including pre-conditions and post-conditions should be embedded in code generation instead of trying to modify the code a-posteriori, as done in this paper. In the source base, nearly 50% of the AUTOSAR software components are generated from TargetLink. Thus, at least 50% of the components, i.e. those that have manually written code, can be easily enhanced with DbC through the use of our approach.

Performance of the approach: For the components we considered performance is acceptable. However, we should better investigate how deployment of DbC scales while considering various attributes/properties of components, such as memory footprint, execution time, etc. This is part of future work.

Summary of strengths and weaknesses: Table 5 shows a summary of strengths and weaknesses of using DbC in AUTOSAR software components.

7 Conclusions and Future Works

This work testifies that DbC can be used for improving the robustness of AUTOSAR software components. In order to apply the approach developers should analyse the documented specification or the stakeholders' requirements carefully to know all the possible values of the input, output and invariant.

However, even though DbC has high potential for industrial deployment, we need further investigations and evaluation results with more complex and real-life applications, e.g. by considering one complete feature such as cruise control. For example, we need to better understand the impact that deploying DbC might have on real-time requirements, memory footprint, computational load, etc. Such investigations will be part of our future work.

Acknowledgements. The work is partially supported by Software Center (http://www.software-center.se).

References

1. Fleming, B.: An overview of advances in automotive electronics [automotive electronics]. IEEE Veh. Technol. Mag. **9**(1), 4–9 (2014)
2. Knauss, E., Pelliccione, P., Heldal, R., Ågren, M., Hellman, S., Maniette, D.: Continuous integration beyond the team: a tooling perspective on challenges in the automotive industry. In: Proceedings of ESEM 2016. ACM (2016)
3. Pelliccione, P., Knauss, E., Heldal, R., Ågren, S.M., Mallozzi, P., Alminger, A., Borgentun, D.: Automotive architecture framework: the experience of volvo cars. J. Syst. Architect. **77**, 83–100 (2017). http://www.sciencedirect.com/science/article/pii/S1383762117300954
4. AUTOSAR, Autosar technical overview v2.2.2 (2012)
5. Meyer, B.: Object-Oriented Software Construction, 1st edn. Prentice-Hall Inc., Upper Saddle River (1988)
6. Meyer, B.: Design by contract, Technical report TR-EI-12/CO, Interactive Software Engineering Inc. (1986)
7. Meyer, B.: Applying "design by contract". Computer **25**(10), 40–51 (1992)
8. Araujo, W., Briand, L.C., Labiche, Y.: Enabling the runtime assertion checking of concurrent contracts for the java modeling language. In: Proceedings of the 33rd International Conference on Software Engineering, ICSE 2011, pp. 786–795. ACM, New York (2011)
9. Araujo, W., Briand, L.C., Labiche, Y.: On the effectiveness of contracts as test oracles in the detection and diagnosis of functional faults in concurrent object-oriented software. IEEE Trans. Software Eng. **40**(10), 971–992 (2014)
10. Liu, Y., Cunningham, H.C.: Software component specification using design by contract. In: Proceeding of the South-East Software Engineering Conference. Tennessee Valley Chapter. National Defense Industry Association (2002)
11. Cheon, Y., Leavens, G., Sitaraman, M., Edwards, S.: Model variables: cleanly supporting abstraction in design by contract. Softw. Pract. Experience **35**(6), 583–599 (2005)

12. Thüm, T., Schaefer, I., Kuhlemann, M., Apel, S., Saake, G.: Applying design by contract to feature-oriented programming. In: Lara, J., Zisman, A. (eds.) FASE 2012. LNCS, vol. 7212, pp. 255–269. Springer, Heidelberg (2012). doi:10.1007/978-3-642-28872-2_18
13. Benveniste, A., Caillaud, B., Nickovic, D., Passerone, R., Raclet, J.-B., Reinkemeier, P., Sangiovanni-Vincentelli, A., Damm, W., Henzinger, T., Larsen, K.: Contracts for systems design, Research Report N.8147, Inria (2012)
14. Jones, M., Haraldsson, J.: D2.4 Dedicate Framework Description (2012)

Modelling for Systems with Holistic Fault Tolerance

Rem Gensh(✉), Ashur Rafiev, Fei Xia, Alexander Romanovsky, and Alex Yakovlev

Newcastle University, Newcastle upon Tyne, UK
{r.gensh,ashur.rafiev,fei.xia,alexander.romanovsky, alex.yakovlev}@newcastle.ac.uk

Abstract. Trade-offs between extra-functional properties, such as performance, reliability and resource utilisation, have been recognised as crucial in system design. The concept of Holistic Fault Tolerance (HFT) is aimed at targeting these trade-offs in run-time system control. Previous work has shown that HFT systems can have significant complexity, which may require sophisticated modelling at the design stage. This paper presents a novel HFT design methodology based on hierarchical modelling and stochastic simulations. The former caters to system complexity and the latter estimates extra-functional properties in the trade-offs. The method is demonstrated with an application example of number plate recognition software.

Keywords: Modelling · Holistic Fault Tolerance · Order Graphs · Stochastic Activity Networks · Extra-functional Properties

1 Introduction

System modelling aims to create an abstract representation of a designed system. This process assists in better understanding of the system and gives a possibility to find and eliminate potential problems at early stages of system development. However, for complex systems, the system model can also be complex and difficult to use. Therefore, it is necessary to ensure that only important parts of the system are studied during the modelling to reduce comprehension complexity.

A well-accepted method of controlling model complexity is the use of hierarchical models. Different models may be constructed for the same system or subsystem at different levels of abstraction. High-level models of high degrees of abstraction tend to be small and easy to analyse, but also include few details and may provide low representative resolution or precision for the quantities or parameters being studied [1]. On the other hand, low-level models of less abstraction may offer finer grain representation of system details and provide higher resolution for studied parameters. However, they may have high degrees of complexity and difficult to work with. Hierarchical modelling provides designers with a means of trading off modelling quality with model usability.

Another popular method of dealing with the model complexity issue and at the same time handling run-time unpredictability is stochastic modelling. Quantities and

A. Romanovsky and E.A. Troubitsyna (Eds.): SERENE 2017, LNCS 10479, pp. 169–183, 2017.
DOI: 10.1007/978-3-319-65948-0_11

parameters under study are assumed to be stochastic and models of manageable size can be used to estimate such quantities without precise knowledge of all the contributing factors such as run-time eventualities [2].

Aspects of study during system design and analysis include functional behaviour and extra-functional parameters. Functional correctness is important, but extra-functional parameters can also be significant contributors of the success or failure of a design. The most interesting extra-functional parameters attracting the attention of system designers include performance, energy consumption and reliability.

In previous studies, we introduced the notion of Holistic Fault Tolerance (HFT) [3] and showed that the HFT architecture can be applied to implement the system, taking into account extra-functional properties, such as reliability, performance and resource utilisation [4]. And finally, maintainability evaluation of the HFT architecture was provided in [5].

In these investigations, it was demonstrated that the HFT approach provides better maintainability of fault tolerance mechanisms. The HFT architecture includes system components, an HFT controller and a number of agents which supports interactions between the components and the HFT controller. The HFT run-time is implemented through control loops that manage the extra-functional parameters through component configuration. However, there remain challenges faced by the HFT developer during the design stage. It is not always clear how to choose the system components, which will be involved in the interaction with the elements of the HFT architecture (essentially the number of control loops). If the designer chooses to involve all system components in the interaction with the HFT elements, i.e. have the maximum number of all possible control loops included, the system would be extremely complex for modelling, implementation and maintenance. On the other hand, unguided control loop reduction would rarely result in optimal system designs.

This study focuses on modelling that supports design-time and run-time system optimisation through the (re)configuration of system components and the efficient use of control loops. At the same time the model should not be very complex for understanding. Iterative top-down design and stochastic representation of extra-functional parameters offer promising solutions.

In this paper we propose a general design method supporting HFT systems. This method makes use of a hierarchical model language, known as order graphs (OGs) [6], which has good representations of horizontality and verticality issues and good support for having different levels of abstraction for different parts of a system model. Also included is an established stochastic model language, known as stochastic activity networks (SANs) [2], which provides facilities such as state-space analysis and simulation engines.

The proposed design workflow is based on the following key points:

- The characterisation of system components leading to SANs models. These SANs models can be used to provide estimates of the extra-functional parameters under study (usually reliability, system utilisation and/or performance) and generate importance costs for potential control loops in the HFT control.
- The concept of controllability is applied to minimise the number of control loops.

- The development of a hierarchical model of the HFT system based on OGs. This model can be used to validate the existence of control loop paths at all levels of model abstraction.

This paper is organised as follows. Section 2 provides the background describing SANs, OGs and HFT. Section 3 explains our modelling methodology. Section 4 describes an HFT case study. Section 5 concludes the paper with discussions.

2 Background

2.1 SANs and Stochastic Modelling

SANs is an extension to general stochastic Petri nets (GSPNs) which are based on Petri nets (PNs) [7]. It inherits the general attributes of PNs including a distributed representation of system states, making it easy to represent parts of a system directly as local subsystems, and more straightforward representations of such important issues as concurrency and synchronisation. A well-established method, it is supported by the mature software tool-kit: Möbius [8].

SANs are capable of representing both deterministic and stochastic events, and event durations in time. The elements used in this work include (a) transitions whose firing speeds (rates) are specified as stochastic, following given distributions, (b) transitions with multiple firing cases with specific probabilities for each case, and (c) input and output gates with predicates and implications specified through logic functions.

The Möbius tool, used in this paper, incorporates a set of solvers including both Monte-Carlo simulation and statespace related solvers. Numerical Markovian solutions can be done for steady-state or time averaged interval rewards, but limited to models with exponentially distributed firing rates. The tool's concept of "rewards" can be easily extended to physical parameters, such as power. In this work we use rewards to evaluate system's extra-functional properties including performance, reliability (defined as success rate), and resource utilisation.

2.2 Order Graphs and Resource Modelling

Hierarchical representations have been used for modelling complex systems for a long time. The idea of separating the "vertical" relation between the layers of abstraction from the "horizontal" knowledge of the system at each particular layer of abstraction has been hinted in [9] and then formally defined in Zoom structures [10] as the concepts of verticality and horizontality. Zoom structures are based on partial orders and are very permissive. In contrast, OGs put a number of constraints on the modelling, which guarantee consistency between the abstraction layers.

An OG is a graph with nodes representing various system resources arranged in tree hierarchies. The hierarchies can be built from the knowledge of the system structure and by similarities of its constituents. The distance from the root relates to the level of abstraction. The formal definition and properties can be found in [6].

The modelling using OGs is an iterative top-down process, starting from the most abstract representation of the system and gradually adding more details, when moving to lower levels. The dependencies between the system's components at the same level of abstraction are represented with "horizontal" arcs in the graph, hence the horizontal paths represent transitive dependencies between the elements in the system. The rigorous definition of OGs provides a built-in capability of consistency checking by preserving the resource dependency paths at each level of abstraction.

OG contains the static knowledge of the system and needs to be paired with a dynamic model to capture the system behaviour (in our case: SANs). The nodes in OG that are included in this model relation form a cut. If the cut goes through different depths in the hierarchy (layers of abstraction), it is called a cross-layer cut. The cut containing all leaves relates to the most concrete (detail) model of the system. Moving up in the abstraction hierarchy, thus grouping multiple nodes into one, represents grouping the corresponding elements in SANs into a single entity by averaging/totalling their parameters (known as black-boxing). This reduces the size of a model, but also introduces inaccuracy. The trade-off between the model complexity and accuracy can be achieved from manipulating cross-layer cuts. This method, called selective abstraction, has been explored in details in [1].

2.3 Holistic Fault Tolerance

The idea of Holistic Fault Tolerance was introduced and developed in [3, 4]. There are two goals of the HFT architecture. The first goal is to provide a method that allows the developer to design and implement computer systems that are efficient in terms of performance and resource utilisation. The second goal is to improve the software maintainability of fault tolerance mechanisms in the system.

A computer system implemented in accordance with the HFT architecture includes functional components that are responsible for main system tasks and the HFT part. The HFT part controls the functional components and ensures reliable and efficient system operation. This part is built around the HFT controller, which is responsible for distribution of computation resources in the application and provides an overarching control over the extra-functional properties, such as system performance. HFT controller also performs a task of re-configuring the system in run-time in case it finds a better operating point.

The HFT controller interacts with the system components through a set of public interfaces. Additionally, the controller is assisted with the HFT agents – auxiliary objects aimed at decreasing the complexity of the HFT architecture. Each HFT agent is responsible for certain extra-functional property of the system. The HFT agents monitor and, when it is required, intervene in the control flow of the critical components. The typical HFT agent can be responsible for one of the following activities: performance monitoring, error handling and gathering of diagnostics information. The structure of an agent can depend on the components it works with, the idea is that the agent incorporates component-dependent code in order to keep HFT as flexible as possible. The data gathered by the HFT agents are translated into a component-independent format and transferred to the HFT controller for dynamic analysis. In case of error handling, the HFT agent requests the HFT controller for a suitable handling action.

It is advised to implement the link between an HFT agent and a functional component implicitly for the component. This approach significantly reduces the dependence of the component on the HFT agent, thus the component would focus on implementing only its functional task without tangling with non-functional activities. In our previous works [4, 5], we used Aspect Oriented Programming [11] in order to improve the development cycle and reduce maintainability effort. In general, the decisions on the structure of HFT agent heavily depend on the software design and the tasks of the system, however the aim of this work is to address the design decisions in a methodological way.

3 Modelling Methodology

In this section, we consider the goal of the modelling, define extra-functional properties of the system, and the context in which these properties are analysed. We also introduce the workflow of the modelling approach.

The goal of the modelling is to provide a method that allows the developer to design and implement the system based on the HFT architecture. It is necessary to guarantee that the system will be efficient with regards to extra-functional properties, such as reliability, performance and resource utilisation. The modelling assists in defining efficient points of the interplay between these extra-functional properties. An *efficient design* allows the developer to implement such a system, which will be efficient in terms of this interplay.

Performance is considered as the amount of work completed per unit time. Faster operation typically requires more resources or can be achieved by reducing the quality of computation. The work performed by the system is measured in *work units*. The processing of each work unit can be finished successfully or unsuccessfully.

Reliability is represented with the success rate, which is defined as the ratio of successfully finished work units to the total amount of work units.

Resource utilisation is the amount of computer resources required to process a certain number of work units. In this context, we define a resource as any facility that enables computation, which may include CPU cores, application threads, memory, energy, etc.

As mentioned in Sect. 2, the system contains functional components that implement the computation. The HFT control for the extra-functional properties is realised using *knobs and monitors*. The knobs are provided by system components as configuration points, and the monitors are instrumentation that provides readings of extra-functional properties at the component level. The system-wide set of knob states is called a *system configuration*. During the system operation, the HFT controller dynamically choses the most suitable system configuration, depending on the history of monitor data.

An instance of such interaction between the HFT elements and the functional system components is defined as a *control loop*. It can be considered as a special interface between the components and the HFT part. The control loop is managed only by the HFT part and is implicit to the system components.

3.1 Workflow of the Modelling Approach

The workflow of the HFT system modelling approach is described in Fig. 1. Each of the steps is described in a subsequent subsection. Note that order graph modelling happens in parallel to the right hand main branch of the workflow.

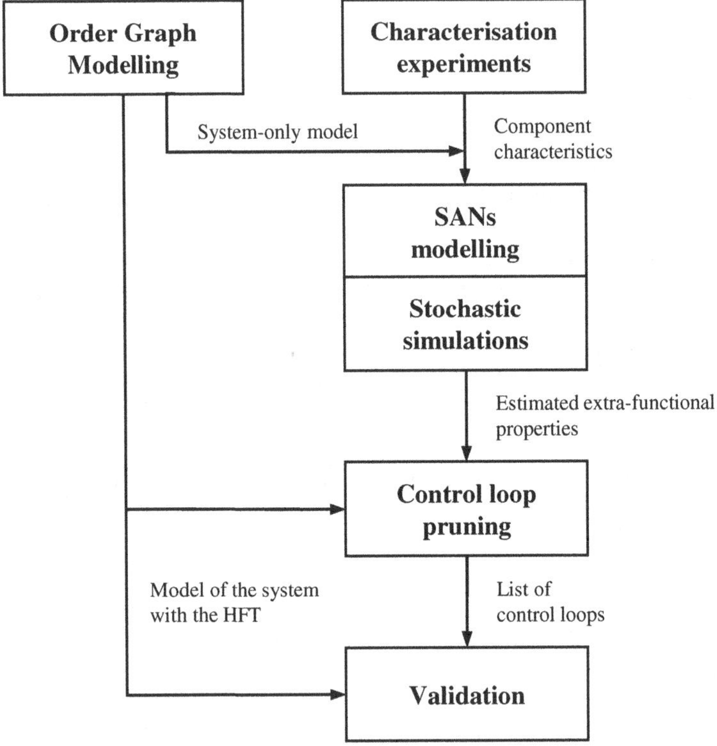

Fig. 1. Workflow diagram

3.2 Characterisation of the System's Extra-Functional Components

The designer should characterise the extra-functional properties of each individual component. If the component supports multiple configurations or algorithms of processing, the characterisation should be done for each individual configuration. The full result of a characterisation pertaining to some component and some extra-functional property describes the value of that property when executing that component. Characterisation is not done beyond component level.

3.3 Building and Simulating the SANs Model of the System

In this step the SAN model of the system is built using component characterisations from the previous step and the system-only OG model. The granularity of the SAN model for any part of the system is determined by the OG modelling step (Fig. 1) and the parameter values are obtained from the characterisation step. The characterisation step usually pertains to the SAN model of the finest detail, because there is no point of developing a SAN model at a finer level of detail than the existing characterisation data. If the OG step suggests a higher level of abstraction, it is possible to derive SAN models of less detail than the characterisation data, for instance by running simulations at the characterisation level of detail then abstracting from the results.

From characterisation to the final SAN model for simulations the approach is bottom-up, but the OG step is usually top-down. There is no conflict because in order to determine the granularity of the final SAN model the entire OG model covering all levels of abstraction needs to have been established. In a way discovering the SAN model is a process of raising the level of abstraction from the bottom traversing the OG until a satisfactory SAN has been found.

The preferred tool for working with SANs is Möbius [8]. The main point of this step is that the SAN system model, assembled from component models, supports system-wide analysis of the modelled extra-functional properties from component-level characterisation data. The most practical analysis method for SAN models of HFT is simulation, as other forms of analysis such as state space studies tend to be restricted to very small models. However, Möbius does provide non-simulation solvers if and when they can and need to be used.

3.4 Control Loop Pruning

The estimated values of system-wide extra-functional properties, obtained from the previous step, can be used to reduce the complexity of the HFT controller, by eliminating unnecessary control loops.

The method is based on the problem of preserving controllability [16] while reducing the number of knobs. It assumes that the number of monitors is both sufficient and necessary to represent the extra-functional properties under study. The monitor values are considered state variables.

We use simulations to build system transfer function [16] relating knobs to monitors. This is achieved by analysing differentials in the estimated monitor values from simulations. Ideally, this requires an exhaustive set of simulation covering all combinations of knob values. However, it is possible to apply known optimisation methods, such as Monte-Carlo [17], to improve the usability of the method.

From this database of state relations, it is possible to determine the smallest set of knobs that maintains controllability.

Although in this paper we deal only with deciding what control loops to include in an HFT system, the off-line design flow described here can yield valuable quantitative data that may be helpful for the detailed design of run-time control. For instance, the

SAN models may provide a set of reference points which may be used in the designs of individual control loops.

3.5 Validation Using OG Hierarchy

As mentioned in Sect. 2, OG modelling provides a top-down workflow that helps the developer to incrementally add the details in the system design. In the proposed workload, the dependencies in the graph represent interactions between the element of the system and provides paths for the control loops. A rigorous path consistency checking between the layers of abstraction guarantees that the designed HFT controller is consistent with the control loops established in the previous steps of the workflow.

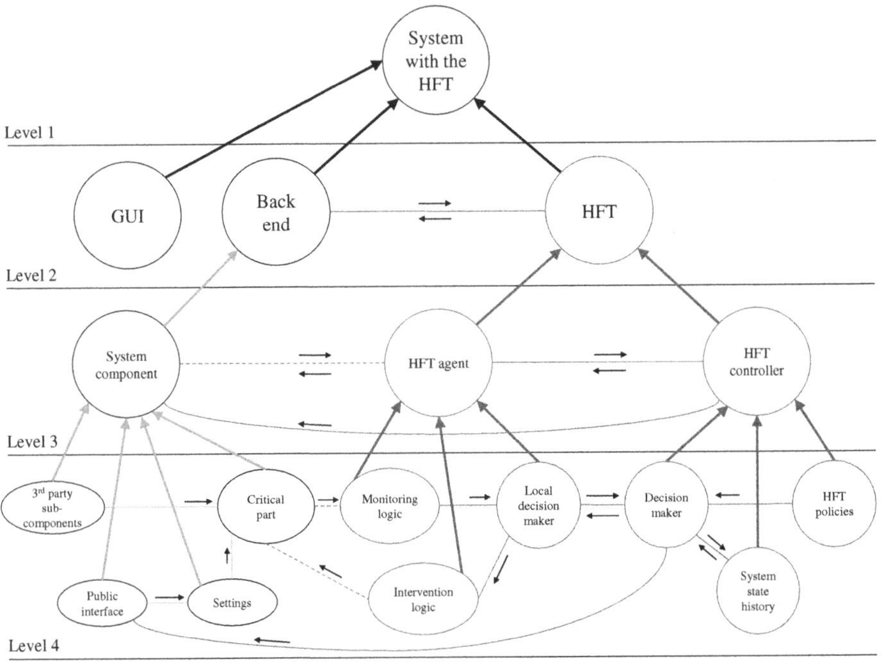

Fig. 2. A general template for HFT Order Graph model

Figure 2 illustrates the hierarchical model of the system with the HFT architecture in three levels of detail. At the top level, there is only the system with the HFT architecture. The second level contains graphic user interface, backend or functional part of the system and HFT part. Information flow between the backend and the HFT is shown in both directions. The next level represents the backend is decomposed to the system components and the HFT part decomposed to the HFT controller and HFT agents. For simplicity, the figure shows only one component and only one agent. At this level, the control loops between the system components and the HFT elements should start to appear.

The most detailed level of the hierarchical model considers the inner structure of the system components and the HFT elements. The system component may include third-party subcomponents, public interfaces, component settings and critical parts. A possible internal structure of an HFT agent consists of monitoring logic, intervention logic and local decision maker. The HFT controller includes the decision maker, the system state history (or dynamic HFT data) and the HFT policies (or static HFT data).

Connections represented by the dashed lines assume that for better maintainability it is preferable to implement this link in such a way that the system component was not aware of implementation details of monitoring and intervention logic in the HFT agent. HFT agents do not directly provide performance of reliability benefits. They were introduced to simplify the developing and improve understanding of the systems with the HFT. It was shown [5] that such configuration supports maintainability of the system. This is the reason why we consider decomposition of the HFT architecture to the HFT controller and the HFT agents.

4 Use Case

4.1 Case Study Application

As a use case, we have chosen the application for the recognition of the UK number plates [4, 5]. The input of the application is a set of images. As an output, the application links each image with recognition results that include the contour of the number plate, recognised string and the probability of correct recognition.

The functional part of the application consists of several components. The Graphical User Interface (GUI) component is the frontend of the application, which allows the user to upload the images. These images are sent to the Initial Image Processing (IIP) component. At this stage, every image undergoes an initial processing, which includes various filters, searching of the number plate on the image, cropping of the number plate from the image and elimination of the perspective skews of the number plate cutout. Two algorithms for number plate search can be applied: OpenCV-based rectangle detection and HAAR cascade [12] trained to recognise the area with the UK number plate. If the number plate is found and cropped it is put to Number Plates Queue (NPQ). When the NPQ is not empty, the Optical Character Recognition (OCR) component takes available number plate cutout and performs the text recognition on the cutout. There are two OCR algorithms in the OCR component: Tesseract [13] and number plate recognition algorithm described in [14]. If the OCR recognises the text on the cutout, this text is checked by the Result Checker (RC) component to ensure compliance of the car number with a national format. These additional algorithms are introduced to provide redundancy and increase reliability of the application.

The UML diagram of the application is shown in Fig. 3. GUI does not participate in the HFT scheme and it should not be considered in details in the model. Interfaces between the functional components (IIP and OCR) and the HFT controller are omitted to make the diagram clearer.

In both IIP and OCR components the images are processed concurrently. The HFT controller specifies the most suitable number of working threads for each component. The Performance agent monitors the execution time of the IIP and OCR components. The Error Handling agent is responsible for handling the errors in the IIP and OCR component. An error implies a deviation from the correct service [15] and it is not necessarily exception only. Impossibility to find the number plate or low probability of the recognition is considered as an error as well. At the same time, not all exceptions are regarded as errors. If the error is detected by Error Handling agent, it requests the HFT controller for a suitable error recovery action, which could vary depending on current system operation.

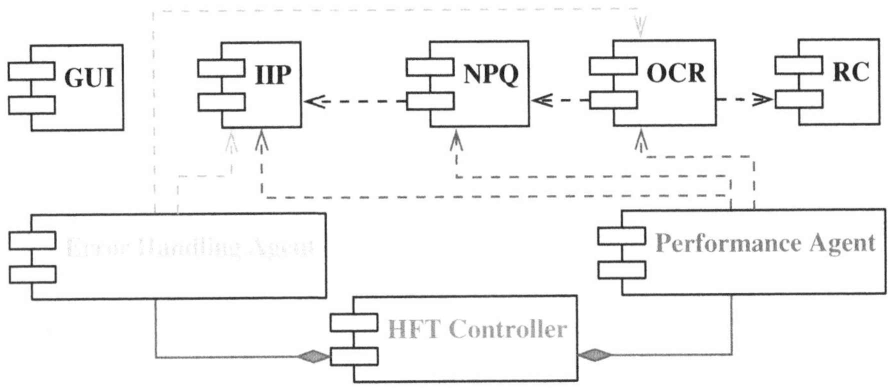

Fig. 3. UML diagram of the use case application

4.2 Characterisation of the Components

For the characterisation, we have chosen the IIP and the OCR components, since they are the most critical components of the application. Characterisation data is presented in Tables 1 and 2. The input data varies significantly for the given application, hence we have chosen three groups of images distinguished by size: small, medium and large. Time and reliability of the image processing significantly depends on the image size.

Table 1. Characterisation of the IIP component

Original image size		Number plate detection algorithm			
		Rectangle detection		HAAR cascade	
		Average time	Average reliability	Average time	Average reliability
Small	<200 KB	20 ms	85%	9.3 ms	77%
Medium	200 KB – 1 MB	85 ms	80%	76 ms	85%
Large	1 MB – 7 MB	143 ms	72%	328 ms	86%

Table 2. Characterisation of the OCR component

Original image size		Optical Character Recognition algorithm			
		OpenCV implementation		Tesseract	
		Average time	Average reliability	Average time	Average reliability
Small	<200 KB	23 ms	70%	33 ms	75%
Medium	200 KB – 1 MB	29 ms	73%	37 ms	78%
Large	1 MB – 7 MB	45 ms	48%	50 ms	62%

4.3 SAN Modelling and Simulations of the System

With this characterisation data, we can build the SAN models in Möbius. A detailed SAN model for the two components IIP and OCR, each in three versions small, medium and large is shown in Fig. 4. The fundamental states for each component version are working and idle. Working means that this component version is in execution and idle means that it is not in execution. The model is simplified to put all idles together. This means that for, e.g. IIP, the IIP_idle place is initialised with the with the number of threads given to the IIP component. This may be known as the IIP capacity of the system. Each completion of an IIP component version puts a token back to this idle place. Each IIP component version has a probability of success P_s and a probability of failure $1-P_s$ and this is represented by the stochastic timed transitions IIP_finish. The OCR component models have the same structure. Between the IIP and OCR blocks, three queues are modelled with the standard SAN representation for queues or buffers. The IIP_start transition on the left generates input images stochastically according to probability functions and rates that can be set in the model.

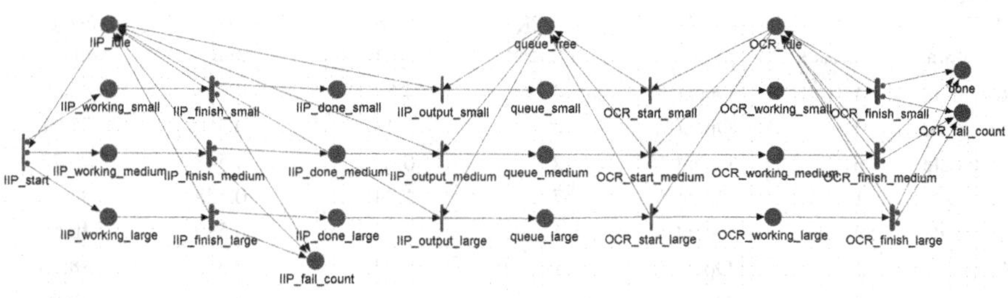

Fig. 4. Detailed SANs model of the use case application in Möbius

The occurrences of failure are tracked by the markings of the failure places and the overall number of successful recognitions is recorded in the final done place at the right end of the net. Running simulations with this model produces success and failure rates, resource utilisation (e.g. the average number of threads being active) and overall performance.

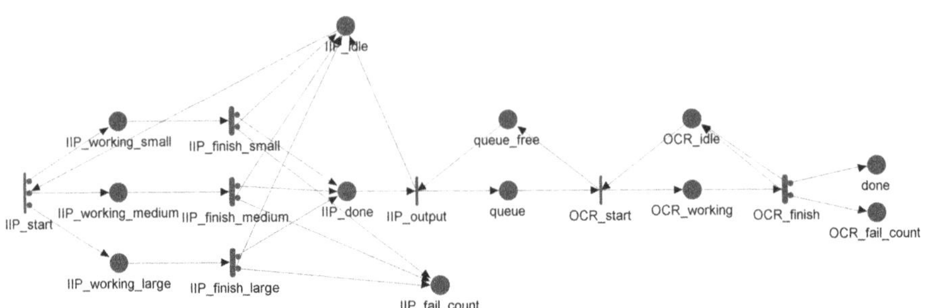

Fig. 5. Reduced SANs model of the use case application in Möbius

This model turns out to require somewhat significant time (more than a few minutes) to simulate. As a result, by making OG analysis and studying the characterisation data, we decided to derive a reduced model, which is shown in Fig. 5.

The reduced model only has a single OCR component version by combining the three different versions in the detailed model into one using the average behaviour. The reason behind this is that the version pertaining to large size is significantly slower than the others, which are very similar. Intuitively, component capacities are used more on the faster processing versions as they tend to grab the token from the idle place more frequently.

The reduced model required simulation times that are an order of magnitude shorter than the detailed model, and they produced very close results with differences within 5% on all the extra-functional properties being studied. Some simulation results are shown in Table 3.

Table 3. Simulation results

Configuration				Estimates		
IIP algorithm	IIP threads	OCR algorithm	OCR threads	Core allocation	Success rate	Image time
Rectangle	4	OpenCV	4	4.55	0.543	44.89
Rectangle	2	OpenCV	6	2.40	0.550	55.91
Rectangle	6	OpenCV	2	6.63	0.548	40.77
Rectangle	1	OpenCV	7	1.24	0.528	87.11
Rectangle	7	OpenCV	1	7.49	0.559	40.68
Rectangle	1	OpenCV	1	1.22	0.529	88.26
Rectangle	3	OpenCV	1	3.40	0.553	48.86
HAAR	4	Tesseract	4	4.53	0.574	90.54
HAAR	2	Tesseract	6	2.36	0.577	116.89
HAAR	6	Tesseract	2	6.57	0.568	77.46
Rectangle	4	Tesseract	4	5.42	0.561	46.23
Rectangle	2	Tesseract	6	2.86	0.564	56.53
Rectangle	6	Tesseract	2	7.27	0.551	41.91
HAAR	4	OpenCV	4	4.26	0.561	90.01
HAAR	2	OpenCV	6	2.20	0.589	117.79
HAAR	6	OpenCV	2	6.31	0.557	76.98

In these particular simulations, we wanted to find out if the relative numbers of IIP and OCR components executed affect the execution time, resource utilisation and reliability. It was found that the reliability stays about the same, but running more IIP components than OCR components improved the overall execution time and resource utilisation (more components get executed simultaneously, pressing more cores and reducing idle time and queue length).

In case if the observed change in reliability is considered insignificant, the reduction of control loops leads to removal of all knobs except the number of IIP threads. This remaining knob provides the control over resource utilisation and performance. On the other hand, if the reliability difference is considered significant, all knobs contribute to controlling the system properties.

4.4 Hierarchical Model of the System

A hierarchical model of the system is built following the general template (Fig. 2) and is shown in Fig. 6.

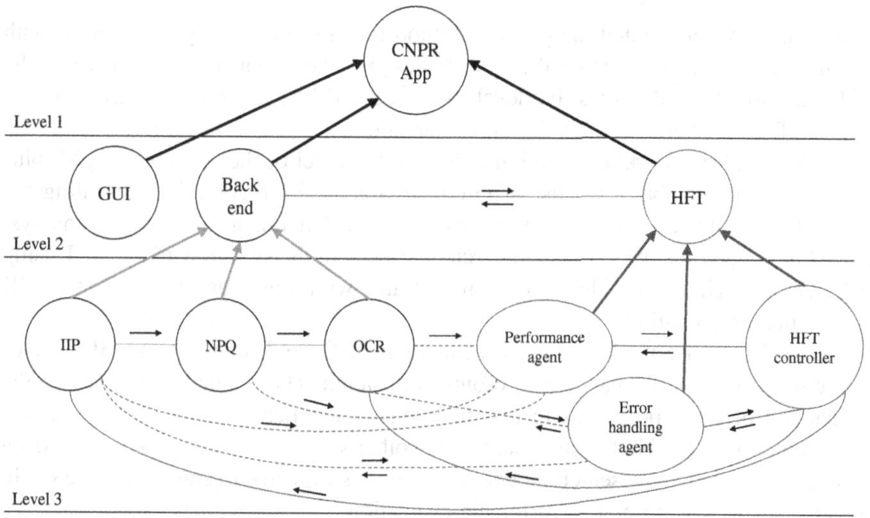

Fig. 6. Hierarchical model of the system

At Level 1 of the system Order Graph there is only one node "Car Number Plate Recognition Application". Level 2 distinguishes between the HFT part of the system and functional part, which is comprised of the GUI and system backend. At Level 3 all crucial components of the system and the HFT part are illustrated. We do not model GUI behaviour, therefore we stop at Level 2 for GUI. We have chosen to decompose the backend to IIP, NPQ and OCR components because it follows the UML structure of the application. The HFT part is decomposed to the HFT controller, Performance Agent and Error Handling Agent. At Level 4 there is further decomposition to the inner structure of the functional components and the HFT elements. Level 4 is not illustrated here due to the number of elements at this level.

There is uni-directional information flow from the IIP, the NPQ and the OCR components to the Performance agent, because this agent only monitors the components, but it does not affect the control flow of the components. In contrast, the Error Handling agent has bi-directional information flow, since it intervenes in the control flow of IIP and OCR components in order to handle the errors. The interfaces between the agents and components are represented by dashed lines because they are implicit for the components. The HFT controller, in turn, utilises public interfaces of the IIP and OCR components to reconfigure the components and performs fault handling of the application. In addition, there are information flows between the HFT controller and the HFT agents. It can be seen that all control loops mentioned in Sect. 4.4 exist in this Order Graph, which validates the correctness of the selected HFT architecture.

5 Conclusion

In this study, we elaborated the general method for modelling computer systems with the HFT at the early stages of the system design. The given method simplifies the modelling process and allows the developer to adjust the system at the early stage to achieve efficient operation after the implementation.

As a part of the workflow, we build the SANs model of the system using Möbius tool. After that we obtain the list of interfaces for the HFT control representing the control loops between system components and extra-functional properties of the system. At the same time, we create a hierarchical model of the system with the HFT using Order Graphs. The method has been demonstrated with a use case application of UK number plate recognition.

Currently we are working on the evaluation of the efficiency of the HFT architecture in terms of performance and resource utilisation. The evaluation is based on the comparison of these properties in two functionally identical systems. One system is implemented with the HFT architecture and another system uses the standard approach to fault tolerance. The presented modelling method is expected to significantly assist in adjusting the system to prepare it for the evaluation.

As a future work we are planning to ensure scalability of the HFT approach, and show that the HFT architecture can be applied for large-scale systems. We propose to introduce the idea of adaptive holistic fault tolerance, that will be able to control the HFT agents in run-time depending on the current system state. To do this the presented modelling approach should be extended to include the reconfiguration of the HFT architecture elements.

References

1. Rafiev, A., Xia, F., Iliasov, A., Gensh, R., Aalsaud, A., Romanovsky, A., Yakovlev, A.: Selective abstraction and stochastic methods for scalable power modelling of heterogeneous systems. In: 2016 Forum on Specification and Design Languages (FDL), pp. 1–7. (2016)
2. Sanders, W.H., Meyer, J.F.: Stochastic activity networks: formal definitions and concepts. In: Brinksma, E., Hermanns, H., Katoen, J.-P. (eds.) EEF School 2000. LNCS, vol. 2090, pp. 315–343. Springer, Heidelberg (2001). doi:10.1007/3-540-44667-2_9
3. Gensh, R., Romanovsky, A., Yakovlev, A.: On structuring Holistic Fault Tolerance. In: Proceedings of the 15th International Conference on Modularity (MODULARITY 2016). ACM, Málaga, Spain (2016)
4. Gensh, R., Rafiev, A., Garcia, A., Xia, F., Romanovsky, A., Yakovlev, A.: Architecting Holistic Fault Tolerance. In: 2017 IEEE 18th International Symposium on High Assurance Systems Engineering (HASE), pp. 5–8 (2017)
5. Gensh, R., Garcia, A., Romanovsky, A.: Experience report: evaluation of Holistic Fault Tolerance. School of Computing Science Technical report Series. School of Computing Science, Newcastle University (2017)
6. Rafiev, A., Xia, F., Iliasov, A., Gensh, R., Aalsaud, A., Romanovsky, A., Yakovlev, A.: Order Graphs and cross-layer parametric significance-driven modelling. In: 2015 15th International Conference on Application of Concurrency to System Design, pp. 110–119. (2015)
7. Peterson, J.L.: Petri Net Theory and the Modeling of Systems. Prentice Hall PTR, Englewood Cliffs (1981)
8. The Möbius modelling tool. https://www.mobius.illinois.edu
9. Zurcher, F.W., Randell, B.: Iterative multi-level modelling - a methodology for computer system design. In: Proceedings IFIP Congress 1968, pp. 138–142 (1968). http://citeseerx.ist.psu.edu/viewdoc/summary?doi=10.1.1.2.4270
10. Ehrenfeucht, A., Rozenberg, G.: Zoom structures and reaction systems yield exploration systems. Int. J. Found. Comput. Sci. **25**, 275–305 (2014)
11. Laddad, R.: AspectJ in Action: Practical Aspect-Oriented Programming. Manning Publications Co., Greenwich (2003)
12. Bradski, G.: The OpenCV Library. Dr. Dobb's J. Softw. Tools **25**(11), 120–123 (2000). https://scholar.google.com/citations?view_op=view_citation%20hl=en%20user=yeDFJgoAAAAJ%20citation_for_view=yeDFJgoAAAAJ:9yKSN-GCB0IC
13. Smith, R.: An overview of the Tesseract OCR engine. In: Ninth International Conference on Document Analysis and Recognition (ICDAR 2007), pp. 629–633 (2007)
14. Baggio, D.L., Emami, S., Escrivá, D.M., Ievgen, K., Mahmood, N., Saragih, J., Shilkrot, R.: Mastering OpenCV with Practical Computer Vision Projects. Packt Publishing Ltd., Birmingham (2012)
15. Avizienis, A., Laprie, J.-C., Randell, B., Landwehr, C.: Basic concepts and taxonomy of dependable and secure computing. Trans. Dependable Secure Comput. **1**, 11–33 (2004)
16. Bubnicki, Z.: Modern Control Theory. Springer-Verlag, Heidelberg (2005). doi:10.1007/3-540-28087-1
17. Metropolis, N., Ulam, S.: The Monte Carlo method. J. Am. Stat. Assoc. **44**(247), 335–341 (1949)

Holistic Processing and Exploring Event Logs

Marcin Kubacki and Janusz Sosnowski(✉)

Institute of Computer Science,
Warsaw University of Technology, Warsaw, Poland
j.sosnowski@ii.pw.edu.pl

Abstract. Computer systems generate large amounts of event logs related to various operational aspects (positive and negative). Extracting from them useful information (e.g. targeted at dependability and resilience issues) is a challenging problem widely discussed in the literature and still needing deeper studies. We have developed a new holistic approach using enhanced event classification (based on original text mining algorithms) combined with multidimensional statistical analysis of various properties in vocabulary (words, phrases), time, spatial, local and global correlations. It has been incorporated in the developed tools and verified on event data sets collected from different computers.

Keywords: Event logs · Anomaly detection · System profiling · Text mining

1 Introduction

Most computer systems provide diverse event logs which are useful traces to detect, diagnose and predict anomalies [2]. Moreover, they characterize on-going processes [15], system workloads and environment interactions. Hence, event log analysis is an important issue in studies of various system dependability and resilience aspects [5].

Publications on event logs are mostly targeted at specific logs and problems, quite often limited to particular systems or a single research issue. Most of them provide methods of detecting system anomalies or security threats basing on searching characteristic classes and patterns of events, etc. ([2–4, 6] and references therein). The presented results neglect the specificity of logs. Identification of event log features is the bases for developing efficient analysis algorithms as well as identifying deficiencies to improve the quality of logs.

Having analyzed event logs from laptops, workstations, and servers we have found the need of deeper studies in relevance to syntactic and semantic features of log reports in order to perform better event classification. In theses studies an important issue is adapting text mining schemes to study lexicological properties of event reports (neglected in the literature). Improving event classification we have introduced word classes and developed some algorithms identifying variable terms which are supported with regular expression specifications. Beyond the data comprised in event reports an important issue is tracing spatial (relevance to software or hardware modules) and time properties (frequency, time distribution and correlations). Time analysis should take into account different observation perspectives (e.g. diurnal, monthly). This can be further extended by correlating event logs with workload and environment characteristics.

A. Romanovsky and E.A. Troubitsyna (Eds.): SERENE 2017, LNCS 10479, pp. 184–200, 2017.
DOI: 10.1007/978-3-319-65948-0_12

We are interested in tracing anomalies and finding characteristics of operational profiles (resource utilization, workload, user behavior), their changes in time, impact of system upgrades, reconfigurations, external environment, etc. To support these processes we have developed special tools with incorporated original algorithms and visualization capabilities. All this results in a holistic approach to log analysis not encountered in the literature. The efficiency of the proposed methodology has been verified using event repositories of many systems.

Basic features of event logs and the related works are presented in Sect. 2. Section 3 describes original lexicological analysis. New event classification algorithms are introduced in Sect. 4. Spatial and temporal properties are discussed in Sect. 5, final conclusions are summarized in Sect. 6.

2 Event Log Features and Related Work

Event logs depend upon system architecture and software. Windows systems provide four kinds of logs: setup, system, application and security logs. Setup logs comprise information on actions that occur during installation (small number of different and short messages, less than 100 words). System logs register events describing system operation, services, states, erroneous situations. These events are categorized as critical (the highest severity problem), error, warning and information. Application logs deliver information (up to several hundreds of words) on application execution (severity levels: error, warning and information). Security logs relate to log on attempts (success and failure categories). In Unix systems events are provided by syslog daemon (started and stopped at boot and shut down). Syslog receives event records from applications, kernel or other units (e.g. printing system, mail agent) and writes to one or more output files or forwards the logs via UDP to a collection host. Here, seven severity levels can be distinguished (increasing order of severity): debug, info, notice, warning, error, critical, alert, emergency. In practice, the specified severity level can be misleading or not meaningful, so deeper analysis is needed.

Depending upon the system we may have event reports in more or less structured form. Windows logs are based on XML structure and can refer to various templates which specify divers elements (fields), e.g.: time stamp, event provider (name or source), event identifier, severity level, keywords, user ID, event ID, operation which raised the event, textual description of the event (message). Hence, an important issue is extracting meaningful information [14]. Log reports can be treated as a plain text comprising constant and variable parts (terms). Usually, constant parts are predefined by the event generator. Variable parts appear in correlation with the constant parts as some differing character strings generated dynamically. Variable parts refer to time stamps, port numbers, IP addresses, file paths, memory addresses, etc.

Event log analysis can be targeted at characterization of system/application behavior (operational profile and external interactions), detection of anomalies [9] or predictions [7, 16] of their potential occurrences. In general, such analysis bases on extracting characteristic log features. Here, we can distinguish three steps: log parsing, feature extraction and evaluation (e.g. anomaly detection). Log parsing (clustering or heuristic approaches [2, 8, 12, 14]) produces event templates describing their structure and information contents (constant and variable parts, message signature). Feature extraction is targeted at finding characteristic properties related to semantical contents of reports (occurrence time, source and destination IP, user information, etc.), event classification, their spatial and time distribution, etc. In particular, we can generate event count vector [9] which describes the occurrence number of each event (or event class) and define these vectors for subsequent groups (chunks) of event sequences obtained by dividing the log set into time windows (fixed, sliding, session).

Log analysis depends upon the goal. The simplest techniques base on searching events with specific known keywords (e.g. error, fail, crash, denied access, overflow, congestion) or patterns defined by experts. Further we can look at some baseline features [3]. They can relate to exceeding specified thresholds, e.g. success and failures of log in (or log off), restarts, recovery, transmission retries, log message type per source or day [16]. In practice, more sophisticated techniques are needed. Here we can distinguish supervised and unsupervised anomaly detection. Supervised methods base on labeled training data with specified normal and abnormal cases [9]. They use logistic regression (statistic model), decision trees or SVM (Supervised Vector Machine) learning method. Non supervised methods detect outlier cases within the observed events. Typically, they use log clustering [12], methods with big dimension data reduction (Principal Component Analysis [20]), invariant mining [13], frequent sequence and rare events mining [3, 14]. A comparative study is given in [8, 9].

In [2] log clustering is performed basing on combining similar messages. Log reports are compared using Levenstein ratio defined as the Levenstein distance between two compared strings (minimum number of edits needed to transform one string into another) divided by the length of the longer one. The modified ratio attributes different weights to subsequent words (decreasing from the message beginning). Other metric is introduced in [19]. It takes into account the number of matched and non matched terms (words) between two compared reports. Measuring and understanding log features is also an important issue in system resilience evaluation [5, 7, 18].

Most papers on event logs are targeted at detection of specific anomalies (e.g. cyber attacks, program problems) or specific log datasets (e.g. from telephony [2]). They base usually on single aspect features, describe at some general level the used methodology and present summarized results on accuracy and precision in relevance to specific systems. Quite often they are hard to interpret and do not provide intuitive insights. In our practice we observed the need of looking not only at anomalies but also deriving system properties, their changes in time, workload and environment interaction. We are interested in finding known and unknown features. We have noted that there is a lack of deeper text mining and lexicological analysis of event logs as well as unsatisfactory event classification. Moreover, the analysis should take into account multiple aspects of logs (holistic approach). To deal with these problems we have developed new event classification algorithms and implemented tools which are integrated with specially adapted event log data base. They assure log collection, parsing, filtering, reformatting, statistical and other analyses. This approach has been verified on real data log sets. It provides a better knowledge on system operation and possible logging improvements.

3 Textual Log Analysis

Event reports can be treated as textual documents and submitted to classical text mining processes. They can be targeted at various aspects characterizing the contents of the reports. The text mining problem is widely discussed in the literature in the context of classical documents comprising a big amount of natural language text, e.g. publications, web page contents [1]. This approach is neglected in event log analysis. We analyzed event message texts using classical mining techniques such as: identifying keywords [1], novelty mining, word statistics, sentimental analysis (positive or negative notion of text - [11] and references therein), etc. In most cases the results were not satisfactory due to specificity of short event massage texts comprising many terms (words) beyond natural language. Hence, we decided to analyze in detail text properties using the developed LogMiner tool.

Event reports comprise relatively short texts with natural language words and many other words expressing various numerical and specific technical terms. Moreover, grammatical rules of composing the text are vague and many informal specifications are encountered. Textual descriptions can comprise scanty or imprecise phrases, technical acronyms, text shortcuts, etc. Hence, an important issue is statistical characterization of event texts. We have performed such analysis for a representative sample of event logs related to Unix and Windows oriented systems.

Analyzing texts comprised in event logs we base on appropriate dictionaries, e.g. WordNet base (http://wornet.princton.edu) comprises a set of English words dictionaries specified in XML format. Here, we have separate dictionaries for nouns, verbs, adjectives, adverbs, etc. Words are grouped according to their meanings. Having performed a manual preliminary analysis of event log records we have found the need of specifying some additional dictionaries to facilitate text mining. In particular, we have introduced the following dictionaries: negative nouns (13), negative verbs (49), negative adjectives (2118), negative adverbs (437). These words have been verified and supplemented with others selected manually (by referring to negative word dictionaries, e.g. [11]). Moreover, we have added dictionaries of technical terms related to hardware, software, internet, file formats or others related to the analysis goals.

Basing on classical dictionaries we deal with words comprising only letters. In event logs we have also more complex words, e.g. comprising numerical or special characters (file paths, process names, etc.). Hence, developing a special tool for text mining (LogMiner) we have admitted two options of word analysis: (i) related to standard lexical words, (ii) enhanced with partitioning complex words into elementary words. In the last case we deal with complex words comprising elementary words concatenated by numerical or special characters (e.g. /). Despite a significant extension of word definition LogMiner does not classify all words, hence the word class "unknown" is usually large. This group comprises various acronyms, words comprising numbers, etc. Classification of such words needs more complex algorithms and can be combined with the developed process of deriving variables and classifying event logs (Sect. 4). The semantics of event logs on one hand bases on natural language phrases or word meaning and on the other hand it comprises some technical terms both of general widely used meaning (e.g. task termination) or a very narrow meaning close to the specificity of the considered system (e.g. cron.daily, cron.weekly, USER=root; error (grandchild #6367 failed with exit status 1), COMMAND=/bin/ps]). Moreover, some information can be presented in an encoded form (e.g. COMMAND=/bin/kill -9 21657, TTY=pts/2). Application logs usually show high diversity in formats.

The developed LogMiner facilitates text mining. Using this tool we have derived some interesting properties within the collected event logs. For an illustration we give statistics of word classification within logs (message fields) collected from Neptun server covering 6 months – over 100 000 events. These statistics include words selected from complex words (option (ii) of LogMiner). Cancelling this extension (option (i)) we have got much smaller number of identified words, i.e. only 12 600 nouns as opposed to 472 519 in the first case. This confirms that log messages comprise much more specialized complex words than regular English words. Such words can be analyzed with regular expressions and referring to various dictionaries. We use classical dictionaries and predefined dictionaries of specialized terms, acronyms, words of negative meaning, etc. For an illustration we give distribution of words in the considered Neptun server (with introduced acronyms):

adjectives (AD - 460), negative adjectives (NAD - 129), adverbs (ADV - 129433), computer acronyms (ACR - 38467), hardware (HW - 1984), internet (INT - 1013), nouns (N - 422519), negative nouns (NN - 142), software (SW 144050), verbs (V 327682), negative verbs (NV - 77).

All words not included in considered dictionaries are classified as unknown words (UW - 199664). More interesting is the distribution of different (unique) used words (cardinality of used dictionaries). For an illustration we give word cardinalities for logs of two Unix servers: Neptun and Catalina:

- Neptun: UW - 548, AD - 219, NAD - 14, ADV - 71, ACR - 51, HW - 48, INT - 20, N - 606, NN - 4, SW - 47, V - 301, NV - 9
- Catalina: UW - 125, AD - 40, NAD - 3, ADV - 14, ACR - 7, HW - 6, INT - 9, N - 130, NN - 1, SW - 15, V - 55, NV - 1

Similarly, we analyzed logs from laptops and workstations (Windows systems). These logs (collected within 1–4 years from 8 systems) comprised in total 621118 events, 14 747 358 words (57 642 unique words). We have identified only 1335 and 1083 unique English and Polish words, and 48 IT words. Total numbers of these words in the logs were 10329591, 3432139 and 2724503, respectively. Within other unique word categories dominated hex values (17280), path specifications (12216), integer numbers 8861, globally unique identifiers (8861), other categorized words (web addresses, files with exe, dll, etc.) ranged from 45 to 700, uncategorized (12216).

Typically, the used English vocabulary in event logs is relatively poor (several hundreds or thousands of words) as compared with classical documents analyzed with text mining. Nevertheless, we should comment here that this analysis does not take into account so called non regular words, i.e. words comprising numbers, concatenated words (with special characters). In particular, in this group we can have file paths, port numbers or such specifications as: error1, user5, server#11. These words as well as words classified in dictionary of unknown words (e.g. specific acronyms, user names) can be analyzed with the available classification algorithms and regular expressions (Sect. 4).

Different event logs have different text properties, word statistics, vocabularies, etc. For an illustration the access log of Catalina server and syslog of Neptun server used about 280 and 1200 unique English words, respectively. However, Catalina event records comprised more words than Neptun (many of them non regular or not classified). The semantical diversity here was also much lower. Having identified log properties we have to adapt appropriately the analysis.

Using more advanced text mining we have studied so called Inverse Document Frequency (IDF(t)) which measures importance of the considered word t [1]:

$$IDF(t) = \log\{|D|/|[d \in D: t \in d]|\}$$

where D is the set of documents (event reports in our case). This function assumes lower values for less significant words, in particular those which appear frequently (e.g. stop words). For natural languages the plot of IDF values in deceasing order has the shape of a logarithmic curve.

For the considered Neptun server and analyzed 1184 words we got a logarithmic shape of IDF parameter (values 1–5). The x-axis covered unique words from 11 dictionaries, however we should notice that some words appeared in different dictionaries (e.g. adjectives and negative adjectives, noun and verb, etc.). In classical text mining IDF parameter is helpful in identifying interesting words (e.g. keywords), as those with high IDF value. In our case we had many words with high IDF, so it was not sufficient criteria for selecting interesting event records. So some other criteria should be added. In particular, we have decided to check IDF for negative words and here we have received interesting results. From the 219 used adjectives 13 have been defined as negative, for 11 of them IDF was in the range 2.62–5.01, similarly 3 negative nouns: fault, warning, error achieved IDF 2.96, 3.58 and 4.53, respectively. Event records comprising such words (e.g. recovery, retry, backup, unavailable, permission, cancel) are interesting for the users. Distribution of IDF for access logs of Catalina server (Fig. 1) was quite different (close to linear decrease) with only 40 words with IDF exceeding 2.8 (as opposed to over 1000 in the case of Neptun server).

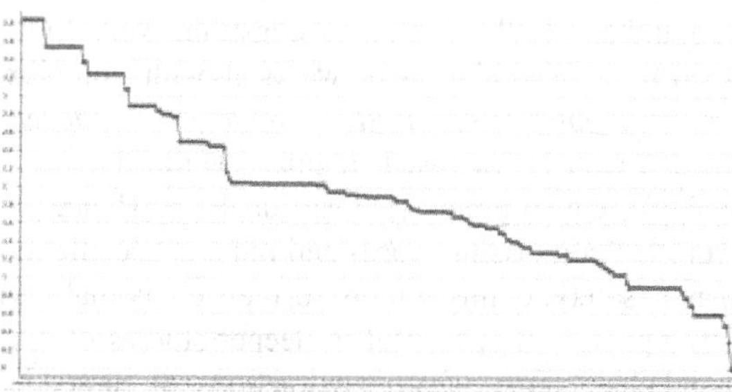

Fig. 1. Distribution of IDF for Catalina server (x-axis: 286 unique words, y-axis: 0–3.8)

We have extended this analysis for word phrases (treating them as generalized words). LogMiner has several options dedicated for this purpose. In particular, we can select phrase length (2–6 words), various filtering (e.g. phrases comprising words belonging to specified dictionaries). This allowed us to select interesting log entries. Dealing with IDF we should be prepared for situations with bursts of replicated events within some time window. In the case of anomalous situations this may happen quite frequently. This effect decreases IDF of words appearing in bursts, so it is reasonable to filter them out appropriately in calculations.

For an illustration we give interesting phrases (for Neptun syslog) composed of 4 words with relatively high values of IDF: [link is not ready] – IDF = 4.71, [file could not be] – IDF = 4.71, [not provided by any] – IDF = 4.41. In Catalina access log usually event messages were relatively long, so we searched even for longer phrases. For example, the phrase [non clean shutdown detected on] attained IDF = 2.5 and it related to interesting events, e.g.:

2012-09-27 16:11:45 INFO: Non clean shutdown detected on log [/opt/apache-tomcat-7.0.16/data/passim-entity/nioneo_logical.log.1]. Recovery started ...

This event related to incorrect closing of a library by an application.

Looking for logs related to critical or dangerous situations we have defined dictionaries of critical words (based on statistical analysis discussed above). They included such words as no, not, error, fail, unavailable, false, kill, exception, panic, failover, recovery, heartbeat, shutdown, timeout, missing, etc. In fact more interesting were phrases comprising these words. So we analyzed k-word phrases (k-grams) comprising negative words (typically k in the range 2–6). For illustration we give some statistics (occurrence numbers) of such phrases for the considered Windows logs presented above: i) two word phrases (bigrams) comprising “failed”: *failed to* (3830), *failed for* (656), *driver failed* (794), *service failed* (555), *reason failed* (419), *login failed* (419); ii) 4 word phrases with failed: *failed to be changed* (1802), *failed to load for* (794), *service failed to start* (553), *failed to open the* (419). Phrases comprising word “not” were more populated. Here are some examples of 3 word phrases (trigrams): *not always available* (31267), *not available key* (1767), *name not available* (1766), *response not available* (1079), *did not start* (601), *not start because* (593). Please note that the occurrence numbers of these phrases constitute very low percentage of all events (about 700 000). In a similar way we deal with complex words, e.g. *unable_to_retest, unexpected_job_state, job_stuck, node_dead, packet_drop.*

Relatively limited numbers of used regular words in logs makes effective lexical/linguistic analysis, e.g. n-grams (phrase) analysis. Hence, we can create and validate “smoke” word list comprising words and phrases specific to the analysis goals targeted at performance, safety, configuration, resilience, anomaly issues, etc. This list can be systematically updated. It is helpful in deeper studies of event logs involving event classification and characteristic feature extractions, discussed in the sequel. In the analysis we have to take into account misspelling words as well as mixing words from other languages (e.g. Polish in our case).

4 Event Classification

While analyzing event logs an important issue is to identify their classes (clustering). This process can be simplified by identifying events comprising the same fixed terms and differing on variable terms (parameters). Here, we outline two developed heuristic algorithms. Algorithm A1 uses preliminary operations which calculate the number of occurrences of each word W on position P in event log records, this results in a list LC of counters with elements *count [W][P]*. The sorted list LC provides its median element. In the case the word W occurs on position P more or equally frequently (condition >=) than the median it is qualified as a constant term. Another variant takes into account sharp condition (>).

```
for every line (record) LE in the log do
{create a list L of subsequent words in LE
 if length(L) <= 1 then continue
sum_global = 0
   for every word W1 on position P1 in L do
   {for every word W2 on position P2 != P1 in L do
      {if P2 > P1 then W = W1 ~ W2 else W = W2 ~ W1
      sum_global = sum_global + count[W]}}
threshold = sum_global / (length(L) * (length(L)-1))
   for every word W1 on position P1 in L do
   {sum = 0
      for every word W2 on position P2 != P1 in L do
      {if P2 > P1 then W = W1 ~ W2 else W = W2 ~ W1
      sum = sum + count[W]}
avg = sum / (length(L)-1)
 if avg >= threshold  then  W1 is a fixed element in the line LE
 else W1 is parameter (variable)
add W1 to R # result record }}
```

Fig. 2. Identification of variable terms – algorithm A2

More complex is algorithm A2 (Fig. 2), because it takes into account the word context. Here, we check word successions. In the preliminary phase for every word W1 on position P1we count the occurrence of word W2 on position P2 (P2 > P1). In this way we create a list L of subsequent words (pairs) with elements *count[W]* comprising the number of these occurrences, where W is the concatenation of W1 and W2 (W1 $\sim$ W2). Between W1 and W2 other words can occur. In the first phase algorithm A2 finds a threshold of occurrences for the further discrimination. For each pair of words we take the number of succession occurrences. Taking into account summing N (N – 1) operations (where N is the number of words in the event report – length L) we have to divide the obtained *sum_gobal* by this value. Event lines with no more than one word are skipped. In the second phase we check whether the average number of word pair occurrences, exceeds the calculated threshold, i.e. *sum* divided by N – 1 (variable *avg* in Fig. 2). In the positive case W1 is qualified as a fixed term and stored in result record R with this specification.

The developed algorithms have been verified for different log data sets. They provided reasonable results. Taking into account over 100 000 event logs of Neptun server and rejecting fields with time stamp and process ID (they are replaced by symbol (*)) we received 3036 event classes which have been submitted to processing by algorithms A1 and A2. The number of obtained event classes were 694, 332 and 473 for algorithm A1 with conditions >, >= and algorithm A2, respectively. Identified variables in the events have been replaced by symbols (…). Examples and quality of this classification will be discussed later.

```
findMostSimilarWordClass(words: list of string)
returns WordClass
{maxWCSim = 0
 mostSimilarWC = EMPTY
   for each WordClass wc in wordClasses (list of WordClass) do
   { wcSim = 0
   for each string word in words do
   {maxPatternsSim = 0
      for each WordPattern wp in wc.wordPatterns
      { patternsSim = matchDegree(word, wp)
         if patternsSim > maxPatternsSim
         maxPatternsSim = patternsSim}
wcSim = wcSim + maxPatternsSim}
wcSim = wcSim / length(words)
if wcSim > maxWCSim and wcSim >= similarityThreshold
   { maxWCSim = wcSim
   mostSimilarWC = wc}}
return mostSimilarWC}
```

Fig. 3. Word class identification – algorithm A3

The derived event classes may comprise variables denoted with non informative symbols (…), however related to a set of words. Quite often different events comprise variables of the same type (e.g. IP addresses). To improve event class visibility we have developed algorithm A3 (Fig. 3) which identifies word classes correlated with variable terms (not encountered in literature). It finds word classes describing a set of words related to variable terms. It bases on initially defined or found word classes and tries to add to the known class words from a new class by checking their similarity. Initially variable *mostSimilarWC* is empty, variable *wcSim* is used to calculate class similarity in relevance to considered set of words (initially set to 0). For every word within the list words of analyzed words we calculate similarity between every word pattern *wp* and string word using *matchDegree* method (*maxPatternSim* stores the found maximal similarity of this word), *wp* covers string word to some degree, e.g. 60% of characters. Asymmetric function *matchDegree(p1, p2)* gives the length of the longest match in p1 divided by its length and multiplied by the number of used characters of p2 in the longest match divided by the length of p2. Word patterns p1 and p2 can be both plain words or regular expressions. For example p2 = abcd([0-9]+) contains a regular expression that matches all characters of p1 = d1234, but since only 9 out of 12 of its characters are used, the result is 9/12 = ¾. Average value of the maximal similarities (*wcSim/length(words)*) is compared with predefined *similarityThreshold* to add the words satisfying this condition to the created class of words *mostSimilrWC*. Many experiments confirmed the selected 75% threshold as some optimum. Other similarity metrics can also be used.

Each class is labeled in a general way as ${WordClass_<no>} with subsequent numbers <no> or can be renamed according to the semantical meaning, e.g. ${USERS_NAME} and can be attributed to identified variable terms in events. Analyzing event data set of Neptun server with algorithm A2 we have got 473 event classes, 323 of them comprised at least one variable term. Analyzing the set of these terms we have identified 568 word classes. Unfortunately, some of the identified terms in fact are constant (imperfection of algorithm A2). Eliminating them we have got 375 word classes. Further reduction of word classes is possible by consolidation algorithm A4 (Fig. 4) which generalizes smaller classes in bigger ones.

```
consolidate(wordPatterns: set of string)
{ resultSet = wordPatterns
tmpResultSet = resultSet
hasChanged = true
   while hasChanged == true do
   {hasChanged = false
      for each p1 in resultSet do
         {for each p2 in resultSet do
            {if p1 == p2 then continue
            sim12 = matchDegree(p1, p2)
            sim21 = matchDegree(p2, p1)
            if sim12 == sim21 then
               { if length(p1) < length(p2) then merged = merge(p1, p2)
               else merged = merge(p2, p1) }
            else if sim12 > sim21 then merged = merge(p1, p2)
               else merged = merge(p2, p1)
            if merged is not NULL then
               {remove(tmpResultSet, p1)
               remove(tmpResultSet, p2)
                  if tmpResultSet doesn't contain merged then
                  {insert(tmpResultSet, merged)
                  hasChanged = true }}
         }}
      resultSet = tmpResultSet}
   return resultSet }
```

Fig. 4. Word class consolidation – algorithm A4

The basic algorithm A3 may be not sufficiently effective and a new word may not be matched with a set of words. Moreover, in event processing it may be more convenient to deal with regular expressions describing identified variables instead of explicit set of the word class. For this purpose we have developed consolidation algorithm A4. It generates regular expressions and allows us to eliminate redundant word classes. Word classes can be also specified partially by regular expression and partially explicitly. Generalization of word classes enables matching them to more variables (e.g. different sets of IP addresses). Algorithm A4 transforms word classes into *WordPatterns* defined by a set of regular expressions. It consolidates word patterns, e.g. a set of timestamps can be presented as a small set of regular expressions. Hence, a variable covering log files: */var/log/messages-2012-08-14; /var/log/messages-2012-12-13; /var/log/messages-2012-10-22* may be replaced with the expression */var/log/messages-<date>*, where *<date>* is defined by expression 2012-([0-9]+)-([0-9]+). Merging word patterns (p1, p2) we have to check their similarity (*matchDegree*). In the merging process of word patterns it is possible to replace an expression specifying a narrow class of words by a wider expression (pattern promotion). This extension is realized by successive attempts using wider regular expressions, e.g. according to the following order: ([0-9]+), ([a-f]+), ([A-F]+), ([a-z]+) ([A-Z]+), ([a-f0-9]+), ([A-F0-9]+), ([a-zA-Z]+), ([a-z0-9]+), ([A-Z0-9]+), ([a-fA-F0-9]+), ([a-zA-Z0-9]+), i.e. starting from digits, small letters, etc. We can also take into account sequences of expressions, e.g. a([0-9]+) ([a-f]+) which can be promoted to ([a-f0-9]+) or more sophisticated ones with special or non alphanumeric characters.

The main consolidating function (A4) is given in Fig. 4. It runs till no possibilities of merging any pattern. At the beginning each pair of patterns p1 and p2 (within the set of all *wordPatterns*) is checked for matching possibility, in the positive case a new pattern is generated and replaces patterns p1 and p2. In the case when p1 matches p2 and reciprocally we chose the shorter pattern. It is important to note that the introduced matching function allows to analyze similarity of character strings comprising also regular expressions (this is not assured by Levenstein based similarity metrics). For an illustration let us consider the following events:

MKub executed command from host: 1.2.3.4 at 2016-04-14 02:15
JSos executed command from host: 2.68.2.2 at 2015-12-12 01:03
RPod executed command from host: 123.1.5.1 at 2014-17-14 11:17

Algorithms A1–2 identify 4 fields with variables (denoted by (…)) and create a generalized message with word classes (labelled with $) which can be defined by regular expressions generated by algorithm A4 (notation as in Qt) related to user name, host IP, date and time:

(…) executed command from host: (…) at (…) (…)
${USER_NAME} executed command from host: ${HOST_IP} at ${DATE} ${TIME}
${USER_ NAME}=([a-z]+); ${HOST_IP}=([0-9]+).([0-9]+).([0-9]+).([0-9]+)
${DATE}=201([0-9]+)-([0-9]+)-([0-9]+); ${TIME}=([0-9]+):([0-9]+)

The developed EventAnalyser tool is correlated with a database comprising the considered event logs. It allows us to visualize registered raw events as well as the derived classes of events. We can select events related to specified time period, matching specified keywords, smoke words or phrases (Sect. 3), specified character strings (e.g. using regular expressions), events of specified priority (severity), IDs, etc. Complex selections with multiple conditions are also possible. Moreover, we can perform event selection in a hierarchical way and submit to classifications only selected subsets, etc. This gives high flexibility in drilling down event properties. Especially, in the case of logs with predefined templates we can select events according to event providers, opcodes (e.g. installation, service start, reboot, state change), assigned tasks (e.g. log on, audit, logging, recovery), keywords (e.g. failure, helper audit success, exhaustion of system limit). Dealing with event classes we can display (or extract) all events within such classes. Similarly, we can display all values of used variables (word classes) within event classes. This is quite useful to identify all user names which had problems with log in attempt, names of hosts for which this occurred, memory addresses for which errors have been notified, etc.

Event classification and consolidation processes can be performed iteratively and validated. In particular, we can verify the word class cardinality and compatibility within identified variables, as well as their context. Word classes with low cardinality are suspicious and can be easily verified or rejected. Too many variables not separated with constant phrases or words need also verification. Analyzing Neptun event logs with algorithms A2 and A4 we have got 54% of event classes without variables (except dates and time), 26.4% with a single variable, 5% with double separated variables, and 14.6% of classes comprising many variables with no separation words. Further analysis iterations of the last group resulted in splitting them into real classes with variables and classes with no variables. For most variables regular expressions have been derived automatically. Event classes with variables cover most events of the log. Event classification can be combined with textual analysis. In particular, we can classify subsets of events comprising interesting words or n-grams. Moreover, we can also use partial results of log analysis obtained with other tools.

Having analyzed many logs we have created a knowledge database comprising disclosed or well-known event patterns related to cyber-attacks, failures, system initialization, software updates, etc. This database is systematically updated. Most discovered anomalies related to configuration, HW/SW compatibility inconsistencies or not allowed user activities for the specified laboratory. Most events are not interesting so we can identify such neutral classes and skip them in further analysis. These classes relate only to normal system and application activities (suspected situations may appear if related event frequencies deviate in some aspect). Identified event classes can simplify calculations within algorithms. In the case of big logs we can optimize the analysis taking into account log subsets and then merging the results (parallel and distributed processing). Typically, analyzing a sample of logs (e.g. related to a few weeks or months) we identify most event classes (then we can look for new ones).

5 Temporal and Correlational Analysis

Semantical and syntactical event log analysis allows us to derive characteristic events specifying critical situations, characterize system operation trends, etc. This analysis has to be enhanced with temporal, spatial and correlation analysis of logs. Within the temporal analysis we can distinguish:

1. Distribution in time of the number of registered events (summarized view), this can be further drilled down by taking into account specified event classes (individual view), distribution of events depending upon their severity level. Some results for a cluster system we give in [17].
2. Distribution of times between subsequent events summarized or local view (all or specified classes)
3. Aggregated distribution profiles – monthly, weekly, daily perspectives: for each time interval (e.g. 24 h intervals) of the selected perspective (e.g. daily) we sum up events from the considered observation period (e.g. one year)
4. Event density plots: x axis shows event frequencies, y-axis gives the number of time intervals related to the specified event frequency (density spikes are suspicious and can be verified)
5. Trend analysis based on identifying distribution properties within subsequent periods (e.g. months, weeks), percentage of events of different severity levels.

Analyzing trends of specific events or their classes we can preview critical situations, e.g. in a laptop we observed increased frequency of event 8219 (crossing time limit of disc service), it appeared sporadically for 10 weeks and than stabilized at the level 35–72 events/week in 3 subsequent weeks and resulted in disc crash (normal situation can be assumed 0–7 events per month).

Table 1. Monthly distribution of negative words in event logs for two servers

Server	Word	1	2	3	4	5	6
Neptun	Error	34	0	0	40	2	37
	Warning	3	0	1	20	2	1
	Fault	0	0	3	0	0	0
Catalina	Exhausted	0	0	0	2	0	2
	Stopped	51	101	132	147	521	192
	Unregistered	33	25	50	174	29	46

In Table 1 we give monthly distribution of registered events comprising "negative smells". Excessive number of events with "*error*" appeared in 3 months (Neptun server), events with "*stopped*" word (Catalina server) showed some visible increase in time. Words *error, warning* and *fault* related to some minor deficiencies in SNMP demon generated by applications running in GUI (configuration inconsistencies) – found by correlating events with application usage log. Other negative words *warn* and *fail* correlated with Bluetooth problem and system restarting. In Catalina server events with *stopped* word related to the problem of removing threads which lead to memory leakage. Very high level of these events on the 5-th month related to high activity of performed tests and imports of data (in this period we have also observed higher rate of other negative words). Similar analysis has been performed for other negative and "smoke" words/phrases. Some trend of increasing the frequency of events with negative words resulted from system operational changes crossing its resilience capabilities. These problems disappeared after system reconfiguration. Hence, getting knowledge on normal level of these events is useful to predict various problems (preventive actions).

Another issue is studying various internal and external correlations. Internal correlations relate to events within the same log, external correlations relate to different logs (e.g. system and application, system and performance logs [10]) or event logs with workload and environment characteristic (profiles), seasonal parameters, etc. Spatial distribution of events is correlated with specified event sources, e.g. computer node or module, application, storage or network usage.

We can track normal and deviation patterns of some activities, e.g. user logins taking into account frequency per day or week, login times (working hours) correlated with holidays, sick days, instances where users log outside of their typical sites or beyond normal hours. Monitoring our laboratory systems we take into account laboratory schedules, used applications, course attendees, etc. We have observed different event profiles and sometimes some outlying patterns, e.g. references to not previewed web pages, so we detect not allowed student activities. Too frequent warning events produced on some stations showed lack of programming skills of some students, etc.

Analyzing various correlations we should take into account their support and confidence:

$$Supp(E{:}\ COR) = |E{:}\ COR|$$
$$Conf\,(E{:}\ COR) = Supp(E{:}\ COR)/Supp\ (E)$$

where Supp(…) is the number of occurrences of the specified rule in brackets, E: COR denotes a set of registered events E satisfying condition COR (e.g. appearing before some other event), Supp(E) denotes the number of all occurrences of event E in a specified observation time period T_{COR}. E can stand also for an event class.

Quite valuable is tracking occurrence of event sequences (double, three, etc.) and select those with high confidence. Events with high support usually related to normal activities (e.g. system restart). More interesting are low support and high confidence events mostly related to some anomalies. For event pairs with high support and confidence <e1, e2> it is reasonable searching complimentary pairs <e1, ei> with ei different from e2 (or vice versa) which can relate to abnormal situations, e.g. in one Windows computer we have identified within its application log (about 500000 events) event pairs <MI: 11707, MI: 1033> with support 148 and confidence 1, and other complimentary pairs were <MI: 11708, MI: 1033> and <MI: 11722, MI; 1033> with support 19 and 1, respectively (confidence 1), MI is the source of the event (Msinstaller). The latter pairs related to unsuccessful and faulty installation (installation is specified by event 1033). Similar situation related to program updates, product configurations, automatic virus scanning, etc. Further we can derive ordered (e.g. by confidence) pairs comprising initial event ei and create event adjacency matrices or profile graphs. Disturbances in dominating pairs or other event sequences (e.g. lack or replacement of previewed event) can be drilled down. Some events show seasonal behavior, e.g. intensive disc writes in a specified time interval every day. This periodicity can be attributed to daily backups, etc. Lack of some seasonal operations can be a signature of some problems, similarly excessive duration of such activities, etc.

Identified critical events can be further classified to correlate them with problem sources by searching additional keywords in messages, e.g. hardware, software, node, storage, blade, network, I/O, partition. Diverse software and hardware dependability mechanisms can be triggered by the same fault source and generate various events. Hence, an important issue is to correlate (in time, space and context) theses events with fault sources. This can be combined with semantic merging different logs. Correlating events within a specified time window we should be conscious of possible overlapping of two or more faults.

Text mining of identified critical event messages facilitates diagnosing fault types, e.g. related to processors, peripheral devices, memory, network, data base, operating system, file system, application. In most cases fault types can be pointed out by referring to the appropriate word or phrase categories (e.g. defined in a specially constructed technical dictionary). This enhances evaluation of system and application level resilience including measuring mean time between detected problems, duration of system outages, application hangouts, etc. Identifying (based on event logs) failover operations we can drill down their effectiveness. In practice, failure tolerance at the system level may impact applications or disrupt workload. Deriving characteristic features and various statistics of event logs (e.g. related to dropped packets, missing modules or files, wrong permissions, timeouts) we can track the impact of workload and environment changes.

The identified problems (event classes, event sequences, their statistical and timing features) can be correlated with resiliency attributes: *robustness* (security and sensitivity to stressful external situations), *recoverability* (time, scope and effectiveness of system or application recovery) and *resourcefulness* (availability of resources). Systematic system monitoring and log analysis can contribute to collecting event traces (signatures) characterizing resiliency (confirmation or disapproval). This process can be supported by interactions with system administrators and users to explain discovered anomalies or suspicious situations.

6 Conclusion

Deriving system operation features from event logs needs holistic analysis targeted at structural, contextual, time, spatial and semantic issues. This has been assured by the developed algorithms and tools (LogMiner, LogAnalyser). The identified properties should be submitted to correlation studies taking into account context of the environment, workload, executed applications, etc. Such approach enables finding sources of anomalies and detecting occurring or imminent resilience/dependability problems.

The presented lexicological analysis facilitates event message interpretation and classification. Nevertheless, ambiguous and not precise event reports occur. Hence, it is reasonable to support system logging with administrator and user logs. Designing logs (especially for newly developed applications) we should take into account requirements to facilitate automatic text mining. An important issue is to update the analytical methods taking into account the gained experience with detected anomalies or other interesting event features (e.g. derived critical patterns, regular expressions, word classes, statistical properties of different aspects). For this purpose we create thesaurus of interesting keywords and phrases (in relevance to the analysis goals).

Future research is targeted at checking the impact of fault injections (focused on system, application and user activities) on log contents [4]. This can be followed by developing recommendations to improve logging infrastructure and event description (compare [21]).

References

1. Berry, M.W., Kogan, J.: Text Mining Applications and Theory. Wiley, Chichester (2010)
2. Chen, C., Singh, N., Yajnik, D.: Log analytics for dependable enterprise telephony. In: Proceedings of 9th European Dependable Computing Conference, pp. 94–101 (2012)
3. Chuvakin, A., Schmid, K., Phillips, C., Moulder, P.: Logging and log management, the authoritative guide to understanding the concepts surrounding logging and log management. Elsevier (2013). http://dx.doi.org/10.1016/B978-1-59-749635-3.00024-5
4. Cinque, M., Cotroneo, D, Della, Corte, R., Pecchia, A.: Assessing direct monitoring techniques to analyze failures of critical industrial systems. In: Proceedings of IEEE 25th International Symposium on Software Reliability Engineering, pp. 212–222 (2014)
5. Di Martino, C., Kalbarczyk, Z., Kramer, W., Iyer, R.: Measuring and understanding extreme-scale application resilience: a field study of 5,000,000 HPC application runs. In: IEEEE/IFIP International Conference on Dependable Systems and Networks, pp. 25–36 (2015)
6. Fu, X., Ren, R., Zhan, J., Zhou, W., Jia, Z., Lu, G.: Logmaster: mining event correlations in logs of large-scale cluster systems. In: Proceedings of the 31st IEEE Symposium on Reliable Distributed Systems, pp. 71–80 (2012)
7. Gainaru, A., Cappelo, F., Snir, M., Kramer, W.: Fault prediction under the microscope: a closer look into HPC systems. In: Proceedings of the International Conference for High Performance Computing, pp 1–12 (2012)
8. He, P., Zhu, J., He, S., Li, J., Lyu, M.R.: An evaluation study on log parsing and its use in log mining. In: Proceedings of the 46th Annual IEEE/IFIP International Conference on Dependable Systems and Networks, pp. 654–661 (2016)
9. He, S., Zhu, J., He, P., Lyu, M.R.: Experience report: system log analysis for anomaly detection. In: Proceedings of the International Symposium on Software Reliability Engineering (ISSRE), pp 207–218 (2016)
10. Kubacki, M., Sosnowski, J.: Multidimensional log analysis. In: Proceedings of European Dependable Computing Conference, pp. 193–196 (2016)
11. Law, D., Gruss, R., Abrahams, A.S.: Automated defect discovery for dishwasher appliances from online consumer reviews. Expert Syst. Appl. **67**, 84–94 (2017)
12. Lin, Q., Zhang, H., Lou, J.G., Zhang, Y., Chen, X.: Log clustering based problem identification for online service systems. In: Proceedings of the 38th International Conference on Software Engineering (2016)
13. Lou, J., Fu, Q., Yang, S., Xu, Y., Li, J.: Mining invariants from console logs for system problem detection. In: Proceedings of the USENIX Annual Technical Conference (2010)

14. Makanju, A., Zincir-Heywoodet, A.N., Milios, E.E.: A lightweight algorithm for message type extraction in system application logs. IEEE Trans. Knowl. Data Eng. **24**(11), 1921–1936 (2012)
15. Nagappan, M., Robinson, B.: Creating operational profiles of software systems by transforming their log files to directed cyclic graphs. In: Proceedings of the 6th International Workshop on Traceability in Emerging Forms of Software Engineering, pp. 54–57. ACM (2011)
16. Peccia, A., Cinque, M., Carrozza, G., Cotroneo, D.: Industry practices and event logging: assessment of a critical software development process. In: Proceedings of the IEEE/ACM 37th IEEE International Conference on Software Engineering, pp. 169–178 (2015)
17. Sosnowski, J., Kubacki, M., Krawczyk, H.: Monitoring event logs within a cluster system. In: Zamojski, W., Mazurkiewicz, J., Sugier, J., Walkowiak, T., Kacprzyk, J. (eds.) Complex Systems and Dependability. AINSC, vol. 170, pp. 259–271. Springer, Heidelberg (2013). doi:10.1007/978-3-642-30662-4_17
18. Stearley, J., Oliner, A.: Bad words: finding faults in spirit's syslogs. In: Proceedings of International Conference on Cluster Computing and the Grid (2008)
19. Tang, L., Li, T., Perng, C.-S.: LogSig: generating system events from raw textual logs. In: Proceedings of the 20th ACM International Conference on Information and Knowledge Management, pp. 785–794 (2011)
20. Xu, W., Huang, L., Fox, A., Patterson, D., Jordon, M.I.: Detecting large-scale system problems by mining console logs. In: Proceedings of the ACM Symposium on Operating Systems Principles, pp. 117–132 (2009)
21. Zhu, J., He, P., Fu, Q., Zhang, H., Lyu, R., Zhang, D.: Learning to log: helping developers make informed logging decisions. In: Proceedings of the 37th International Conference on Software Engineering, pp. 415–424 (2015)

Author Index

Printed in the United States
By Bookmasters